$3 Slow-Cooked Meals

Delicious, Low-Cost Dishes from Both Your Slow Cooker and Stove

Ellen Brown

The Lyons Press
Guilford, Connecticut
An imprint of The Globe Pequot Press

This book is dedicated to Kim Montour, my dearest friend, whose questions prompted the idea for the dual cooking instructions in this book.

To buy books in quantity for corporate use
or incentives, call **(800) 962–0973**
or e-mail **premiums@GlobePequot.com.**

The Lyons Press is an imprint of The Globe Pequot Press.

Designed by Sheryl P. Kober

Library of Congress Cataloging-in-Publication Data
Brown, Ellen.
  $3 slow-cooked meals : delicious, low-cost dishes from both your slow cooker and stove / Ellen Brown.
      p. cm.
  ISBN 978-1-59921-823-6
1. Electric cookery, Slow. 2. Low budget cookery. I. Title. II. Title: Three dollar slow-cooked meals.
  TX827.B745 2009
  641.5'884--dc22
                                        2009017990

Printed in the United States of America

10 9 8 7 6 5 4 3 2 1

Contents

Learn how to become a savvy shopper, with money left in your wallet at the end of a shopping trip. It's all about planning, and you'll see how easy it is to do it.

The slow cooker is a simple appliance that can revolutionize your cooking because it cooks all day while you're out. This chapter explains how it operates and how to convert your favorite recipes to use it.

Eggs are as versatile as the chickens from which they come to create scrumptious dishes that are low in cost and high in protein. This chapter's recipes encompass forms like frittatas and stratas that are great ways to cook for a crowd.

Filling meals of hearty, steaming soups are a wonderful way to enjoy a warming meal on a chilly night, and this chapter contains recipes for the stocks on which they're based. With homemade stocks, meals don't get less expensive than these!

From our old friend, that can of tuna in the pantry, to the schools of aquatic species you can now find at a reasonable price in the supermarket, fish creates wonderful meals in relatively little time.

Chapter 6: From the Coops: Chicken and Turkey Entrees 113

The long process of cooking poultry in the slow cooker produces wonderfully moist chicken that has absorbed all flavors from the sauce. There are also some international ways to create casseroles in the oven from leftover poultry.

Chapter 7: From the Farms and Plains: Beef and Pork Dishes with International Flavors 156

The slow cooker takes less tender and far less expensive cuts of meat and turns them meltingly tender. Stew and pot roasts are the recipes you'll be cooking from this chapter, including a few slow-cooked dishes made with ground meat.

Chapter 8: From the Vegetable Patch: Hearty Vegetarian Entrees 201

It's not surprising that the slow cooker produces delectable bean dishes; it's based on an old-fashioned bean pot. The dishes in this chapter prove that vegetarian can be hearty, too.

Chapter 9: $1 Sweet Endings: Desserts That Are Easy on the Budget 231

The $3 figure includes dessert, and there are a range of options from homey bread puddings and pudding cakes to old-fashioned cheesecake and French baba au rhum.

Acknowledgments

While writing a book is a solitary endeavor, its publications is always a team effort. My thanks go to:

Ed Claflin, my agent, who offers constant support and a great sense of humor as well as his expertise to all my projects.

Eugene Brissie of The Lyons Press, for his faith in me and my ideas, and who launched me on the road to slow cooking many years ago.

Ellen Urban of The Lyons Press, editor extraordinaire, for her guidance and help all through the production process, and Jessie Shiers for her eagle-eyed copy editing.

My many friends who shared their culinary wisdom and tips for saving money.

Tigger and Patches, my furry companions, who personally endorse all fish and seafood recipes.

Preface

There's no singular cause for the astronomical rise in food costs during the past few years, and the factors—like many of the economic crises we're facing—are global, not national, in scope. You can cite reasons ranging from the growth of the middle class in India and China to the restrictions placed on soybean exports from Argentina, as well as the diversion of America's corn crop to ethanol and the rise in the cost of gasoline to transport foods from producers to supermarkets. All are pertinent, and it's likely that none will soon be ameliorated.

That's where *$3 Slow-Cooked Meals,* and the other titles in this series, enter your life and kitchen. We can't fight the fact that food is taking a bigger bite out of our budgets. But we can enjoy delicious meals at the end of a day that stretch that budget and never deprive our taste buds of both flavor and nutrition. Best of all, the "secret ingredient" to most of these delectable dishes is probably in your house—if not out on your counter.

It's a slow cooker, aka Crock-Pot™. These simple and safe electrical appliances that use about the same energy as a 60-watt bulb are now found in 83 percent of American kitchens, which is the same percentage of homes that have coffee pots. And with good reason! The slow cooker sets you free; it tends to its contents all by itself.

The slow cooker watches over your cooking so you can leave for work—or go to a movie with a friend—with a clear conscience, and the reassurance that a tantalizing and healthful meal will await you.

The mouth-watering aroma that greets you when you walk into your house at the end of the day is the first benefit of a slow cooker. Although the food is barely simmering, it's been cooking for long enough that the innate flavors of all the ingredients have blended together and fill the air with their fragrance. By the time a dish is ready, it has been simmering for some time. Like a puff of smoke coming up from a genie's bottle, it lures you right to the kitchen.

There's nothing new about slow cooking; it's been around for centuries, even before there were kitchens, or houses for that matter. The first slow cooking was done in pottery, as it still is today. By the fifth century BCE, iron pots holding simmering food were left to cook all day and all night in the fire's embers. Although slow cooking was a necessity in the past, today it's a choice. With some advance preparation, busy people can enjoy a delicious, homemade meal that cooks without anyone around to watch it. That's a freedom not listed in the Bill of Rights, but a freedom it certainly is!

This book could be called "Confessions of a Former Slow Cooker Snob," and if you have been reticent to use a slow cooker because you visualize with horror cans of "cream of something" soup in your shopping cart, you're not alone. The primary reason I resisted using my slow cooker extensively for a few *decades* was that the recipes I saw written for the slow cooker were full of processed foods, and by extension, chemicals. But the recipes in *$3 Slow-Cooked Meals* will demonstrate that slow cookers can produce delicious meals made totally with fresh ingredients.

There are differences between cooking in a slow cooker and cooking conventionally, and you'll learn all about those in this book. A slow cooker can't produce crispy fried chicken or a crunchy chocolate chip cookie. But it can produce thick and healthful bean dishes, myriad hearty soups, luscious meat and poultry stews, and sinfully rich bread puddings—both savory ones for brunch and sweet ones for dessert.

What differentiates *$3 Slow-Cooked Meals* from other cookbooks devoted to the slow cooker—including my own previous books—is that most recipes in this book give you instructions for how to make the dish conventionally as well as in the slow cooker, either simmered on top of the stove or baked in the oven.

Why? Because it expands your options and gives you more flexibility. Once you've cooked a dish successfully and garnered rave reviews from your family and friends, you're more likely to want to cook it again. But what if you decide to cook it at 5:00 on a Sunday afternoon, and the minimum time for a slow cooker to complete the cooking is five hours? Maybe that recipe could be dinner for the next night, but not the Sunday supper you envisioned.

Or, what to do when you liked a dish so much that you want to make it for a dinner party of 20 guests next week? There's a finite limit to the size of a batch of food you can make in the slow cooker; it's the size for which the recipe is written. But it's always possible to produce larger batches of food when cooking conventionally; you just use a larger pot or roasting pan. All of my labor testing these dishes both in the slow cooker and with a conventional stove gives you a chance to decide how you would like to cook them.

There are some dishes in *$3 Slow-Cooked Meals* that fall within the universal description of *slow* cooking—cooking that takes time—rather than slow *cooker* cooking. These include many innovative ways to utilize the leftovers from cooking—a cost-effective turkey dish when it's not Thanksgiving, or corned beef on a day other than St. Patrick's Day. Not to mention desserts like a classic cheesecake or a homey carrot cake that can be made for mere cents a serving at home but garner high price tags in bakeries. You'll learn to make them from the recipes in this book, too.

So dust off your slow cooker, if it's been banished to the basement. And get ready for some exotic aromas, followed by fabulous flavors.

Stick with me and the recipes in *$3 Slow-Cooked Meals* and dazzle your family and friends with the array of delicious dishes coming forth from your slow cooker.

Happy cooking!

—Ellen Brown
Providence, Rhode Island

Introduction

This book is about spending very little time in the kitchen—but enjoying all the aromas, flavors, and textures from foods that did. And you don't even have to be home to monitor the progress of the cooking, because these delicious dishes are simmering away in your slow cooker.

You can be at work, taking the kids for a romp in the park, or at a movie. And when you walk into your house you're greeted by a nutritious, healthful meal that satisfies all your senses—and doesn't stretch your limited food budget. You'll be eating like a prince on a pauper's budget, but budget is hardly synonymous with boring. Frugal food can be exciting and fun. Plus, it's easy to prepare.

The recipes in *$3 Slow-Cooked Meals* encompass comfort food classics, like meatloaf and pot roast, but no one culture or cuisine owns comfort food. What's a stew in Boston is a *daube* in Bordeaux and a *cazuela* in Buenos Aires. So along with American favorites are recipes drawn from cuisines around the world. But all the ingredients can be found in your supermarket—and at a reasonable cost.

While flexibility and freedom are two of the slow cooker's trump cards, there are others, too:

- Slow cookers don't scorch thick stews and bean dishes that tend to stick to the bottom of a pan placed over the direct heat of a stove burner.

- Slow cookers provide a third hand for party prep. Use a slow cooker to free up the oven for food that needs higher heat. Plus, a slow cooker can be left alone.

- Slow cookers don't heat up the kitchen, so they're perfect for summer cooking.

- Slow cookers keep food warm so family members can eat at different times, if necessary, and the food remains hot while not drying out.

To fully appreciate the wonders of the slow cooker, you need to understand some of the basics of food chemistry underpinning its operation. How all food is cooked is divided into two camps; there's "wet heat" and there's "dry heat." The slow cooker is the champ for making "wet heat" foods, while roasting in a hot oven or over glowing coals are the way we cook "dry heat" foods.

Every cuisine has less-tender cuts of meat—which, fortuitously, are also less expensive—that are simmered in flavorful liquid for many hours until they're tender. We call it braising if it's big pieces of food, and stewing if the pieces are smaller. We describe the end result of the process as "fork tender," and that's what braising is about—tenderness.

Braising is a low-heat method because the meat is the same temperature as the simmering liquid, 212°F. This simmering converts the collagen of the meat's connective tissue to gelatin, which makes the meat tender. There's no fear of the outside drying out, as in high-heat dry roasting, because the food is covered with a liquid that produces a moist heat. That's also why it takes almost as long to cook a stew, in which the meat is cut into small pieces, as it does to braise a large roast. The only difference is the time the meat takes to reach the same temperature as the liquid.

The tougher the piece of meat, the more connective tissue it has, so the more tender it will become after braising. Conversely, if an innately tender cut of meat, such as a tenderloin or rib roast, is braised, it will become tough because there is no collagen to convert. But we don't have to concern ourselves with beef tenderloin; it's clearly not within the definition of a $3 meal.

What you'll learn reading—and cooking from—this book is how far your finite food budget can stretch. The goal of *$3 Slow-Cooked Meals,* as well as other books in the *$3 Meals* series, is an ambitious one; this small amount of money—less than the cost of a large fast food burger or a slice of gourmet pizza—is for your *whole meal!*

That includes the greens for your tossed salad, and the pasta or rice you cook to enjoy all the gravy from a stew. And it includes a sweet treat for dessert. So unlike many books that promise cost-conscious cooking, this book really means it.

In addition to eating wonderfully, you'll also be eating more healthfully. It may not be by accident that *convenience* and *chemical* start with the same letter. Chemicals are what convenience foods are all about; they are loaded up with them to increase their shelf life, both before and after opening. The recipes in this book don't contain such unhealthy ingredients as trans-fats and high fructose corn syrup, which can be hidden in processed foods, too.

One of the rules of economical cooking is that the more processed a food is, the more expensive it is. These recipes are made with foods that are ingredients; at one time they grew from the earth, walked upon it, or swam in its waters. The most processing that has taken place is the milk of animals having been transformed into natural cheeses. So when you're cooking from *$3 Slow-Cooked Meals*, you're satisfying your body as well as your budget.

There's another reason why cooking the recipes in this book is good for your health; it's because of the low, gentle heat with which slow cookers accomplish their task. Some compounds called "advanced gly-cation end products" (AGEs) are formed when sugars, fats, and pro-teins are heated at high temperatures by grilling, broiling, or even using a microwave oven. These AGEs irritate cells and may be a factor in the formation of heart disease and cancer. Foods cooked in the slow cooker contain fewer AGEs.

In addition to not taking shortcuts with ingredients, *$3 Slow-Cooked Meals* also does not take preparation shortcuts that can damage the resulting dish. While many books aimed at slow cooker cooking do not utilize any conventional cooking techniques—like sautéing onions to mellow their flavor or browning meats to add richness to the sauce— that is not the case with the recipes in this book. While no dish takes more than 20 minutes of your active time before you turn on the slow cooker, most of the recipes do include some steps accomplished by conventional cooking.

There are a few ingredient compromises made to trim costs; how-ever, these shortcuts trim preparation time, too. For my series of *$3 Meals* books, I've used bottled lemon and lime juice in recipe develop-ment rather than freshly squeezed juices from the fruits themselves; I discovered it took a bit more juice to achieve the flavor I was after, but with the escalated cost of citrus fruits this was a sacrifice that I chose to make. The same is true with vegetables; many of these recipes call for cost-effective frozen vegetables rather than fresh. For vegetables such as the chopped spinach added to a soup or casserole, or the peas added to many dishes, using frozen produce doesn't affect the quality of the finished recipe.

I've also limited the range of herbs and spices specified to a core group of less than a dozen. There's no need to purchase an expensive dried herb that you may never use again.

On the other hand, there are standards I will never bend. I truly believe that unsalted butter is so far superior to margarine that any minimal cost savings from using margarine is not worth the trade-down in flavor. Good quality Parmesan cheese, freshly grated when you need it, is another ingredient well worth the splurge. You use very little of it, because once grated it takes up far more volume than in a block, and its innate flavor is far superior.

You'll also find that the dishes in *$3 Slow-Cooked Meals* offer a wide range of flavors, and are dishes that are satisfying to the soul.

Chapter 1:
Saving Money at the Supermarket

You might want to mark February 10 on your calendar as an annual occasion; that's the date by which you've earned enough money to pay your food bills for the year. But with the current rise in food costs, spring flowers may be in bloom by the time you've amassed the same sum next year.

Next to housing and auto expenses, food is Americans' major annual expense, as it is around the world. The fact that Americans spend about a 12 percent chunk of disposable income on food still remains the envy of most people living in the industrialized world. Just across the border in Canada the figure is 14 percent, while in Mexico it is more than 25 percent.

But we know that the cost of a dozen eggs, a quart of milk, and a pound of beef is higher than it's ever been, and this chapter will help you become a savvier shopper. You'll be able to stretch your food dollar like a sheet of pasta dough—the cost of which has also gone up. Planning and shopping are the cornerstones to trimming the fat out of your food bills, and you'll learn how to do both.

PLAN *BEFORE* YOU SHOP

The most important step to cost-effective cooking is to decide logically and intelligently what you're going to cook for the week. That may sound simple, but if you're in the habit of deciding when you're leaving work at the end of the day, chances are you've ended up with a lot of frozen pizza or Chinese carry-out. While this section on how to plan is very detailed, it really takes but minutes to compile your master plan once you've gotten in the habit.

A master plan is more important for a book like *$3 Slow-Cooked Meals* than many others because most dishes require many hours of cooking. You can't "whip up" a beef stew or a pot of split pea soup on a whim.

First, look at the week, and what activities are listed. How many nights will you actually be home? Are there guests invited for any meals? How about the kids? Do they have activities that mean that the family won't be eating dinner together? Is there a sporting event on television that everyone will want to see, so eating may be on laps instead of a table? These are all questions to ponder before putting pen to paper.

The next step is to shop in your own house first. Look and see what's still in the refrigerator, and how that food—which you've already purchased and perhaps also cooked—can be utilized. Let's say you roasted a chicken a few days earlier, so look at the recipes in "The Second Time Around" section in Chapter 6 to see some exciting ideas. What about Turkey and Spinach Enchilada Bake? You can use chicken instead of turkey, and that also uses up the leftover spinach from the other night. Or what if, in addition to the chicken, you've also got some mashed potatoes? Sounds like Turkey Shepherd's Pie is a plan, and it uses up the leftover vegetables, too.

Now look and see what foods you have in the freezer. Part of savvy shopping is stocking up on foods when they're on sale; in fact, sales of free-standing freezers have grown by more than 10 percent during the past few years, while sales of all other major appliances have gone down. And with good reason—a free-standing freezer allows you to take advantage of sales.

But preparing food for the freezer to ensure quality is important. Never freeze meats, poultry, or seafood in the supermarket wrapping alone. To guard against freezer burn, double-wrap food in freezer paper or place it in heavy resealable plastic bags. Mark the purchase date on raw food, and the date when frozen on cooked items, and use them within three months.

Also, part of your strategy as a cook is to cook only a few nights a week; that means when you're making recipes that can be doubled—like a pasta sauce or stew—you make larger batches and freeze a portion. Those meals are "dinner insurance" for nights you don't want to cook. Those are the nights that you previously would have brought in the bucket of chicken or the box of pizza, and spent more money for less nutrition.

The other factor that enters into the initial planning is looking at your depletion list, and seeing what foods and other products need to be purchased. A jar of peanut butter or a bottle of dishwashing liquid might not factor into meal plans, but they do cost money—so they have to be factored into your budget. Some weeks you might not need many supplies, but it always seems to me that all of the cleaning supplies seem to deplete the same week.

THAT FRUGAL FRAME OF MIND

The first step to savvy shopping is to get into a frugal frame of mind. You're out to save money on your food budget, but not feel deprived. You're going to be eating the delicious dishes in this book.

Think about where your food budget goes other than the grocery store. The cost of a few "designer coffee" treats at the local coffee shop is equal to a few dinners at home. Couldn't you brew coffee and take it to work rather than spend $10 a week at the coffee cart? And those cans of soft drinks in the vending machine are four times the cost of bringing a can from home.

Bringing your lunch to work does increase your weekly supermarket tab, but it accomplishes a few good goals. It adds funds to the bottom line of your total budget, and it allows you to control what you're eating—and when. If you have a pressured job, chances are there are days that you end up eating from snack food vending machines or fast food at your desk. By bringing your lunch you know what it will be— even if you don't know when. And almost every office has a microwave oven, so lunch can frequently be leftovers from dinner the night or two before, so the extra cost is minimal.

STRATEGIES FOR SHOPPING

It's a new world out there. You're going to the supermarket and you're going to buy what's on your list. Here's the first rule: stick to that list. Never go shopping when you're hungry; that's when non-essential treats wind up in your basket.

The next time you are at the market, have a pad and pen with you. Take note of what is located where, such as "baking supplies (flour, sugar, chocolate chips) in aisle 2," and create a master form for your shopping list according to the layout of your market. Divide a sheet of paper into three columns, starting with the meats, fish, and other protein, and then make listings for dairy products and shelf-stable pantry items by aisle number. After a few times, this system becomes so familiar that you will probably not be referring to your master guide.

Supermarkets are almost all designed to funnel traffic first into the produce section; that is the last place you want to shop. Begin with the proteins, since many items in other sections of your list relate to the entrees of the dinners you have planned. Once they are gathered, go through and get the shelf-stable items, then the dairy products (so they will not be in the cart for too long) and end with the produce. Using this method, the fragile produce is on the top of the basket, not crushed by the gallons of milk.

The last step is packing the groceries. If your grocery store gives you the option of packing them yourself, place items stored together in the same bag. That way all of your produce can go directly into the refrigerator, and canned goods destined for the basement will be stored in one trip.

Bargain Shopping 101

Every grocery store has weekly sales, and those foods are the place to start your planning for new purchases. And almost every town has competing supermarket chains that offer different products on sale. It's worth your time to shop in a few venues, because it will generate the most savings. That way you can also determine which chain offers the best store brands, and purchase them while you're there for the weekly bargains. Here are other ways to save:

- **Clip those coupons.** And use them! The best deal you can find is a coupon for an item that is being offered on a "buy one, get one free" promotion in the supermarket. Large companies publish coupons in every Sunday newspaper, and other companies send them at bulk rate with your mail delivery. You can save substantially by spending some time looking at the coupons. I found a $5 off coupon for a premium cat food my finicky cats liked in a local paper, which cost 50 cents. It was worth it to buy four copies of the paper; I spent $2 but I then netted an $18 savings on the cat food.

- **"Junk mail" may contain more than junk.** Don't toss those Valpack and other coupon envelopes that arrive in the mail. Look through them carefully, and you'll find not only coupons for food products, but for many services, too.

- **Spend a stamp to get a rebate.** Many large manufacturers are now sending out coupon books or cash vouchers usable in many stores to customers who mail in receipts demonstrating that they have purchased about $50 of products. For example, Procter &

Gamble, the country's largest advertiser and the company for which the term "soap opera" was invented, is switching millions of dollars from airwaves to these sorts of promotions.

- **Find bargains online.** It's difficult for me to list specific Web sites because they may be defunct by the time you're reading this book, but there are hundreds of dollars worth of savings to be culled by printing coupons from Web sites, and for high-end organic products, it's the only way to access coupons. Ones I use frequently are www.couponmom.com and www.coupons.com, and I also look for the coupon offers on such culinary sites as www.epicurious.com. Also visit manufacturers' Web sites; they offer both coupons and redemption savings.

- **Find coupons in the store.** Look for those little machines projecting out from the shelves; they usually contain coupons that can be used instantly when you check out. Also, don't throw out your receipt until you've looked at it carefully. Frequently, there are coupons printed on the back. The cashier may also hand you other small slips of paper with your cash register receipt; most of them are coupons for future purchases of items you just bought. They may be from the same brand or they may be from a competing brand. Either way, they offer savings.

- **Stock up on cans.** Even if you live in a small apartment without a basement storage unit, it makes sense to stock up on canned goods when they're on sale. The answer is to use every spare inch of space. The same plastic containers that fit under your bed to hold out-of-season clothing can also become a pantry for canned goods.

- **Shuffle those cards.** Even if I can't convince you to clip coupons, the least you can do for yourself to save money is take the five minutes required to sign up for store loyalty cards; many national brands as well as store brands are on sale only when using the card. While the current system has you hand the card to the cashier at the checkout, that will be changing in the near future. Shopping carts will be equipped with card readers that will generate instant coupons according to your purchasing habits. I keep my stack of loyalty cards in the glove box of my car; that way they don't clutter my purse but I always have them when shopping.

- **Get a bargain buddy.** There's no question that supermarkets try to lure customers with "buy one, get one free" promotions, and sometimes one is all you really want. And those massive cases of paper towels at the warehouse clubs are also a good deal—if you have unlimited storage space. The answer? Find a bargain buddy with whom you can split large purchases. My friends and I also swap coupons we won't use but the other person will. Going back to my example of the cat food savings, there were dog food coupons on the same page, so I turned them over to a canine-owning friend.

Learning the Ropes

The well-informed shopper is the shopper who is saving money, and the information you need to make the best purchasing decision is right there on the supermarket shelves. The shelf tag gives you the cost per unit of measurement. The units can be quarts for salad dressing, ounces for dry cereal, or pounds for canned goods. All you have to do is look carefully.

But you do have to make sure you're comparing apples to apples and oranges to oranges—or in this example, stocks to stocks. Some stocks are priced by the quart, while others are by the pound.

- **Check out store brands.** Store brands and generics have been improving in quality during the past few years, and according to *Consumer Reports,* buying them can save anywhere from 15 to 50 percent. Moving from a national brand to a store brand is a personal decision, and sometimes money is not the only factor. For example, I have used many store brands of chlorine bleach, and have returned to Clorox time and again. But I find no difference between generic corn flakes and those from the market leaders.

- **Compare prices within the store.** Many foods—such as cold cuts and cheeses—are sold in multiple areas of the store, so check out those alternate locations. Sliced ham may be less expensive in a cellophane package shelved with the refrigerated foods than at the deli counter.

- **Look high and low.** Manufacturers pay a premium price to shelve products at eye level, and you're paying for that placement when you're paying their prices. Look at the top and bottom shelves in aisles like cereal and canned goods. That's where you'll find the lower prices.

- **Buy the basics.** When is a bargain not a bargain? When you're paying for water or you're paying for a little labor. That's why even though a 15-ounce can of beans is less expensive than the same quantity of dried beans (approximately a pound), you're still better off buying the dried beans. One pound of dried beans makes the equivalent of four or five cans of beans. In the same way, a bar of Monterey Jack cheese is much less expensive per pound than a bag of grated Monterey Jack cheese. In addition to saving money, the freshly grated cheese will have more flavor because cheese loses flavor rapidly when grated. And pre-cut and pre-washed vegetables are truly exorbitant.

Waste Not, Want Not

We're now going to start listing exceptions to all the rules you just read, because a bargain isn't a bargain if you end up throwing some of it away. Remember that the goal is to waste nothing. Start by annotating your shopping list with quantities for the recipes you'll be cooking. That way you can begin to gauge when a bargain is a bargain. Here are other ways to buy only what you need:

- **Don't overbuy.** Sure, the large can of diced tomatoes is less per pound than the smaller can. But what will you do with the remainder of the can if all you need is a small amount? The same is true for dairy products. A half-pint of heavy cream always costs much more per ounce than a quart, but if the remaining three cups of cream will end up in the sink in a few weeks, go with the smaller size.

- **Ring that bell!** You know the one; it's always in the meat department of supermarkets. It might take you a few extra minutes, but ask the real live human who will appear for *exactly* what you want. Many supermarkets do not have personnel readily available in departments like the cheese counter, but if there are wedges of cheeses labeled and priced, then someone is in charge. It might be the deli department or the produce department, but find out who it is and ask for a small wedge of cheese if you can't find one the correct size.

- **Check out the bulk bins.** Begin buying from the bulk bins for shelf-stable items,like various types of rice, beans, dried fruits, and nuts. Each of these departments has a scale so you can weigh ingredients like dried mushrooms or pasta. If a recipe calls for a quantity rather than a weight you can usually "eyeball" the quantity. If you're unsure of amounts, start by bringing a 1-cup measure with you to the market. Scoop contents from the bin into the measuring cup rather than directly into the bag. One problem with bulk food bags is that they are difficult to store in the pantry; shelves were made for sturdier materials. Wash out plastic deli containers or even plastic containers that you bought containing yogurt or salsa. Use those for storage once the bulk bags arrive in the kitchen. Make sure you label your containers of bulk foods both at the supermarket and, if you're transferring the foods to other containers, at home so you know what they are, especially if you're buying similar foods. Arborio and basmati rice look very similar in a plastic bag, but they are totally different grains and shouldn't be substituted for each other.

- **Shop from the salad bar for tiny quantities.** There's no question that supermarkets charge a premium price for items in those chilled bins in the salad bar, but you get exactly what you need. If you don't see how you're going to finish the $4 pint of cherry tomatoes, then spend $1 at the salad bar for the handful you need to garnish a salad.

SUPERMARKET ALTERNATIVES

All of the hints thus far in this chapter have been geared to pushing a cart around a supermarket. Here are some other ways to save money:

- **Shop at farmers' markets.** I admit it; I need a 12-step program to help me cure my addiction to local farmers' markets. Shopping *al fresco* on warm summer days turns picking out fruits and veg- etables into a truly sensual experience. Also, you buy only what you want. There are no bunches of carrots; there are individual carrots sold by the pound. The U.S. Department of Agriculture began publishing the *National Directory of Farmers' Markets* in 1994, and at that time the number was fewer than 2,000. That figure has now doubled. To find a farmers' market near you, go to www.ams.usda.gov/farmersmarkets. The first cousins of farmers' markets for small quantities of fruits are the sidewalk vendors in many cities. One great advantage to buying from them is that their fruit is always ripe and ready to eat or cook.

- **Shop at ethnic markets.** If you live in a rural area this may not be possible, but even moderately small cities have a range of ethnic markets, and that's where you should buy ingredients to cook those cuisines. Dried corn husks to make tamales are far less expensive than in the Hispanic aisle of the supermarket, and such ethnic enclaves as a city's "Little Italy" almost always contain some grocery stores with great prices for Mediterranean foods— and the fresh produce used to make them, too.

- **Shop alternative stores.** Groceries aren't only at grocery stores; many "dollar stores" and other discount venues stock shelf-stable items. Also, every national brand of drugstore—including CVS and Walgreen's—carries grocery products and usually has great bar- gains each week. In the same way that food markets now carry much more than foods, drug stores stock thousands of items that have no connection to medicine.

- **Shop online.** In recent years it's become possible to do all your grocery shopping online through such services as Peapod and Fresh Express. While there is frequently a delivery charge involved, for housebound people this is a true boon. If you really hate the thought of pushing the cart, you should explore it; it's impossible to make impulse buys. There are also a large number of online retailers for ethnic foods, dried herbs and spices, premium baking chocolate, and other shelf-stable items. Letting your cursor do the shopping for these items saves you time, and many of them offer free shipping at certain times of the year.

So now that you're becoming a grocery guru, you can move on to find myriad ways to save money on your grocery bill while eating wonderfully. That's what *$3 Slow-Cooked Meals* is all about.

Chapter 2:
Slowly Does It!

It seems almost an oxymoron to say that hours of cooking in a slow cooker are totally consistent with our fast-paced world. But that is the case. Slow cookers provide the flexibility to be gone for hours at a time without fear of ruined food or—perish the thought—a fire.

And what greets you after being away for hours is instant gratification; your slow cooker has produced a healthful, economical dish that is better for your body *and* your budget than nutritionally bankrupt fast food. Perhaps that's the reason that slow cookers are now found in 83 percent of American kitchens; that's the same percentage that own electric coffee pots.

Slow cookers operate by cooking food using indirect heat at a low temperature for an extended period of time. Direct heat is the power of a stove burner underneath a pot; indirect heat is the overall heat that surrounds food in the oven.

Think of it this way: If you're standing on a hot sidewalk, you're feeling direct heat on the soles of your feet, but the heat you feel all over your body when you're lounging on the beach under the sun is indirect heat.

While in many households slow cookers are banished when screens replace storm windows, in my kitchen at least one lives on the counter year round because the range of dishes it produces is so large, and during the warm summer months it doesn't raise the kitchen temperature by even a degree. Slow cookers save on your utility bill as well as your grocery budget—they use about as much electricity as a 60 watt bulb.

And the analogy does not end there. Slow cookers are as easy to use as turning on a light switch, and even though some now come with many programmable features and other bells and whistles, the vast majority remains both easy and affordable. In this chapter you'll learn about slow cookers and how to achieve the best results from them.

Rival introduced the first slow cooker, the Crock-Pot, in 1971, and the introductory slogan remains true more than 35 years later: It "cooks all day while the cook's away." Like such trademarked names as Kleenex for paper tissue or Formica for plastic laminate, Crock-Pot has almost become synonymous with the slow cooker. However, not all slow cookers are Crock-Pots, so the generic term is used in this book.

ANATOMY OF A SLOW COOKER

Slow cookers come in both round and oval shapes, and which one you select should be dependent on how you plan to use it most often. I find that the oval slow cookers are better for large roasts; they hold the shape of most pot roasts. However, round slow cookers are preferable for stews and bean dishes because they bring the temperature of food in the center of the slow cooker up more evenly; I also recommend the round versions for dishes such as bread puddings for the same reason.

Regardless of shape, the parts and operation remain constant. Food is assembled in a pottery insert that fits inside a metal housing and is topped with a clear glass or plastic lid. As you'll learn below, removing the lid is not a good idea, so manufacturers make them clear, or they become clear when you jiggle them so that steam and condensation fall back into the pot.

What actually cooks the food are the wrap-around heating elements encased between the slow cooker's outer and inner layers of metal. The coils never directly touch the crockery insert. As the element heats, it gently warms the air between the two layers of metal, and it is the hot air that touches the crockery. This construction method eliminates the need for stirring because no part of the pot gets hotter than any other.

On the front of this metal casing is the control knob. All slow cookers have Low and High settings. Some also have a Stay Warm position. Some new machines have a programmable option that enables you to start food on High, and then the slow cooker automatically reduces the heat to Low after a programmed time. Since I never figured out how to program a VCR, and sophisticated functions of any remote control elude me, all of my slow cookers are simple (and less expensive) ones. You can purchase a slow cooker for as little as $20 at a discount store; the top-of-the-line ones sell for close to $300. And they all function in the same simple way.

The largest variation in slow cookers is their size, which ranges from tiny 1-quart models that are excellent for hot dips and fondue but fairly useless for anything else, to gigantic 7-quart models that are excellent for large families and large batches.

With few exceptions—such as a few meat dishes—all recipes in this book were written for and tested in a 4- or 5-quart slow cooker; that is what is meant by "medium." Either of those sizes makes enough for four to eight people, depending on the recipe.

None of the pots currently on the market can be programmed by the clock, and that is important for food safety. They will cook the food once programmed, and then either turn off or turn to the Stay Warm setting, but you can't program them to start at noon when it's 8:00 a.m. The reason is that food could spoil in the intervening hours, as you'll read later in this chapter.

CARING FOR YOUR SLOW COOKER

Even though slow cookers do not require a lot of power to operate, they are electrical appliances, and the same safety rules apply as with any electrical appliance. Be careful that the cord is not frayed in any way, and plug the slow cooker into an outlet that is not near the sink.

Cooking in glazed pottery and at low temperatures means that food rarely sticks. To ensure easy cleanup, spray the inside of the insert with vegetable oil spray before adding the food. If food does stick, which rarely happens, soak the insert in hot soapy water and then wash it clean. Try not to use an abrasive pad on the slow cooker insert because it can scratch the surface of the glaze, which would allow food to stick.

Another option for easy cleanup is to buy plastic bag insert liners; they're shelved with the other paper and plastic goods in the supermarket. They're expensive, however, so I don't recommend them. But, more importantly for the safety of your food, don't substitute any old plastic bag for an insert liner. The insert liners are made from a special material that will not transfer chemicals to your food; they're similar to the oven bags sold for roasting turkeys.

Glass lids for slow cookers, as well as the inserts, can be washed in the dishwasher. If the lid is plastic, however, consult the manufacturer's instructions.

Modern slow cookers heat slightly hotter than those made thirty years ago; the Low setting on a slow cooker is about 200°F, while the High setting is close to 300°F. If you have an older appliance, it's a good idea to test it to make sure it still has the power to heat food sufficiently. Leave 2 quarts water at room temperature overnight, then pour the water into the slow cooker in the morning. Heat it on Low for 8 hours. The temperature should be 185°F after 8 hours. Use an instant-read thermometer to judge it. If it is lower, any food you cook in this cooker might not pass through the danger zone of 40 to 140°F rapidly enough.

SLOW COOKERS AND FOOD SAFETY

The question I am asked most often when being interviewed about slow cookers concerns food safety. The Food Safety and Inspection Service of the U.S. Department of Agriculture approves slow cooking as a method for safe food preparation. The lengthy cooking and the steam created within the tightly covered pot combine to destroy any bacteria that might be present in the food.

While fruits and vegetables can contain some bacteria, it's far more common for food-borne illness to be caused by meat, poultry, and seafood. Begin by storing these perishable foods on the bottom shelves of your refrigerator so their juices cannot accidentally fall on other foods. And keep these foods refrigerated until just before they go into the slow cooker. Keep in mind at all times that bacteria multiply more rapidly at room temperature.

It's not wise to cook whole chickens or cuts of meat larger than those specified in the recipes in this book because during slow cooking, these large items stay too long in the bacterial "danger zone"—between 40 and 140°F. It is important that food reaches the higher temperature in less than two hours and remains at more than 140°F for at least 30 minutes.

If you want to cook large roasts, brown them under the oven broiler or in a skillet on top of the stove over direct heat before you place them into the slow cooker. This will help the chilled meat heat up faster, as well as producing a dish that is more visually appealing.

Getting a jump start on dinner while you're preparing breakfast may seem like a Herculean task, and it is possible to prep the ingredients destined for the slow cooker the night before—with some limitations. If you cut meat or vegetables in advance, store them separately in the refrigerator and layer them in the slow cooker in the morning.

Do not store the cooker insert in the refrigerator, because that will also increase the amount of time it takes to heat the food to a temperature that kills bacteria.

Concern about food safety extends to after a meal is cooked, and the leftovers are ready for storage. As long as the temperature remains 140°F or higher, food will stay safe for many hours once it's done cooking in the slow cooker. Leftovers, however, should never be refrigerated in the crockery insert because it will take them too long to go through the "danger zone" in the other direction—from hot to cold.

Freeze or refrigerate leftovers in shallow containers within two hours after a dish has finished cooking. Also, never reheat food in the slow cooker because it takes too long for chilled food to reheat; bacteria can be a problem on cooked food as well as raw ingredients. Once food has been reheated on the stove or in the microwave, it can be kept warm in the slow cooker—without the fear of burning it—until serving time.

One of the other concerns about food safety and the slow cooker is loss of power in the house—especially if you don't know when it occurred in the cooking process. If you're home, and the amount of time that the power was out is minimal, add it back into your end time. Or if the time is more than 30 minutes, finish the food by conventional cooking, adding more liquid, if necessary.

However, if you set the slow cooker before you left for work, and realize from electric clocks that power was off for more than an hour, it's best to discard the food, even if it looks done. You have no idea if the power outage occurred before the food passed through the danger zone.

Use "better safe than sorry" as a motto.

SLOW COOKER HINTS

Cooking in a slow cooker does not require any culinary techniques beyond the basics that you've used for years. You're slicing and dicing food, sometimes browning it, and measuring other ingredients accurately. But slow cookers can be perplexing if you're not accustomed to using one. Here are some general tips to help you master slow cooker conundrums:

- Remember that cooking times are wide approximations—within hours rather than minutes! That's because the age or power of a slow cooker, and the temperature of ingredients, must be taken into account. Check the food at the beginning of the stated cooking time, and then gauge if it needs more time, and about how much time. If carrots or cubes of potato are still rock-hard, for example, turn the heat to High if cooking on Low, and realize that you're looking at another hour or so.

- Foods cook faster on the bottom of a slow cooker than at the top because there are more heat coils and they are totally immersed in the simmering liquid.

- Appliance manufacturers say that slow cookers can be left on either High or Low unattended, but use your own judgment. If you're going to be out of the house all day, it's advisable to cook food on Low. If, on the other hand, you're going to be gone for just a few hours, the food will be safe on High.

- Use leaf versions of herbs such as thyme and rosemary rather than ground versions. Ground herbs tend to lose potency during many hours in the slow cooker.

- Don't add dairy products except at the end of the cooking time, as noted in the recipes. They can curdle if cooked for too long.

- Season the dishes with pepper at the end of cooking, because it can become harsh.

- If you want a sauce to have a more intense flavor, you can reduce the liquid in two ways. If cooking on Low, raise the heat to High, and remove the lid for the last hour of cooking. This will achieve some evaporation of the liquid. Or, remove the liquid either with a bulb baster or by straining it from the solids, and reduce it in a saucepan on the stove.

HINTS FOR SPEEDING UP SLOW COOKING

Remember that one hour of cooking on High achieves the same results as two hours on Low. Here are some ways to speed up food in the slow cooker:

- The first few hours of cooking on Low, and at least one hour if cooking on High, are spent bringing the liquid to a simmer. You can trim hours off a slow-cooked meal by adding liquid that is boiling, rather than at room temperature or chilled. To test how much time can be trimmed, place the amount of liquid in the slow cooker and see how long it takes to come to a boil on High. Don't subtract that entire time, because when cooking there will be other ingredients, too; so subtract half the time.

- If you'll be at home, or if you have a programmable slow cooker, start it for at least one hour on High before reducing the temperature to Low. This speeds up the course through the bacterial "danger zone."

SLOW COOKER CAUTIONS

While using a slow cooker is not nuclear physics by any measure, there are actions that you should not take with them:

- Never leave a slow cooker plugged in when not in use. It's all too easy to accidentally turn it on and not notice until the crockery insert cracks from overheating with nothing in it.

- As a corollary, do not preheat the empty insert while you're preparing the food because the insert could crack when you add the cold food.

- Never submerge the metal casing in water, or fill it with water. While the inside of the metal does occasionally get dirty, the best you can do is clean it with an abrasive cleaner and wipe it with a damp cloth or paper towel. While it's not aesthetically pleasing, do remember that food never touches the metal, so if there are a few drips here and there it's not really important.

- Always remember that the insert is fragile; it's not made from metal or heavy plastic. While not dropping it is the most obvious caution to keep it in one piece, also don't put a hot insert onto a cold counter; that could cause it to break, too. The reverse is also true; while you can use the insert as a casserole in a conventional oven (assuming the lid is glass and not plastic), it cannot be put into a preheated oven if chilled.

- Resist the temptation to look and stir. Every time you take the lid off the slow cooker you need to add 10 minutes of cooking time if cooking on High and 20 minutes if cooking on Low to compensate. Certain recipes in this book, especially those for fish, instruct you to add ingredients during the cooking time. In those cases the heat loss from opening the pot has been factored into the total cooking time.

- Always fill a slow cooker between one-half and two-thirds full for food safety as well as proper cooking. A slow cooker should always be at least half full so it can generate the necessary steam to kill bacteria. You also don't want it more than two-thirds full or the food in the center will not pass through the "danger zone" quickly enough.

- Don't add more liquid to a slow cooker recipe than that specified in the recipe. Even if the food is not submerged in liquid when you start, foods such as meats and vegetables give off liquid as they cook; in the slow cooker, that additional liquid does not evaporate.

- You'll notice that slow cooker recipes do not call for hot red pepper sauce or cayenne except at the very end of cooking; these foods become very bitter in the slow cooker.

- Always thaw food before placing it in the slow cooker. This is another maxim to follow to ensure that the trip from 40 to 140°F is accomplished quickly and efficiently. While adding a package of frozen green beans will slow up the cooking, starting with a frozen pot roast or chicken breast will make it impossible for the low temperature of the slow cooker to accomplish its task.

HIGH ALTITUDE ADJUSTMENT

Rules for slow cooking, along with all other modes of cooking, change when the slow cooker is located more than 3,000 feet above sea level. At high altitudes the air is thinner, so water boils at a lower temperature and comes to a boil more quickly. The rule is always to cook on High when above 3,000 feet; use the Low setting as a Keep Warm setting.

Other compensations are to reduce the liquid in a recipe by a few tablespoons, and add about 5 to 10 percent more cooking time. The liquid may be bubbling, but it's not 212°F at first.

CONVERTING CONVENTIONAL RECIPES

Not all dishes can easily be converted to slow-cooked dishes. Even if a dish calls for liquid, if it's supposed to be cooked or baked uncovered, chances are it will not be successfully transformed to a slow cooker recipe, because the food will not brown and the liquid will not evaporate.

But, if a dish is cooked covered in a conventional oven or simmered covered over low heat on top of the stove, it can be cooked in a slow cooker—as long as the quantity of the recipe is appropriate. A huge batch of stew that will fill the insert more than two-thirds full, or a small amount of sauce that only covers the bottom of the insert by a few inches, is not a good candidate. If this is the case, fiddle with the batch size to make it appropriate for the slow cooker.

The easiest way to convert your recipes is to find a similar one in this book and use its cooking time for guidance. When looking for a similar recipe, take into account the amount of liquid specified as well as the quantity of food. The liquid transfers the heat from the walls of the insert into the food itself, and the liquid heats in direct proportion to its measure. You should look for similar recipes as well as keeping in mind some general guidelines:

- Most any meat or poultry stew or roast takes 8 to 12 hours on Low or 4 to 6 hours on High.

- Chicken dishes cook more rapidly. Count on 6 to 8 hours on Low or 3 to 4 hours on High.

- Quadruple the time from conventional cooking to cooking on Low, and at least double it for cooking on High.

- Cut back on the amount of liquid used in stews and other braised dishes; the amount will depend on the recipe. Unlike cooking on the stove or in the oven, there is little to no evaporation in the slow cooker. If the food isn't totally covered with liquid when you start to cook, don't worry. Ingredients like meat, chicken, and many vegetables give off their own juices as they cook.

- For soups, cut back on the liquid by $1/4$ if the soup is supposed to simmer uncovered, and cut back by a few cups if the soup is simmered covered. Even when covered, a soup that is simmering on the stove has more evaporation than one cooked in the slow cooker.

- Add tender vegetables like tomatoes for only the last 45 minutes of cooking time.

DRESSING UP YOUR DISHES

One aspect many cooks perceive as a downside of the slow cooker is that most food is soft and has a uniform texture when it finishes cooking.

Now that you've mastered the basics of slow cooking and how to prepare foods, here are some ideas to help those delicious dishes garner a "Wow!" when they appear on the table:

- Instead of adding cheese to a dish for the last part of the cooking time, sprinkle it on top of the food right before you serve it. This is especially good with hard cheeses like Parmesan and feta.

- For an unexpected crunch, add toasted croutons to the tops of stews and soups before serving.

- Garnish with sprigs of the same fresh herbs used while cooking to add color.

- Toast nuts like slivered almonds and chopped walnuts in a 350°F oven for 5 minutes and sprinkle on stews before serving.

- Crumbled bacon is a good garnish for pork stews and hearty soups.

THE RATIONALE OF ROASTING

While most recipes in this book are made in the slow cooker, many give options for conventional cooking. That's where the science of roasting meats and poultry comes in. Large roasts—especially pork loins, hams, and turkeys—are a superb value in the cost per pound of edible meat. And you will find many recipes later in this book that give them second lives; those recipes are in sections called "The Second Time Around."

Roasting, as we use the term, is really oven baking, not roasting in the classic fashion, which is turning the meat on a spit over fire. Roasting depends on the air in the oven to transfer heat from the oven walls, which are heated by the gas flame or electric heating element.

Air, when compared with water or oil, is an inefficient heat carrier, so regardless of the temperature at which the oven is set, it will take a long time for the heat to transfer from the air to the meat's fibers and cook them.

It's a good rule of thumb that the further a cut of meat is from the animal's hoof or horn, the more tender it will be. The muscles in the legs and shoulders of animals are far more developed than those around their sides. For all animals, the loin, tenderloin, and rib sections are the most tender and the ones that should be roasted. Roasting the shoulder of a young animal, such as pork or lamb, is fine, but not for beef.

ROASTING RIGHT

Bring meat to room temperature before roasting. When you take them out of the refrigerator, rub them with salt and pepper, as well as with herbs, garlic or other flavorings, so that as they warm they will be absorbing flavor.

Microwave the meat on the defrost setting or Low (20 percent power). If using the defrost setting, enter into the microwave half the weight of the meat; if using the Low setting, the meat should be at room temperature in 2 to 5 minutes depending on the size. Check and repeat in 1-minute intervals until it reaches room temperature.

The key pieces of equipment for a roast are a low-sided baking pan and an instant-read meat thermometer. The roast should be placed in the pan so that it has 3 inches of space on all sides. If the pan is too large, the juices will burn during cooking. If it is too small or too deep, the meat will steam rather than roast.

Insert the instant-read thermometer into the center of the meat an equal distance from each end. Leave it in for 20 seconds, and then take the reading. Keep in mind that foods continue to cook after they are out of the oven; that's why the reading should be 5 to 10 degrees lower than the temperature you actually want. Here is a list of actual temperatures for different meats, so judge accordingly:

- Beef and lamb: 120°F—Rare; 125 to 130°F—Medium-Rare; 135°F—Medium

- Pork: 145 to 150°F

- Chicken and turkey: 165°F

It is only in the past year that the Food Safety and Inspection Service announced a change in the "Single Minimum Internal Temperature Established for Cooked Poultry." The new cooking recommendation is as follows:

"A whole turkey (and turkey parts) is safe when cooked to a minimum internal temperature of 165°F as measured with a food thermometer. Check the internal temperature in the innermost part of the thigh and wing and the thickest part of the breast. For reasons of personal preference, consumers may choose to cook turkey to higher temperatures."

This new cooking temperature is a change from previous 180°F for a whole turkey and 170°F for turkey breast. The same temperature is now used for whole chickens as well.

Chapter 3:
Egg-cetera: Great Dishes for Brunch or Light Supper

All cooking is based on food science. In this case, eggs remain tender if they are cooked at a low temperature. So, enter the slow cooker to make your egg dishes exceptional!

The protein in an egg becomes hard at 165°F, which is just about what the slow cooker heats to on Low. Eggs should be cooked to that temperature to make them totally safe and bacteria-free. The scientific reality is that if eggs are cooked at a high temperature, they toughen. That might be the objective if you're making fried eggs, because you need them to be hard enough that you can flip them in the pan without breaking them. But the recipes in this chapter are tender egg dishes, and the slow cooker treats them kindly.

In addition to the relatively low cost, a great reason to serve eggs is that they are almost like the chicken from which they come. Eggs are mildly flavored; they are like a blank canvas that absorbs flavor from seasoning and additional ingredients. There is an almost endless variety of both forms and flavors.

There are a number of recipes in this chapter for an easy and inexpensive family of dishes called strata, which is a fancy name for a savory bread pudding. Like their sweet relatives, strata developed as a great way to use up stale bread; in fact, they are better with it. So rather than buying fresh bread at the bakery, look for the area with the discounted baked goods. Every supermarket has one, and the cost is usually half or less than half of the fresh options.

There's no need to trim the crusts from bread when making a strata. These are rustic dishes, and the crusts provide some texture as well as color diversity in the finished dish. Cutting crusts is not only time-consuming, but it's also wasteful.

Another category of recipes you'll find in this chapter is frittatas; these are Italian-style omelets that are made in minutes and feed a crowd. It's easier to make one frittata—either in the slow cooker or with a combination of actions with a conventional stove—than to make individual omelets. They don't require turning, and—like strata—are open to endless variation.

EGGS 101

While the cost of eggs has risen along with every other food, they still represent an excellent value because they are considered nutrient dense; they provide excellent protein and a wide range of vitamins and minerals in proportion to their 75 to 80 calories per egg.

Egg protein is a complete protein and contains all the essential amino acids in a pattern that matches very closely the pattern the body needs. There are 5 grams of fat found in the yolk of a large egg, of which 2 grams are saturated and 3 grams are unsaturated; while egg yolks are high in cholesterol, about 275 mg per egg, the whites contain virtually no fat or cholesterol.

Eggs have gotten a bad nutritional reputation because of the fat and cholesterol in the yolk, not the white. The white is what gives eggs their ability to bind, and it is made up primarily of protein and water.

If you want to be judicious about cutting cholesterol, you can use any of the egg substitute products on the market; the best known one is Egg Beaters. Those products are essentially egg whites tinted yellow. But you can also make your own by using two egg whites for each whole egg, or if a recipe calls for several eggs, use two egg whites and one whole egg for every two whole eggs listed.

The sizes of eggs (Jumbo, Extra Large, Large, Medium, and Small) are determined by how much the eggs weigh per dozen. Most egg recipes call for Large or Extra Large eggs, so they are the ones stocked most often in supermarkets. The color of shells and yolks may vary, but color has nothing to do with egg quality, nutritive value, cooking characteristics, or shell thickness. The shell color comes from pigments in the outer layer of the shell, and varies from white to deep brown; it's determined by the breed of hen that lays the egg. Breeds with white ear lobes lay white eggs and breeds with red ears lay brown eggs.

Never buy cracked eggs because harmful bacteria can enter through the crack, so check them carefully. Once home, store eggs on a shelf in the refrigerator. When they are stored on the door, they can be harmed by the temperature fluctuations caused by opening and closing the door, and slamming the door can cause breakage.

Store eggs in the carton they come in to help prevent moisture loss, and to keep the eggs from picking up other odors. Never rinse eggs before using them since the water makes the shells porous and can cause the eggs to spoil faster and allow bacteria to enter.

Fresh, uncooked eggs can be kept for 4 to 5 weeks beyond their pack date if refrigerated in their cartons. Eggs age more in one day at room temperature than they would in one week in the refrigerator. In fact, properly handled eggs rarely "spoil," but instead are more likely to dry up.

If you're using Small eggs, increase the number by 1 for every 4 Large eggs specified in a recipe. If you're using Medium eggs, increase the number by 1 for every 6 Large eggs. On the other side, decrease the number of eggs called for by 1 for every 4 Jumbo eggs used instead of Large eggs, and by 1 for every 8 Extra Large eggs used instead of Large eggs.

Perfect Scrambled Eggs for a Crowd

I developed this recipe while running Nantucket Cuisine, a catering service on Nantucket, where Sunday brunch was a popular form of entertaining. It's foolproof and means you can serve hot scrambled eggs to a large group without being trapped in the kitchen. And any ingredient you would use to fill an omelet can be folded into these eggs.

Yield: 12–16 servings | **Active time:** 5 minutes | **Start to finish (minimum time, slow cooker):** 2 hours | **Start to finish (conventional):** 30 minutes

  4 tablespoons (½ stick) unsalted butter, sliced
  2 dozen large eggs
  ½ cup half-and-half
  ¼ cup sour cream
  Salt and freshly ground black pepper to taste

1. Place butter in the slow cooker, and cook on High for 15–20 minutes, or until butter melts.
2. Whisk eggs with half-and-half and sour cream, and season to taste with salt and pepper. Use a pastry brush to spread melted butter up the sides of the slow cooker, and then pour in egg mixture.
3. Reduce the heat to Low, and cook for 2–4 hours, or until eggs are set. Stir eggs after 1½ hours of cooking to break up the cooked egg portion. Serve immediately.

If cooking conventionally: Preheat the oven to 325°F, and place butter in a 10 x 14-inch baking pan. Place the pan in the oven while it heats for 3–5 minutes, or until butter melts. Whisk eggs as described in Step 2 above. Cover the pan with aluminum foil, and bake for 15 minutes. Remove the pan from the oven, and scrape the sides and bottom with a wooden spoon to dislodge cooked portion of eggs, breaking up any clumps. Recover the pan, bake another 10 minutes, and repeat procedure. Break up lumps with the spoon, and add any optional ingredients. Return the pan to the oven for 5 minutes, then serve immediately.

Note: The eggs can be prepared for baking up to 1 day in advance and refrigerated, tightly covered.

Variations:
- Add 1 cup grated cheddar, Monterey Jack, or Swiss cheese.
- Add ¼ cup chopped fresh herbs, such as a combination of chives, parsley, and basil.
- Add 1 cup sautéed onion and green bell pepper.
- Add 1 cup chopped baked ham, crumbled bacon, or cooked and crumbled sausage.

While eggs are marked with an expiration date, there's a simple test to determine how fresh they are. Place the eggs in a bowl of cold water. Eggs develop air pockets as they age, so if they sit on the bottom of the bowl, they're fresh. If they float on the surface of the bowl, they're getting old.

Salami and Spinach Frittata

I've discovered that Italian salami is a great low-cost substitute for expensive prosciutto, and it adds both flavor and color to this frittata, which is also punctuated with bits of olive.

Yield: 4–6 servings | **Active time:** 15 minutes | **Start to finish (minimum time, slow cooker):** 2¼ hours in a medium slow cooker | **Start to finish (conventional):** 30 minutes

 2 tablespoons olive oil
 1 medium onion, peeled and chopped
 2 garlic cloves, peeled and minced
 ⅓ pound Genoa salami, finely chopped
 8 large eggs
 3 tablespoons whole milk
 ¾ cup frozen chopped spinach, thawed and drained well
 ¼ cup chopped pimiento-stuffed green olives
 ¼ cup freshly grated Parmesan cheese
 2 tablespoons chopped fresh parsley
 ½ teaspoon dried thyme
 Salt and freshly ground black pepper to taste
 Vegetable oil spray or melted butter

If cooking conventionally:
 2 tablespoons (¼ stick) unsalted butter

1. Heat olive oil in a small skillet over medium-high heat. Add onion, garlic, and salami, and cook, stirring frequently, for 3–5 minutes, or until onion softens. Allow mixture to cool for 5 minutes.
2. Whisk eggs with milk in a mixing bowl. Stir in salami mixture, spinach, olives, Parmesan, parsley, thyme, and vegetable mixture. Season to taste with salt and pepper.
3. Grease the inside of the slow cooker insert liberally with vegetable oil spray or melted butter. Fold a sheet of heavy-duty aluminum foil in half, and place it in the bottom of the slow cooker with the sides of the foil extending up the sides of the slow cooker. Pour egg mixture into the slow cooker.
4. Cook on High for 2–2½ hours, or until eggs are set. Run a spatula around the sides of the slow cooker. Remove frittata from the slow cooker by pulling it up by the sides of the foil. Slide it gently onto a

serving platter, and cut it into wedges. Serve immediately, or at room temperature.

If cooking conventionally: Preheat the oven to 425°F. Follow the recipe to the end of Step 2. Heat butter in a large, ovenproof skillet over medium heat. Add egg mixture and cook for 4 minutes, or until bottom of cake is lightly brown. Transfer the skillet to the oven, and bake for 10–15 minutes, or until top is browned. Run a spatula around the sides of the skillet and under the bottom of the cake to release it. Slide cake gently onto a serving platter, and cut it into wedges. Serve immediately, or at room temperature.

Note: The vegetable mixture can be cooked up to 1 day in advance and refrigerated, tightly covered. Reheat the vegetables to room temperature in a microwave-safe dish, or over low heat, before completing the dish.

Variations:
- Substitute chopped baked ham for the salami.
- Substitute chopped broccoli, cooked according to package directions, for the spinach.

There are two ways to extract all the liquid from frozen spinach. For a whole package, place it in a colander and press with the back of a spoon. For a small amount, pick it up in your hand and squeeze it.

Bacon, Tomato, and Potato Frittata

Here's a frittata that's a whole meal in itself; it has some crispy potatoes included along with luscious cheese and tomatoes.

Yield: 4-6 servings | **Active time:** 20 minutes | **Start to finish (minimum time, slow cooker):** 2½ hours in a medium slow cooker | **Start to finish (conventional):** 40 minutes

½ pound bacon, cut into 1-inch lengths
2 large redskin potatoes, scrubbed and cut into ¼-inch dice
1 large onion, peeled and diced
6 large eggs
3 tablespoons half-and-half
2 ripe plum tomatoes, rinsed, cored, seeded, and chopped
½ cup grated sharp cheddar cheese
Salt and freshly ground black pepper to taste
Vegetable oil spray or melted butter

If cooking conventionally:
2 tablespoons unsalted butter

1. Place bacon in a skillet over medium-high heat. Cook for 5–7 minutes, or until bacon is crisp. Remove bacon from the pan with a slotted spoon, drain on paper towels, and set aside.

2. Discard all but 3 tablespoons bacon fat from the skillet. Add potatoes, and cook for 5 minutes, or until potatoes are tender, scraping them occasionally with a heavy spatula. Add onion to the skillet, and cook for 5 minutes, stirring occasionally, or until onion is soft. Allow mixture to cool for 5 minutes.

3. Whisk eggs with half-and-half in a mixing bowl. Stir in bacon, potato mixture, tomatoes, and cheese, and season to taste with salt and pepper.

4. Grease the inside of the slow cooker insert liberally with vegetable oil spray or melted butter. Fold a sheet of heavy-duty aluminum foil in half, and place it in the bottom of the slow cooker with the sides of the foil extending up the sides of the slow cooker. Pour egg mixture into the slow cooker.

5. Cook on High for 2–2½ hours, or until eggs are set. Run a spatula around the sides of the slow cooker. Remove frittata from the slow cooker by pulling it up by the sides of the foil. Slide it gently onto a

serving platter, and cut it into wedges. Serve immediately, or at room temperature.

If cooking conventionally: Preheat the oven to 425°F. Follow the recipe to the end of Step 3. Heat butter in a large, ovenproof skillet over medium heat. Add egg mixture and cook for 4 minutes, or until bottom of cake is lightly brown. Transfer the skillet to the oven, and bake for 10–15 minutes, or until top is browned. Run a spatula around the sides of the skillet and under the bottom of the cake to release it. Slide cake gently onto a serving platter, and cut it into wedges. Serve immediately, or at room temperature.

Note: The vegetable mixture can be cooked up to 1 day in advance and refrigerated, tightly covered. Reheat the vegetables to room temperature in a microwave-safe dish, or over low heat, before completing the dish.

Variations:
- Substitute Swiss cheese for the cheddar cheese.
- Substitute chopped baked ham for the bacon, and use 3 tablespoons vegetable oil to sauté vegetables.

> If your skillet has a plastic handle, wrap the handle with heavy-duty foil (or a double layer of regular foil) before placing it in the oven.

Mushroom and Italian Sausage Frittata

It's only fitting to include a few Italian recipes in this section; after all, frittatas are an Italian form! This one contains mushrooms in addition to sausage and cheese, and it's always a crowd-pleasing dish.

Yield: 4–6 servings | **Active time:** 20 minutes | **Start to finish (minimum time, slow cooker):** 2½ hours in a medium slow cooker | **Start to finish (conventional):** 30 minutes

    ½ pound bulk sweet or hot Italian sausage
    1 medium onion, peeled and diced
    1 garlic clove, peeled and minced
    ¼ pound mushrooms, wiped with a damp paper towel, trimmed,
      and thinly sliced
    8 large eggs
    ¼ cup half-and-half
    ½ cup grated mozzarella cheese
    1 teaspoon Italian seasoning
    Salt and freshly ground black pepper to taste
    Vegetable oil spray or melted butter

    If cooking conventionally:
    2 tablespoons unsalted butter

1. Place sausage in a skillet over medium-high heat. Cook for 5–7 minutes, breaking up lumps with a fork, or until sausage is browned. Remove sausage from the pan with a slotted spoon, drain on paper towels, and set aside.
2. Discard all but 2 tablespoons sausage fat from the skillet. Add onion, garlic, and mushrooms, and cook for 5 minutes, or until mushrooms are tender. Allow mixture to cool for 10 minutes.
3. Whisk eggs with half-and-half in a mixing bowl. Stir in sausage, vegetable mixture, cheese, and Italian seasoning, and season to taste with salt and pepper.
4. Grease the inside of the slow cooker insert liberally with vegetable oil spray or melted butter. Fold a sheet of heavy-duty aluminum foil in half, and place it in the bottom of the slow cooker with the sides of the foil extending up the sides of the slow cooker. Pour egg mixture into the slow cooker.

5. Cook on High for 2–2½ hours, or until eggs are set. Run a spatula around the sides of the slow cooker. Remove frittata from the slow cooker by pulling it up by the sides of the foil. Slide it gently onto a serving platter, and cut it into wedges. Serve immediately, or at room temperature.

If cooking conventionally: Preheat the oven to 425°F. Follow the recipe to the end of Step 3. Heat butter in a large, ovenproof skillet over medium heat. Add egg mixture and cook for 4 minutes, or until bottom of cake is lightly brown. Transfer the skillet to the oven, and bake for 10–15 minutes, or until top is browned. Run a spatula around the sides of the skillet and under the bottom of the cake to release it. Slide cake gently onto a serving platter, and cut it into wedges. Serve immediately, or at room temperature.

Note: The vegetable mixture can be cooked up to 1 day in advance and refrigerated, tightly covered. Reheat the vegetables to room temperature in a microwave-safe dish, or over low heat, before completing the dish.

Variation:
- Substitute ¼ pound thinly sliced zucchini or yellow squash for the mushrooms.

A fast and easy way to slice mushrooms—and make sure they are the same size—is with an egg slicer.

Southwestern Frittata

There are two types of chorizo: a raw bulk sausage and a hard, ready-to-eat sausage. This brightly flavored frittata uses raw chorizo, and its spicy flavor permeates the dish to deliver eggs with a punch.

Yield: 4–6 servings | **Active time:** 20 minutes | **Start to finish (minimum time, slow cooker):** 2¼ hours in a medium slow cooker | **Start to finish (conventional):** 40 minutes

> ½ pound bulk chorizo sausage
> 1 medium onion, peeled and chopped
> 2 garlic cloves, peeled and minced
> ½ green bell pepper, seeds and ribs removed, and chopped
> 1 tablespoon ground cumin
> 1 teaspoon dried oregano
> 8 large eggs
> ¼ cup half-and-half
> ½ cup grated jalapeño Jack cheese
> 1 (4-ounce) can chopped mild green chiles, drained
> ¾ cup canned red kidney beans, drained and rinsed
> Salt and freshly ground black pepper to taste
> Vegetable oil spray or melted butter

If cooking conventionally:
> 2 tablespoons unsalted butter

1. Place chorizo in a skillet over medium-high heat. Cook for 5–7 minutes, breaking up lumps with a fork, or until sausage is browned. Remove sausage from the pan with a slotted spoon, drain on paper towels, and set aside.
2. Discard all but 2 tablespoons fat from the skillet. Add onion, garlic, and green bell pepper, and cook for 5 minutes, or until vegetables soften. Add cumin and oregano, and cook for 1 minute, stirring constantly. Allow mixture to cool for 5 minutes.
3. Whisk eggs with half-and-half in a mixing bowl. Stir in chorizo, vegetable mixture, cheese, chiles, and beans, and season to taste with salt and pepper.
4. Grease the inside of the slow cooker insert liberally with vegetable oil spray or melted butter. Fold a sheet of heavy-duty aluminum foil in half, and place it in the bottom of the slow cooker with the sides of

the foil extending up the sides of the slow cooker. Pour egg mixture into the slow cooker.

5. Cook on High for 2–2½ hours, or until eggs are set. Run a spatula around the sides of the slow cooker. Remove frittata from the slow cooker by pulling it up by the sides of the foil. Slide it gently onto a serving platter, and cut it into wedges. Serve immediately, or at room temperature.

If cooking conventionally: Preheat the oven to 425°F. Follow the recipe to the end of Step 3. Heat butter in a large, ovenproof skillet over medium heat. Add egg mixture and cook for 4 minutes, or until bottom of cake is lightly brown. Transfer the skillet to the oven, and bake for 10–15 minutes, or until top is browned. Run a spatula around the sides of the skillet and under the bottom of the cake to release it. Slide cake gently onto a serving platter, and cut it into wedges. Serve immediately, or at room temperature.

Note: The vegetable mixture can be cooked up to 1 day in advance and refrigerated, tightly covered. Reheat the vegetables to room temperature in a microwave-safe dish, or over low heat, before completing the dish.

Variation:

- For a milder dish, substitute Monterey Jack for the jalapeño Jack, and omit the chiles.

Basic Cheese Strata

Here is your master recipe for a classic strata; it's loaded with cheese, and puffs almost like a soufflé while it cooks. As for other master recipes in this book, many general variations to dress it up follow.

Yield: 4–6 servings | **Active time:** 10 minutes | **Start to finish (minimum time, slow cooker):** 4¼ hours in a medium slow cooker | **Start to finish (conventional):** 1 hour

> 6 large eggs
> 2½ cups whole milk
> Salt and freshly ground black pepper to taste
> ½-pound loaf French or Italian bread, cut into ½-inch slices
> 1½ cups grated cheese (it can be cheddar, smoked cheddar, Swiss, Gruyère, whole-milk mozzarella, or a combination of any of these cheeses with freshly grated Parmesan)
> Vegetable oil spray or melted butter

1. Combine eggs, milk, salt, and pepper in a large mixing bowl. Whisk well. Add bread pieces to the bowl, and stir so bread absorbs egg mixture. Add cheese to bread mixture, and stir well. Allow mixture to sit for 10 minutes.

2. Grease the inside of the slow cooker insert liberally with vegetable oil spray or melted butter. Transfer bread mixture to the slow cooker. Cook on Low for 4–6 hours, or until puffed and an instant-read thermometer inserted in the center registers 165°F. Serve immediately.

If cooking conventionally: Preheat the oven to 350°F, and grease a 10 x 14-inch baking dish with vegetable oil spray or melted butter. Follow the recipe to the end of Step 1, and transfer mixture to the prepared pan. Cover the baking pan with aluminum foil, and bake in the center of the oven for 30 minutes. Remove the foil, and bake for an additional 15–20 minutes, or until puffed and an instant-read thermometer inserted in the center registers 165°F. Serve immediately.

Note: Using either cooking method, the strata can be baked up to 2 days in advance; reheat it in a 325°F oven, covered, for 20–25 minutes, or until hot.

Variations:

- Add 1–2 cups chopped or diced cooked ham, turkey, or chicken.
- Add ½ pound bacon, cooked, drained, and crumbled.
- Add ½ cup diced tomato.
- Add herbs, such as 1 teaspoon dried thyme, oregano, basil, or rosemary.
- Substitute olive bread, herb bread, or any flavored bread for the French bread.
- Add 1 cup sautéed onions and/or green bell peppers.

If you're cooking conventionally, you can hurry up baking a strata if you bake the bread mixture individually in muffin cups. Cover the muffin tin for 15 minutes, and then bake uncovered for 15 minutes.

Italian Sausage Strata

This is a hearty strata perfect for a fall or winter brunch or supper. It includes some vegetables along with the flavorful sausage. If serving it for supper, try spooning some marinara sauce over it.

Yield: 4–6 servings | **Active time:** 15 minutes | **Start to finish (minimum time, slow cooker):** 4¼ hours in a medium slow cooker | **Start to finish (conventional):** 1 hour

> 6 large eggs
> 2½ cups whole milk
> Salt and freshly ground black pepper to taste
> 1 cup grated mozzarella cheese
> ¼ cup chopped fresh parsley
> 2 teaspoons Italian seasoning
> ½-pound loaf French or Italian bread, cut into ½-inch slices
> ½ pound bulk sweet Italian sausage
> 1 large onion, peeled and diced
> 2 celery ribs, rinsed, trimmed, and chopped
> Vegetable oil spray or melted butter

1. Combine eggs, milk, salt, and pepper in a mixing bowl, and whisk well. Stir in cheese, parsley, and Italian seasoning. Add bread slices to the mixing bowl, and press them down so the bread will absorb liquid. Allow mixture to sit for 10 minutes.
2. Heat a large skillet over medium-high heat. Add sausage and cook, breaking up lumps with a fork, for 5–7 minutes, or until sausage is browned. Remove sausage from the skillet with a slotted spoon, transfer it to the bowl with bread, and discard all but 2 tablespoons sausage grease. Reduce the heat to medium, add onion and celery, and cook, stirring frequently, for 5–7 minutes, or until vegetables are soft. Stir vegetables into bread mixture.
3. Grease the inside of the slow cooker insert liberally with vegetable oil spray or melted butter. Transfer bread mixture to the slow cooker. Cook on Low for 4–6 hours, or until puffed and an instant-read thermometer inserted in the center registers 165°F. Serve immediately.

If cooking conventionally: Preheat the oven to 350°F, and grease a 10 x 14-inch baking dish with vegetable oil spray or melted butter. Follow the recipe to the end of Step 2, and transfer mixture to the prepared pan. Cover the baking pan with aluminum foil, and bake in the center of the oven for 30 minutes. Remove the foil, and bake for an additional 15-20 minutes, or until puffed and an instant-read thermometer inserted in the center registers 165°F. Serve immediately.

Note: Using either cooking method, the strata can be baked up to 2 days in advance; reheat it in a 325°F oven, covered, for 20–25 minutes, or until hot.

Variations:
- Substitute fresh fennel for the celery.
- Substitute herbes de Provence for the Italian seasoning.
- Substitute ground pork for the sausage for a milder dish.

> All sausages should be considered a "convenience food" because they add so much flavor to dishes with no additional ingredients listed in the recipe. Feel free to substitute sausage for ground meat in any recipe.

Jalapeño Jack Strata with Chorizo and Vegetables

Jalapeño Jack, which is a Monterey Jack cheese that comes already imbedded with flecks of fiery pepper, is not a convenience food; it's a real cheese and it's the same price as its mild cousin. But it is a convenience to have the peppers included, and they really enliven this strata.

Yield: 4-6 servings | **Active time:** 15 minutes | **Start to finish (minimum time, slow cooker):** 4¼ hours in a medium slow cooker | **Start to finish (conventional):** 1 hour

> 6 large eggs
> 2½ cups whole milk
> Salt and freshly ground black pepper to taste
> 1 cup grated jalapeño Jack cheese
> ½-pound loaf French or Italian bread, cut into ½-inch slices
> ⅔ cup chorizo or linguiça sausage, chopped
> 1 medium onion, peeled and diced
> 2 garlic cloves, peeled and minced
> ½ green bell pepper, seeds and ribs removed, and chopped
> 2 celery ribs, rinsed, trimmed, and chopped
> 1 (10-ounce) package frozen corn, thawed and drained
> Vegetable oil spray or melted butter

1. Combine eggs, milk, salt, and pepper in a mixing bowl, and whisk well. Stir in cheese, add bread slices to the mixing bowl, and press them down so that bread will absorb liquid. Allow mixture to sit for 10 minutes.

2. Heat a large skillet over medium-high heat. Add chorizo and cook for 5-7 minutes, or until chorizo is browned. Remove sausage from the skillet with a slotted spoon, add to the mixing bowl with bread, and discard all but 2 tablespoons sausage grease. Reduce the heat to medium, add onion, garlic, green bell pepper, and celery, and cook, stirring frequently, for 5-7 minutes, or until vegetables are soft. Stir vegetables and corn into bread mixture.

3. Grease the inside of the slow cooker insert liberally with vegetable oil spray or melted butter. Transfer bread mixture to the slow cooker. Cook on Low for 4-6 hours, or until puffed and an instant-read thermometer inserted in the center registers 165°F. Serve immediately.

If cooking conventionally: Preheat the oven to 350°F, and grease a 10 x 14-inch baking dish with vegetable oil spray or melted butter. Follow the recipe to the end of Step 2, and transfer mixture to the prepared pan. Cover the baking pan with aluminum foil, and bake in the center of the oven for 30 minutes. Remove the foil, and bake for an additional 15–20 minutes, or until puffed and an instant-read thermometer inserted in the center registers 165°F. Serve immediately.

Note: Using either cooking method, the strata can be baked up to 2 days in advance; reheat it in a 325°F oven, covered, for 20–25 minutes, or until hot.

Variations:
- For a milder dish, substitute Monterey Jack instead of the jalapeño Jack.
- Substitute chopped baked ham or cooked chicken for the chorizo.

Green bell peppers are specified for the recipes in this book because they are always less expensive than red bell peppers. Green bell peppers are immature red bell peppers that are not as perishable to ship, which is why they're less expensive. If you can find red bell peppers on sale, use them. They're sweeter.

Ham, Smoked Cheddar, and Sun-Dried Tomato Strata

The olive or antipasto bar in supermarkets is a wonderful bargain for foods like sun-dried tomatoes; you don't need that many and they don't weigh much. The same is true for different types of olives, and roasted red bell peppers. This is one of my favorite types of strata. The smoky taste of the cheese when joined to the ham and tomatoes is fantastic.

Yield: 4–6 servings | **Active time:** 15 minutes | **Start to finish (minimum time, slow cooker):** 4¼ hours in a medium slow cooker | **Start to finish (conventional):** 1 hour

> 6 large eggs
> 2½ cups whole milk
> Salt and freshly ground black pepper to taste
> 1 teaspoon herbes de Provence
> 1 cup grated smoked cheddar cheese
> ½-pound loaf French or Italian bread, cut into ½-inch slices
> ¾ pound baked ham, fat trimmed and chopped
> ½ cup sun-dried tomatoes, finely chopped
> Vegetable oil spray or melted butter

1. Combine eggs, milk, salt, pepper, and herbes de Provence in a mixing bowl, and whisk well. Stir in cheese, add bread slices to the mixing bowl, and press them down so that bread will absorb liquid. Allow mixture to sit for 10 minutes.
2. Stir ham and sun-dried tomatoes into bread mixture.
3. Grease the inside of the slow cooker insert liberally with vegetable oil spray or melted butter. Transfer bread mixture to the slow cooker. Cook on Low for 4–6 hours, or until puffed and an instant-read thermometer inserted in the center registers 165°F. Serve immediately.

If cooking conventionally: Preheat the oven to 350°F, and grease a 10 x 14-inch baking dish with vegetable oil spray or melted butter. Follow the recipe to the end of Step 2, and transfer mixture to the prepared pan. Cover the baking pan with aluminum foil, and bake in the center of the oven for 30 minutes. Remove the foil, and bake for an additional 15–20 minutes, or until puffed and an instant-read thermometer inserted in the center registers 165°F. Serve immediately.

Note: Using either cooking method, the strata can be baked up to 2 days in advance; reheat it in a 325°F oven, covered, for 20–25 minutes, or until hot.

Variations:
- Substitute smoked Gouda for the smoked cheddar.
- Substitute ½ cup sautéed green bell pepper for the sun-dried tomatoes.

If using sun-dried tomatoes packed in oil, always save the oil and use it in salad dressings.

Spinach and Swiss Cheese Strata

If you like creamed spinach, then this is the brunch dish for you, and because it uses frozen spinach it's incredibly easy to make.

Yield: 4–6 servings | **Active time:** 15 minutes | **Start to finish (minimum time, slow cooker):** 4¼ hours in a medium slow cooker | **Start to finish (conventional):** 1 hour

> 6 large eggs
> 2½ cups whole milk
> ½ teaspoon dried thyme
> Salt and freshly ground black pepper to taste
> ½-pound loaf French or Italian bread, cut into ½-inch slices
> 1 cup grated Swiss cheese
> 2 tablespoons unsalted butter
> 1 small onion, peeled and chopped
> 1 garlic clove, peeled and minced
> 1 (10-ounce) package frozen chopped spinach, thawed
> Vegetable oil spray or melted butter

1. Combine eggs, milk, thyme, salt, and pepper in a large mixing bowl. Whisk well. Add bread pieces to the bowl, and stir so bread absorbs egg mixture. Stir in Swiss cheese. Allow mixture to sit for 10 minutes.
2. Heat butter in a small skillet over medium-high heat. Add onion and garlic, and cook, stirring frequently, for 3 minutes, or until onion is translucent. Remove the pan from the heat, and set aside.
3. Place spinach in a colander and press with the back of a spoon to extract as much liquid as possible. Add onion mixture and spinach to bread mixture, and stir well.
4. Grease the inside of the slow cooker insert liberally with vegetable oil spray or melted butter. Transfer bread mixture to the slow cooker. Cook on Low for 4–6 hours, or until puffed and an instant-read thermometer inserted in the center registers 165°F. Serve immediately.

If cooking conventionally: Preheat the oven to 350°F, and grease a 10 x 14-inch baking dish with vegetable oil spray or melted butter. Follow the recipe to the end of Step 3, and transfer mixture to the prepared pan. Cover the baking pan with aluminum foil, and bake in the center of the oven for 30 minutes. Remove the foil, and bake for an additional 15–20 minutes, or until puffed and an instant-read thermometer inserted in the center registers 165°F. Serve immediately.

Note: Using either cooking method, the strata can be baked up to 2 days in advance; reheat it in a 325°F oven, covered, for 20–25 minutes, or until hot.

Variations:
- Substitute 1 (10-ounce) package frozen chopped broccoli for the spinach; cook it according to package directions before adding it to the bread mixture.
- Substitute cheddar cheese for the Swiss cheese.

Spinach and corn are the only two frozen vegetables that can be added to dishes just thawed rather than cooked. That's because both of them are quick-cooking, and the heat during the baking process is all that's needed to cook them thoroughly.

Ham and Vegetable Cornbread Strata

The cornbread base makes this a more homey strata than most, and a great accompaniment is some fried green tomatoes. While there is ham in the recipe, feel free to omit it, or serve slices of baked ham on the side.

Yield: 4-6 servings | **Active time:** 20 minutes | **Start to finish (minimum time, slow cooker):** 4¼ hours in a medium slow cooker | **Start to finish (conventional):** 1 hour

6 large eggs
2½ cups whole milk
Salt and freshly ground black pepper to taste
2 teaspoons dried sage
1 cup grated Monterey Jack cheese
6 cups firmly packed diced cornbread
3 tablespoons unsalted butter
1 medium onion, peeled and diced
1 green bell pepper, seeds and ribs removed, and finely chopped
1 carrot, peeled and finely chopped
1 celery rib, rinsed, trimmed, and finely chopped
¾ pound smoked ham, cut into ½-inch dice
Vegetable oil spray or melted butter

1. Combine eggs, milk, salt, pepper, and sage in a mixing bowl, and whisk well. Stir in cheese, and add cornbread to the mixing bowl, and press them down so that bread will absorb liquid. Allow mixture to sit for 10 minutes.

2. Heat butter in a large skillet over medium heat. Add onion, green pepper, carrot, and celery. Cook, stirring frequently, for 7–10 minutes, or until vegetables are soft. Stir vegetables and ham into bread mixture.

3. Grease the inside of the slow cooker insert liberally with vegetable oil spray or melted butter. Transfer bread mixture to the slow cooker. Cook on Low for 4–6 hours or until the mixture is puffed and an instant-read thermometer inserted in the center registers 165°F. Serve immediately.

If cooking conventionally: Preheat the oven to 350°F, and grease a 10 x 14-inch baking dish with vegetable oil spray or melted butter. Follow the recipe to the end of Step 2, and transfer mixture to the prepared pan. Cover the baking pan with aluminum foil, and bake in the center of the oven for 30 minutes. Remove the foil, and bake for an additional 15–20 minutes, or until the mixture is puffed and an instant-read thermometer inserted in the center registers 165°F. Serve immediately.

When selecting cornbread for this, or any other savory recipe, buy or make one that does not contain sugar, or only a modest amount of sugar. Some cornbread mixes produce a product that is more a cake than bread. That will be too sweet for this savory strata recipe. If the cornbread is very moist, cut back by ¼ cup on the amount of milk in the recipe.

Variation:
- Substitute bulk pork sausage, cooked for 5–7 minutes, or until browned, for the ham.

> Using either cooking method, the strata can be baked up to 2 days in advance; reheat it in a 325°F oven, covered, for 20–25 minutes, or until hot.

Sausage and Apple Strata

American breakfast sausage is one of those foods that can be used as a savory accent in a sweet dish or as the star of a savory dish. In the case of this strata, there's a touch of sweetness from the fruit and maple syrup, and the sausage balances that nicely.

Yield: 4-6 servings | **Active time:** 20 minutes | **Start to finish (minimum time, slow cooker):** 4¼ hours in a medium slow cooker | **Start to finish (conventional):** 1 hour

> 6 large eggs
> 2½ cups whole milk
> 2 tablespoons pure maple syrup
> 2 teaspoons dried sage
> ¾ teaspoon ground cinnamon
> Salt and freshly ground black pepper to taste
> 1 cup grated Monterey Jack cheese
> ½ cup raisins
> ½-pound loaf French or Italian bread, cut into ½-inch slices
> ¾ pound bulk pork breakfast sausage
> 2 tablespoons unsalted butter
> 1 small onion, peeled and diced
> 1 large McIntosh or Golden Delicious apple, peeled, cored, quartered, and chopped
> Vegetable oil spray or melted butter

1. Combine eggs, milk, maple syrup, sage, cinnamon, salt, and pepper in mixing bowl, and whisk well. Stir in cheese and raisins. Add bread slices to the mixing bowl, and press them down so that bread will absorb liquid. Allow mixture to sit for 10 minutes.

2. Place a large skillet over medium-high heat. Add sausage, breaking up lumps with a fork. Cook sausage, stirring frequently, for 5-7 minutes, or until browned and no longer pink. Remove sausage from the skillet with a slotted spoon, and add to bread mixture. Discard sausage grease.

3. Return the skillet to the stove, and reduce the heat to medium. Add butter and onion. Cook, stirring frequently, for 3 minutes, or until onion is translucent. Add apple, and cook, stirring frequently, for 3 minutes, or until apple begins to soften. Stir contents of the skillet into bread mixture.

4. Grease the inside of the slow cooker insert liberally with vegetable oil spray or melted butter. Transfer bread mixture to the slow cooker. Cook on Low for 4–6 hours or until the mixture is puffed and an instant-read thermometer inserted in the center registers 165°F. Serve immediately.

If cooking conventionally: Preheat the oven to 350°F, and grease a 10 x 14-inch baking dish with vegetable oil spray or melted butter. Follow the recipe to the end of Step 2, and transfer mixture to the prepared pan. Cover the baking pan with aluminum foil, and bake in the center of the oven for 30 minutes. Remove the foil, and bake for an additional 15–20 minutes, or until the mixture is puffed and an instant-read thermometer inserted in the center registers 165°F. Serve immediately.

Note: Using either cooking method, the strata can be baked up to 2 days in advance; reheat it in a 325°F oven, covered, for 20–25 minutes, or until hot.

Variation:
- Substitute ripe pear or peach for the apple.

Enchilada Brunch Casserole

This is one of my favorite brunch dishes; the filling is a flavorful corn custard, with cornmeal reinforcing the corn kernels. Then the spicy sausage and cheese add sparkle.

Yield: 6–8 servings | **Active time:** 15 minutes | **Start to finish (minimum time, slow cooker):** N/A | **Start to finish (conventional):** 1¼ hours

½ pound bulk chorizo sausage
6 scallions, white parts and 3 inches of green tops, rinsed, trimmed, and thinly sliced
2 (10-ounce) packages frozen corn, thawed, divided
1 (8-ounce) package cream cheese
½ cup yellow cornmeal
6 large eggs
2 tablespoons granulated sugar
2 cups grated jalapeño Jack cheese, divided
1½ teaspoons dried oregano, preferably Mexican
Salt and cayenne to taste
¾ cup whole milk
8 (6-inch) corn tortillas

1. Preheat oven to 350°F, and grease a shallow 2-quart casserole.
2. Place a medium skillet over medium-high heat. Add chorizo, and cook for 3–5 minutes, stirring occasionally, or until chorizo is lightly browned. Add scallions to the skillet, and cook for 2 minutes, stirring occasionally. Set aside.
3. Combine 1 package of corn, cream cheese, cornmeal, eggs, sugar, 1 cup cheese, oregano, salt, cayenne, and milk in food processor fitted with a steel blade or in a blender. Puree until smooth.
4. Transfer mixture to a mixing bowl, and stir in remaining corn and chorizo mixture. Place 4 tortillas in the bottom of the prepared pan. Layer ½ corn mixture on top of tortillas, and sprinkle top with ½ cup remaining cheese. Repeat with remaining tortillas, corn mixture, and cheese.
5. Cover the pan with aluminum foil, and bake for 30 minutes. Remove the foil, and return casserole to oven for an additional 30 minutes, or until custard is set and top is brown. Allow to stand for 5 minutes before serving.

Note: The dish can be prepared for baking up to 1 day in advance, and refrigerated, tightly covered. Add 15 minutes to covered baking time if chilled.

Variations:
- For a milder dish, substitute Monterey Jack for the jalapeño Jack.
- For a vegetarian dish, substitute 1 (15-ounce) can red kidney beans, drained and rinsed, for the chorizo.

If an egg falls and breaks on the floor, cover the mess with lots of salt and let it stand for 20 minutes. After that time, it should be solid enough to sweep into a dust pan.

Cheddar Grits with Ham

Grits nowadays means hominy grits made from corn that has been ground with steel rollers, which, in essence, cooks the corn. This makes it quicker to cook. However, grits can also be made from wheat or rice. The term refers to any coarsely ground grain.

Yield: 4–6 servings | **Active time:** 15 minutes | **Start to finish (minimum time, slow cooker):** N/A | **Start to finish (conventional):** 1 hour

2 1/2 cups water
2/3 cup quick-cooking white grits
1/2 teaspoon dried thyme
Salt and freshly ground black pepper to taste
1 cup grated sharp cheddar cheese, divided
2 tablespoons unsalted butter, cut into small bits
1/2 pound baked ham, trimmed of fat and cut into 1/2-inch dice
1/2 cup whole milk
3 large eggs, lightly beaten
Vegetable oil spray or melted butter

1. Preheat the oven to 350°F, and grease a 9 x 13-inch baking pan with vegetable oil spray or melted butter.
2. Bring water to a boil in a heavy saucepan over high heat. Stir in grits, thyme, salt, and pepper. Reduce the heat to medium-low, cover the pan, and cook, stirring occasionally, for 15 minutes, or until grits are very thick. Remove the pan from the heat, and stir in 3/4 cup cheddar and butter.
3. Cool 10 minutes, then stir in ham, milk, and eggs. Spoon mixture into the prepared pan. Cover the pan with aluminum foil, and bake for 30 minutes. Uncover the pan, sprinkle with remaining cheese, and bake for an additional 15 minutes, or until set and top is browned. Allow to stand for 5 minutes before serving.

Note: The dish can be prepared for baking up to 1 day in advance, and refrigerated, tightly covered. Add 15 minutes to initial covered baking time if chilled.

Variations:

- Substitute jalapeño Jack for the cheddar cheese for a spicier dish.
- Substitute ½ pound bulk pork sausage, cooked and crumbled, for the ham.

It's always cheaper to buy a large ham when it's on sale and bake it at 325°F for 20 minutes per pound. The price per pound of edible meat is a fraction of what you pay at the deli department.

Chapter 4:
Simmering Soups: Meals in a Bowl

There's an old Spanish proverb that says, "Of soup and love, the first is best." And I tend to agree. A bowl of steaming soup in winter warms you from the inside out, and makes even the harshest day seem better.

Those comforting, filling soups are the recipes you'll find in this chapter, and if you make them with good homemade stocks, they are one of the least expensive meals you can serve—many are only $1 per serving, which eases the strain on your food budget so that another night's meal can be a treat.

Keep in mind that your food budget, regardless of how stringent, is a gross amount for the week. If you eat one of these soups for dinner a few nights a week—and all of them freeze beautifully—then you can splurge on that shrimp dish or grilled steak on another night—especially if one of these luxury foods is on sale.

More than any other category of food, soups are open to endless variation and additions. If it's a vegetable soup, you can add any leftover vegetable you may have from another dinner. If the soup calls for pasta, but you have leftover rice, use it instead.

The serving size for these recipes was calculated based on serving the soup *as* the meal, but if you're serving one of these soups as an appetizer *before* a dinner entrée, you can double or triple the number of people these recipes will feed.

This chapter leads off with many vegetarian recipes that can become the repository for many categories of leftover protein to make them heartier. I've made the Vegetarian Tortilla Soup with everything from cubes of cooked chicken to the trimmings from a pork roast. So feel free to experiment, and always make the whole batch of soup; it's wonderful to have around in your freezer.

STOCKING UP

At the end of this chapter you'll find recipes for basic homemade stocks; these stocks are also referenced in countless recipes for other dishes in this book. Stocks are no more difficult to make than boiling water; all they are is lots of water in which other ingredients simmer for many hours to create water with an enriched flavor.

You may be thinking, "Why should I make stock when there are so many bargain brands on the supermarket shelves?" If that's the case, there are three compelling reasons to make your own: money, health, and flavor. Homemade stock costs virtually pennies to make, and its flavor is far superior to that found in even the highest-priced containers, which are more expensive than a quart of milk or jug of juice—foods you can't make yourself. Additionally, even stocks billed as "low-sodium" contain a lot of it, along with other preservatives.

In the same way that you can utilize bits of leftover vegetables in soups, many of the vegetables that go into stocks would otherwise end up in the garbage can or the compost bin. Save those carrot and onion peelings, parsley stems, the base of a celery stalk, and the dark green scallion tops. All of those foods might not wend their way into cooking a dish, but they're fine for stock!

I keep different bags in my freezer in anticipation of making stock on a regular basis. There are individual ones for chicken trimmings, beef (but not pork) trimmings, fish skin and bones, and vegetables past their prime and their trimmings. When one bag is full, it's time to make stock.

You'll notice that I do not give directions for how to make stocks in the slow cooker, and the reason is that stocks have to simmer for so long to develop flavor that the slow cooker is not efficient to make a large quantity. And a large quantity is what you should make to have it handy at all times.

Once you've cooked your stock—and removed the fat from chicken and beef stock—you should freeze it in containers of different sizes. I do about half a batch in heavy, resealable quart bags; they are the basis for soups. Bags take up less room in the freezer than containers. Freeze them flat on a baking sheet, and you can stack them on a freezer shelf or in the cubbyholes on the freezer door.

I then freeze stock in 1-cup measures and some in ice cube trays. Measure the capacity of your ice cube tray with a measuring table-spoon; it will be somewhere between 1 and 3 tablespoons. Keep a bag of stock cubes for those recipes that require just a small amount.

Vegetarian Tortilla Soup

Filled with healthful vegetables in a tantalizing broth, this soup permeates the kitchen with its aroma as it cooks. It's topped with crispy tortilla strips and buttery avocado for textural interest.

Yield: 4–6 servings | **Active time:** 20 minutes | **Start to finish (minimum time, slow cooker):** 3½ hours in a medium slow cooker | **Start to finish (conventional):** 45 minutes

    2 tablespoons olive oil
    2 medium onions, peeled and diced
    4 garlic cloves, peeled and minced
    1 small jalapeño or serrano chile, seeds and ribs removed, and
        chopped
    1 tablespoon dried oregano
    1 tablespoon chili powder
    1 tablespoon smoked Spanish paprika
    2 teaspoons ground cumin
    1 (14.5-ounce) can diced tomatoes, undrained
    5 cups Vegetable Stock (recipe on page 86) or purchased stock
        (5½ cups if cooking conventionally)
    2 tablespoons tomato paste
    1 celery rib, rinsed, trimmed, and sliced
    1 small zucchini, rinsed, trimmed, and cut into ¾-inch dice
    1 small yellow squash, rinsed, trimmed, and cut into ¾-inch dice
    1 large carrot, peeled and sliced
    1 medium potato, peeled and cut into ½-inch dice
    1 (15-ounce) can kidney beans, drained and rinsed
    Salt and freshly ground black pepper to taste
    ½ cup vegetable oil
    4 corn tortillas, cut into ½-inch strips
    1 ripe avocado, peeled and diced
    ⅔ cup grated Monterey Jack cheese

1. Heat olive oil in a large skillet over medium heat. Add onions, garlic, and chile, and cook, stirring frequently, for 3 minutes, or until onions are translucent. Add oregano, chili powder, paprika, and cumin. Cook for 1 minute, stirring constantly. Add tomatoes, and stir well.
2. Puree mixture in a food processor fitted with a steel blade or in a blender. Scrape puree into the slow cooker, and add stock and tomato

paste. Stir well. Add celery, zucchini, yellow squash, carrot, potato, and beans to the slow cooker.

3. Cook on Low for 6–8 hours or on High for 3–4 hours, or until potatoes are tender. Season to taste with salt and pepper.

4. About 30 minutes before soup will be finished, heat vegetable oil in a medium skillet over high heat. Add tortilla strips, and fry until crisp. Remove strips from the pan with a slotted spatula, and drain on paper towels.

5. To serve, ladle soup into bowls, and garnish each serving with fried tortilla strips, avocado, and cheese.

If cooking conventionally: Follow the recipe to the end of Step 2, assembling the dish in a saucepan, and adding the additional ½ cup stock to the ingredients. Bring to a boil, then reduce the heat to low and simmer soup, covered, for 20–25 minutes, or until potatoes are tender. Season soup to taste with salt and pepper. While soup simmers, heat vegetable oil in a medium skillet over high heat. Add tortilla strips, and fry until crisp. Remove strips from the pan with a slotted spatula, and drain on paper towels. To serve, ladle soup into bowls, and garnish each serving with fried tortilla strips, avocado, and cheese.

Note: Using either cooking method, the soup can be made up to 2 days in advance and refrigerated, tightly covered. Reheat it over low heat, covered. Do not fry the tortilla strips or cut the avocado until just prior to serving.

Variation:

- To make the soup heartier, substitute chicken stock for the vegetable stock, and add ¾ pound of boneless, skinless chicken thighs, cut into ½-inch dice.

Caribbean Sweet Potato Soup

Creamy coconut milk mellows the curry flavor in this thick and hearty chowder made with sweet potatoes and other vegetables. Serve it with a tossed salad and some crusty bread.

Yield: 4–6 servings | **Active time:** 20 minutes | **Start to finish (minimum time, slow cooker):** 3½ hours in a medium slow cooker | **Start to finish (conventional oven):** 45 minutes

> 2 tablespoons olive oil
> 1 medium onion, peeled and chopped
> 2 garlic cloves, peeled and minced
> 1 large carrot, peeled and diced
> 1 green bell pepper, seeds and ribs removed, and diced
> 1 tablespoon curry powder
> 1 tablespoon grated fresh ginger
> 1½ pounds sweet potatoes, peeled and cut into ¾-inch dice
> 3 cups Vegetable Stock (recipe on page 86) or purchased stock
>   (3½ cups if cooking conventionally)
> 1 (14-ounce) can light coconut milk
> Salt and freshly ground black pepper to taste

1. Heat oil in a large skillet over medium-high heat. Add onion, garlic, carrot, and green bell pepper, and cook, stirring frequently, for 3 minutes, or until onion is translucent. Stir in curry powder and ginger, and cook, stirring constantly, for 1 minute. Scrape mixture into the slow cooker.

2. Add sweet potatoes, stock, and coconut milk to the slow cooker. Stir well.

3. Cook soup on Low for 6–8 hours or High for 3–4 hours, or until vegetables are tender.

4. Remove ¼ of solids from soup with a slotted spoon, and place in a food processor fitted with a steel blade or in a blender. Puree until smooth, and stir puree back into soup. Season to taste with salt and pepper, and ladle soup into bowls.

If cooking conventionally: Follow the recipe to the end of Step 2, assembling the dish in a saucepan, and adding the additional ½ cup stock to the ingredients. Bring to a boil, then reduce the heat to low and simmer soup, covered, for 25–35 minutes, or until vegetables are tender.

Remove ¼ of solids from soup with a slotted spoon, and place in a food processor fitted with a steel blade or in a blender. Puree until smooth, and stir puree back into soup. Season to taste with salt and pepper, and ladle soup into bowls.

Note: Using either cooking method, the soup can be made up to 2 days in advance and refrigerated, tightly covered. Reheat it over low heat, covered.

Variations:

- Turn this into a seafood chowder by substituting seafood stock for the vegetable stock, and adding 1 pint of minced clams. Drain the clams and count the clam juice as part of your stock amount. Add the clams 2 hours before the end of cooking on Low, 1 hour on High, or 20 minutes if cooking conventionally.
- Substitute chicken stock for the vegetable stock, and add either 2 cups of cooked and diced chicken at the end of the cooking time, or add ¾ pound boneless, skinless chicken, cut into ½-inch dice, at the start of the cooking time.
- Substitute carrots, peeled and cut into ½-inch slices, for the sweet potatoes if watching your carbohydrates.

Italian Bean and Barley Soup

Barley is an ancient grain, and it creates a thick and robust soup flavored with many vegetables and herbs as well as delicate cannellini beans. Serve it with garlic bread and a tossed salad to complete the meal.

Yield: 4–6 servings | **Active time:** 20 minutes | **Start to finish (minimum time, slow cooker):** 4 hours | **Start to finish (conventional oven):** 1 hour

3 tablespoons olive oil
1 large onion, peeled and diced
3 garlic cloves, peeled and minced
2 celery ribs, rinsed, trimmed, and sliced
2 carrots, peeled and sliced
1 green bell pepper, seeds and ribs removed, and diced
3/4 cup pearl barley, rinsed well
5 cups Vegetable Stock (recipe on page 86) or purchased stock
  (5 1/2 cups if cooking conventionally)
1 (15-ounce) can cannellini beans, drained and rinsed
1 (14.5-ounce) can diced tomatoes, undrained
1 (8-ounce) can tomato sauce
2 tablespoons chopped fresh parsley
1 tablespoon Italian seasoning
1 bay leaf
1 (10-ounce) package frozen leaf spinach, thawed and drained
2/3 cup freshly grated Parmesan cheese
Salt and freshly ground black pepper to taste

1. Heat oil in a large skillet over medium-high heat. Add onion, garlic, celery, carrot, and green bell pepper, and cook, stirring frequently, for 3 minutes, or until onion is translucent. Scrape mixture into the slow cooker.

2. Add barley, stock, beans, tomatoes, tomato sauce, parsley, Italian seasoning, and bay leaf to the slow cooker. Stir well.

3. Cook soup on Low for 6–8 hours or High for 3–4 hours, or until vegetables are tender. If cooking on Low, raise the heat to High. Stir spinach and Parmesan into the slow cooker, and cook for 20–30 minutes, or until cheese melts.

4. Remove and discard bay leaf, season to taste with salt and pepper, and ladle soup into bowls.

If cooking conventionally: Follow the recipe to the end of Step 2, assembling the dish in a saucepan, and adding the additional ½ cup stock to the ingredients. Bring to a boil, then reduce the heat to low and simmer soup, covered, for 35–40 minutes, or until vegetables are tender. Stir in spinach and Parmesan cheese, and cook for 5 minutes. Remove and discard bay leaf, season to taste with salt and pepper, and ladle soup into bowls.

Note: Using either cooking method, the soup can be made up to 2 days in advance and refrigerated, tightly covered. Reheat it over low heat, covered. More stock or water might have to be added if the soup is chilled; the barley keeps absorbing liquid after cooking.

Variations:
- Substitute chicken stock for the vegetable stock, and add ¾ pound boneless, skinless chicken, cut into ½-inch dice, at the start of the cooking time.
- Substitute beef stock for the vegetable stock, and add ¾ pound boneless beef stew meat, cut into ½-inch dice, at the start of the cooking time.

Classic Cuban Black Bean Soup

Black bean soup is synonymous with the best of vegetarian cooking, and this version is replete with flavor from the aromatic spices and vegetables included with the beans in the slow cooker. Try some cheese quesadillas as an accompaniment.

Yield: 4–6 servings | **Active time:** 15 minutes | **Start to finish (minimum time, slow cooker):** 3¼ hours in a medium slow cooker | **Start to finish (conventional):** 50 minutes

¼ cup olive oil
1 large onion, peeled and finely chopped
1 green bell pepper, seeds and ribs removed, and finely chopped
6 garlic cloves, peeled and minced
1–2 jalapeño or serrano chiles, seeds removed, and finely diced
2 tablespoons ground cumin
1 tablespoon ground coriander
5 cups Vegetable Stock (recipe page 86) or purchased stock (5½ cups if cooking conventionally)
4 (15-ounce) cans black beans, drained and rinsed
Salt and freshly ground black pepper to taste
¼ cup chopped fresh cilantro
Sour cream (optional)
Lime wedges (optional)

1. Heat oil in a medium skillet over medium-high heat. Add onion, green bell pepper, garlic, and chiles. Cook, stirring frequently, for 3 minutes, or until onion is translucent. Reduce the heat to low, and stir in cumin and coriander. Cook, stirring constantly, for 1 minute. Scrape the mixture into the slow cooker.
2. Add stock and beans to the slow cooker.
3. Cook soup on Low for 6–8 hours or High for 3–4 hours, or until vegetables are soft.
4. Puree ¾ of soup in a food processor fitted with a steel blade or in a blender, and return puree to the slow cooker. Season to taste with salt and pepper, and stir in cilantro. Ladle soup into bowls, passing sour cream and lime wedges separately, if using.

If cooking conventionally: Follow the recipe to the end of Step 2, assembling the dish in a saucepan, and adding the additional ½ cup stock to the ingredients. Bring to a boil, then reduce the heat to low and simmer soup, covered, for 30–35 minutes. Puree ¾ of soup in a food processor fitted with a steel blade or in a blender, and return puree to the slow cooker. Season to taste with salt and pepper, and stir in cilantro. Ladle soup into bowls, passing sour cream and lime wedges separately, if using.

Note: Using either cooking method, the soup can be made up to 2 days in advance and refrigerated, tightly covered. Reheat it over low heat, covered.

Variation:

• Add 1½ cups diced cooked chicken or ham.

To make a soup with dried beans rather than canned, figure that 1 pound of dried beans equals 4 (15-ounce) cans. The dried beans need to be cooked before using them, however.

Cheddar Potato Chowder

Potatoes and cheese are a natural combination, and they form the centerpiece of this thick and rich chowder. Serve it with some crunchy coleslaw and cornbread.

Yield: 4–6 servings | **Active time:** 20 minutes | **Start to finish (minimum time, slow cooker):** 4 hours in a medium slow cooker | **Start to finish (conventional):** 50 minutes

  3 tablespoons unsalted butter
  1 medium onion, peeled and diced
  1 carrot, peeled and diced
  1 celery rib, rinsed, trimmed, and diced
  1 garlic clove, peeled and minced
  2 pounds redskin potatoes, scrubbed and diced
  4 cups Vegetable Stock (recipe on page 86) or purchased stock
   (4½ cups if cooking conventionally)
  1 teaspoon dried thyme
  1½ cups grated sharp cheddar cheese
  1 cup half-and-half
  Salt and freshly ground black pepper to taste
  3 tablespoons chopped fresh parsley

1. Heat butter in a medium skillet over medium-high heat. Add onion, carrot, celery, and garlic, and cook, stirring frequently, for 3 minutes, or until onion is translucent. Scrape mixture into the slow cooker.

2. Add potatoes, stock, and thyme to the slow cooker. Stir well.

3. Cook on Low for 6–8 hours or on High for 3–4 hours, or until vegetables are tender.

4. If cooking on Low, raise the heat to High. Mash some of vegetables with a potato masher until consistency you want is reached; the more that is mashed the thicker the soup will be. Add cheese and half-and-half, and cook for 30–40 minutes, or until cheese melts and soup simmers. Season to taste with salt and pepper, and ladle soup into bowls, sprinkling each serving with chopped parsley.

If cooking conventionally: Follow the recipe to the end of Step 2, assembling the dish in a saucepan, and adding the additional ½ cup stock to the ingredients. Bring to a boil, then reduce the heat to low and simmer soup, covered, for 25–30 minutes, or until vegetables are tender. Mash some of vegetables with a potato masher until consistency you want is reached; the more that is mashed the thicker the soup will be. Add cheese and half-and-half, and cook for 5–10 minutes, or until cheese melts and soup simmers. Season to taste with salt and pepper, and ladle soup into bowls, sprinkling each serving with chopped parsley.

Note: Using either cooking method, the soup can be made up to 2 days in advance and refrigerated, tightly covered. Reheat it over low heat, covered.

Variations:

- For a Southwestern chowder, add 1 (4-ounce) can diced mild green chiles, and 1 tablespoon ground cumin, and substitute cilantro for the parsley.
- Add 1 (10-ounce) package frozen corn or 1 10-ounce package frozen mixed vegetables, thawed, along with the cream and cheese.
- Substitute Swiss cheese for the cheddar cheese, and add 1 (10-ounce) package frozen chopped spinach, thawed and drained well, along with the cream and cheese.
- Substitute chicken stock for the vegetable stock, and add 1½ cups diced cooked chicken or turkey to the soup.

One of the benefits of using redskin potatoes is that they never need peeling. But if you substitute Russet potatoes, do peel them first.

Southwest Creamy Chicken, Corn, and Sweet Potato Chowder

Chipotle chiles are smoked jalapeño chiles that add a smoky nuance to this creamy chowder that is flecked with corn and other vegetables. Some warm corn tortillas and a salad with avocado work well to complete the meal.

Yield: 4–6 servings | **Active time:** 20 minutes | **Start to finish (minimum time, slow cooker):** 4 hours in a medium slow cooker | **Start to finish (conventional):** 1 hour

4–6 boneless, skinless chicken thighs

3 tablespoons unsalted butter

1 green bell pepper, seeds and ribs removed, and chopped

1 large onion, peeled and diced

2 garlic cloves, peeled and minced

2 large sweet potatoes, peeled and cut into ½-inch dice

4 cups Chicken Stock (recipe on page 84) or purchased stock (4½ cups if cooking conventionally)

2 canned chipotle chiles in adobo sauce, finely chopped

2 teaspoons adobo sauce

1 (15-ounce) can creamed corn

1 cup frozen corn, thawed

1½ cups half-and-half

Salt and freshly ground black pepper to taste

¼ cup firmly packed fresh cilantro leaves

1. Rinse chicken and pat dry with paper towels. Trim chicken of all visible fat, and cut into ½-inch cubes. Place chicken in the slow cooker.

2. Heat butter in a heavy skillet over medium-high heat. Add green pepper, onion, and garlic. Cook, stirring frequently, for 3 minutes, or until onion is translucent. Scrape mixture into the slow cooker. Add sweet potatoes, stock, chipotle chiles, and adobo sauce to the slow cooker. Stir well.

3. Cook on Low for 6–8 hours or on High for 3–4 hours, or until chicken and potatoes are almost tender.

4. If cooking on Low, raise the heat to High. Stir in creamed corn, thawed corn, and half-and-half. Cook for an additional 30–40 minutes, or until corn is cooked and soup is bubbly. Season to taste with salt and pepper, and ladle soup into bowls, sprinkling each serving with cilantro.

If cooking conventionally: Follow the recipe to the end of Step 2, assembling the dish in a saucepan, and adding the additional ½ cup stock to the ingredients. Bring to a boil, then reduce the heat to low and simmer soup, covered, for 30–35 minutes. Add creamed corn, thawed corn, and half-and-half, and simmer for 5 minutes. Season to taste with salt and pepper, and ladle soup into bowls, sprinkling each serving with cilantro.

Note: Using either cooking method, the soup can be made up to 2 days in advance and refrigerated, tightly covered. Reheat it over low heat, covered.

Variation:
- For a less spicy soup, substitute 1 (4-ounce) can chopped mild green chiles, drained, for the chipotle chiles and adobo sauce.

A can of chipotle chiles goes a long way, and here's a method to make sure you don't waste any. Line an ice cube tray with plastic wrap, and place a few chiles and a few teaspoons of sauce in each cup. Once frozen, transfer the cubes to a heavy resealable plastic bag.

Eastern European Chicken and Cabbage Soup

In my opinion, healthful cabbage is a much maligned and underutilized vegetable, and it's always one of the most reasonably priced in the produce department. It becomes silky and smooth in this hearty soup, with a slight nuance of sweet and sour in the broth. Serve it with some crusty peasant bread like pumpernickel and a tossed salad.

Yield: 4–6 servings | **Active time:** 20 minutes | **Start to finish (minimum time, slow cooker):** 4½ hours in a medium slow cooker | **Start to finish (conventional):** 1¼ hours

4–6 boneless, skinless chicken thighs
1 (1-pound) head green cabbage
2 tablespoons vegetable oil
1 large onion, peeled and diced
2 garlic cloves, peeled and minced
5 cups Chicken Stock (recipe on page 84) or purchased stock (5½ cups if cooking conventionally)
1 (14.5-ounce) can diced tomatoes, drained
¼ cup cider vinegar
¼ cup granulated sugar
2 tablespoons chopped fresh parsley
1 teaspoon dried thyme
1 bay leaf
Salt and freshly ground black pepper to taste

1. Rinse chicken and pat dry with paper towels. Trim chicken of all visible fat, and cut into ½-inch cubes. Place chicken in the slow cooker.
2. Discard outer leaves from cabbage. Cut cabbage in half and discard core. Shred cabbage finely, and place it into the slow cooker.
3. Heat oil in a medium skillet over medium-high heat. Add onion and garlic, and cook, stirring frequently, for 3 minutes, or until onion is translucent. Scrape mixture into the slow cooker, and add stock, tomatoes, vinegar, sugar, parsley, thyme, and bay leaf.
4. Cook on Low for 8–10 hours or on High for 4–5 hours, or until cabbage is tender. Remove and discard bay leaf, season to taste with salt and pepper, and ladle soup into bowls.

If cooking conventionally: Follow the recipe to the end of Step 3, assembling the dish in a saucepan, and adding the additional ½ cup stock to the ingredients. Bring to a boil over high heat, then reduce the heat to low and simmer soup, covered, for 45–55 minutes, or until cabbage is tender. Remove and discard bay leaf, season to taste with salt and pepper, and ladle soup into bowls.

Note: Using either cooking method, the soup can be made up to 2 days in advance and refrigerated, tightly covered. Reheat it over low heat, covered.

Variation:
- Substitute red cabbage for the green cabbage, omit the chicken, and use vegetable stock in the recipe for a vegetarian soup.

An easy way to shred cabbage is to cut it into quarters, and core each quarter. At that point, you can flatten the leaves with the palm of your hand into a flat stack that is easy to shred.

Italian White Bean Soup

This thick soup is given a complex flavor from the addition of Italian salami to the stock. Garlic bread and a tossed salad are excellent partners on the table.

Yield: 4–6 servings | **Active time:** 15 minutes | **Start to finish (minimum time, slow cooker):** 5½ hours in a medium slow cooker, including 1 hour to soak beans | **Start to finish (conventional):** 2½ hours, including 1 hour to soak beans

> 2 cups dried navy beans or other small dried white beans
> 3 tablespoons olive oil
> ½ pound stewing beef, cut into ¾-inch cubes
> 1 large onion, peeled and diced
> 6 garlic cloves, peeled and minced
> 1 large carrot, peeled and chopped
> 2 celery ribs, peeled and minced
> 1½ cups shredded cabbage
> 1 (14.5-ounce) can diced tomatoes, drained
> ½ pound Genoa salami or hard salami, chopped
> 6 cups Chicken Stock (recipe on page 84) or purchased stock (6½ cups if cooking conventionally)
> 3 tablespoons chopped fresh parsley
> 2 teaspoons Italian seasoning
> Salt and freshly ground black pepper to taste

1. Rinse beans in a colander and place them in a mixing bowl covered with cold water. Allow beans to soak overnight. Or place beans in a saucepan and bring to a boil over high heat. Boil 1 minute. Turn off the heat, cover the pan, and soak beans for 1 hour. With either soaking method, drain beans, discard soaking water, and begin cooking as soon as possible. Transfer beans to the slow cooker.
2. Heat olive oil in a medium skillet over medium heat. Add beef, and brown well. Remove beef from pan with a slotted spoon, and place in the slow cooker. Add onion, garlic, carrot, and celery to the skillet, and cook, stirring frequently, for 3 minutes, or until onion is translucent. Add mixture to the slow cooker, and stir in cabbage, tomatoes, salami, stock, parsley, and Italian seasoning.

3. Cook on Low for 8–10 hours or on High for 4–5 hours, or until beans are tender. Season to taste with salt and pepper, and ladle soup into bowls.

If cooking conventionally: Follow the recipe to the end of Step 2, assembling the dish in a saucepan, and adding the additional ½ cup stock to the ingredients. Bring to a boil, then reduce the heat to low and simmer soup, covered, for 1–1¼ hours, or until beans are tender. Season to taste with salt and pepper, and ladle soup into bowls.

Note: Using either cooking method, the soup can be made up to 2 days in advance and refrigerated, tightly covered. Reheat it over low heat, covered.

Variation:
- The same basic formulation can also become a Latin American soup. Substitute red kidney beans for the white beans, cilantro for the parsley, and chorizo for the salami. Omit the Italian seasoning and add 1 teaspoon dried oregano and 1 teaspoon ground cumin to the soup.

The inclusion of an acid ingredient, such as tomatoes or wine, causes beans to take longer to soften. That's why this soup—even cooked conventionally—takes more time than others.

Beefy Onion Soup Les Halles

Les Halles was the old market area of Paris known for its cafes that remained open all night serving classic onion soup. This version is even heartier because there's actual beef in the broth, and a gooey cheese and toast topping crowns it all.

Yield: 4–6 servings | **Active time:** 20 minutes | **Start to finish (minimum time, slow cooker):** 8½ hours in a medium slow cooker | **Start to finish (conventional):** 2½ hours

4 tablespoons (½ stick) unsalted butter, cut into small pieces

¼ cup olive oil

3 pounds sweet onions, such as Vidalia or Bermuda, peeled and thinly sliced

1 tablespoon granulated sugar

Salt and freshly ground black pepper to taste

¾ pound boneless chuck roast, cut into ¾-inch cubes

5 cups Beef Stock (recipe on page 85) or purchased stock (5½ cups if cooking conventionally)

¾ cup dry red wine

3 tablespoons chopped fresh parsley

1 bay leaf

1 teaspoon dried thyme

6 slices French or Italian bread, cut ¾ inch thick

⅓ cup freshly grated Parmesan cheese

1 tablespoon cornstarch

2 tablespoons cold water

1½ cups grated Gruyère or Swiss cheese

1. Set the slow cooker on High, and add butter and olive oil. Add onions once butter melts, and add sugar, salt, and pepper. Toss well to coat onions. Cover and cook for 1 hour, remove the cover, and stir onions. Cook for an additional 3–4 hours, or until onions are golden brown.

2. When onions are almost brown, preheat the oven broiler, and line a broiler pan with heavy-duty aluminum foil. Broil beef for 3 minutes per side, or until browned. Set aside. When onions brown, add beef, stock, wine, parsley, bay leaf, and thyme to the slow cooker.

3. Cook on Low for 5–6 hours or on High for 2½–3 hours, or until beef is tender.

4. While soup cooks, preheat the oven to 450°F and cover a baking sheet with aluminum foil. Sprinkle bread with Parmesan cheese, and bake slices for 5–8 minutes, or until browned. Remove, and set aside.
5. Preheat the oven broiler. If cooking on Low, raise the heat to High. Mix cornstarch and cold water in a small cup. Stir mixture into the slow cooker, and cook for an additional 10–20 minutes or until the liquid is bubbling and has slightly thickened. Remove and discard bay leaf, and season to taste with salt and pepper.
6. To serve, ladle hot soup into ovenproof soup bowls and top each with toast slice. Divide Gruyère on top of toast and broil 6 inches from heating element for 1–2 minutes, or until cheese melts and browns. Serve immediately.

If cooking conventionally: Melt butter and oil in a large skillet over medium heat. Add onions, sugar, salt, and pepper, and toss to coat onions. Cover the skillet, and cook for 10 minutes, stirring occasionally. Uncover the skillet, and cook over medium-high heat for 20–30 minutes, or until onions are browned. Scrape onions into a saucepan, and follow Step 2 of recipe, adding the additional ½ cup stock to the ingredients. Bring to a boil, and simmer soup, covered, for 1–1½ hours, or until beef is tender. Follow Steps 4 and 6 above.

Note: Using either cooking method, the soup can be made up to 2 days in advance and refrigerated, tightly covered. Reheat it over low heat, covered. The toasts can be made up to 2 days in advance and kept at room temperature. Do not top with cheese and broil until just before serving.

Variation:
- Omit the beef and substitute vegetable stock to make this a vegetarian dish.

Spicy Jamaican Beef Soup

Spicy chorizo sausage is balanced by creamy coconut milk in this dish inspired by the Caribbean, and healthful Swiss chard punctuates the thick broth. Some stewed black beans are delicious with it as a side dish.

Yield: 4-6 servings | **Active time:** 20 minutes | **Start to finish (minimum time, slow cooker):** 4½ hours in a medium slow cooker | **Start to finish (conventional):** 1½ hours

¼ cup olive oil, divided
1 pound boneless chuck roast, cut into ½-inch cubes
1 large onion, peeled and diced
4 garlic cloves, peeled and minced
1 celery rib, rinsed, trimmed, and thinly sliced
1 carrot, peeled and thinly sliced
½ pound chorizo, finely chopped
1 tablespoon ground cumin
5 cups Beef Stock (recipe on page 85) or purchased stock (5½ cups if cooking conventionally)
1 (14.5-ounce) can diced tomatoes, undrained
1 cup coconut milk, well stirred
4 cups firmly packed rinsed, stemmed, and thinly sliced Swiss chard
½-1 teaspoon hot red pepper sauce, or to taste
Salt and freshly ground black pepper to taste

1. Heat one half of olive oil in a medium skillet over medium-high heat. Add beef and cook, stirring frequently, until beef is browned. Scrape mixture into the slow cooker.
2. Heat remaining olive oil, and add onion, garlic, celery, and carrot. Cook, stirring frequently, for 3 minutes, or until onion is translucent. Add chorizo and cumin, and cook, stirring frequently, for 2 minutes. Scrape mixture into the slow cooker.
3. Add stock, tomatoes, and coconut milk to the slow cooker, and stir well.
4. Cook on Low for 6-8 hours or on High for 3-4 hours, or until vegetables are almost tender.

5. If cooking on Low, raise the heat to High. Add Swiss chard, and cook for 1–1½ hours, or until Swiss chard wilts. Add hot red pepper sauce, season to taste with salt and pepper, and ladle soup into bowls.

If cooking conventionally: Follow the recipe to the end of Step 3, assembling the dish in a saucepan, and adding the additional ½ cup stock to the ingredients. Bring to a boil, then reduce the heat to low and simmer soup, covered, for 1 hour. Add Swiss chard, and cook for 15 minutes, or until Swiss chard wilts. Add hot red pepper sauce, season to taste with salt and pepper, and ladle soup into bowls.

Note: Using either cooking method, the soup can be made up to 2 days in advance and refrigerated, tightly covered. Reheat it over low heat, covered.

Variation:
- Substitute chicken stock for the beef stock and use ¾ pound boneless pork loin, cut into ½-inch dice, instead of the beef.

> Hot red pepper sauce, and all members of the pepper family, should always be added to slow-cooked dishes at the end of the cooking time.

Hearty Mexican Meatball Soup (*Sopa de Albondigas*)

Meatball soups are popular in Spain and Latin America, and this one contains incredibly flavorful meatballs made from a mixture of beef and spicy chorizo bound with cornmeal in a spicy broth. Serve some flour or corn tortillas with it.

Yield: 4-6 servings | **Active time:** 20 minutes | **Start to finish (minimum time, slow cooker):** 3½ hours in a medium slow cooker | **Start to finish (conventional):** 1 hour

1 pound lean ground beef
¼ pound bulk chorizo sausage
¼ cup yellow cornmeal
¼ cup whole milk
1 large egg, lightly beaten
2 tablespoons chili powder, divided
Salt and freshly ground black pepper to taste
Vegetable oil spray
2 tablespoons olive oil
1 large onion, peeled and diced
4 garlic cloves, peeled and minced
1 large jalapeño or serrano chile, seeds and ribs removed, and
   chopped
1 tablespoon ground cumin
2 teaspoons dried oregano
1 (28-ounce) can diced tomatoes, undrained
2½ cups Beef Stock (recipe on page 85) or purchased stock (*3
   cups if cooking conventionally*)
¼ cup chopped fresh cilantro

1. Preheat the oven to 450°F. Line a baking sheet with heavy-duty aluminum foil, and spray the foil with vegetable oil spray.

2. Combine beef, chorizo, cornmeal, milk, egg, 1 tablespoon chili powder, salt, and pepper in a mixing bowl, and mix well. Form mixture into 1-inch balls, and place them on the greased foil. Spray tops of meatballs with vegetable oil spray. Brown meatballs in the oven for 10 minutes, or until lightly browned.

3. While meatballs brown, heat olive oil in a medium skillet over medium-high heat. Add onion, garlic, and chile, and cook, stirring frequently, for 3 minutes, or until onion is translucent. Reduce the heat to low

and stir in remaining 1 tablespoon chili powder, cumin, and oregano. Cook for 1 minute, stirring constantly. Scrape mixture into the slow cooker.

4. Stir tomatoes and stock into the slow cooker, and stir well. Transfer meatballs to the slow cooker with a slotted spoon.

5. Cook on Low for 6–8 hours or on High for 3–4 hours, or until vegetables are tender. Season to taste with salt and pepper, and ladle soup into bowls, sprinkling each serving with cilantro.

If cooking conventionally: Follow the recipe to the end of Step 4, assembling the dish in a saucepan, and adding the additional ½ cup stock to the ingredients. Bring to a boil, then reduce the heat to low and simmer soup, covered, for 30–40 minutes, or until meatballs are cooked through. Season to taste with salt and pepper, and ladle soup into bowls, sprinkling each serving with cilantro.

Note: Using either cooking method, the soup can be made up to 2 days in advance and refrigerated, tightly covered. Reheat it over low heat, covered.

Variations:
- For a lighter soup, substitute chicken stock for the beef stock, and substitute 1¼ pounds ground chicken or ground turkey for the beef and chorizo.
- Substitute 2 tablespoons canned chopped mild green chile, drained, for the fresh chile for a milder dish.
- Add a garnish of diced avocado or strips of fried corn tortillas.

Szechwan Hot and Sour Pork Soup

Hot and sour soup was one of the first spicy dishes to gain favor in America's Chinese restaurants in the middle part of the last century. It is very easy to make, and also very healthful. If you want some crunch, sprinkle a few chow mein noodles on top.

Yield: 4–6 servings | **Active time:** 20 minutes | **Start to finish (minimum time, slow cooker):** 3³/₄ hours in a medium slow cooker | **Start to finish (conventional):** 50 minutes

12 large dried shiitake mushrooms *
1 cup boiling water
³/₄ pound boneless pork loin
5 cups Chicken Stock (recipe on page 84) or purchased stock (5¹/₂ cups if cooking conventionally)
¹/₂ pound firm tofu, well drained and cut into ¹/₂-inch dice
1 (8-ounce) can sliced water chestnuts, drained and rinsed
¹/₃ cup rice vinegar
2 tablespoons soy sauce
1 tablespoon Asian sesame oil *
¹/₂ teaspoon freshly ground black pepper, or to taste
3 tablespoons cornstarch
2 tablespoons cold water
2 large eggs, lightly beaten
Salt to taste
4 scallions, white parts and 3 inches of green tops, rinsed, trimmed, and thinly sliced

1. Soak shiitake mushrooms in boiling water for 10 minutes, pressing mushrooms down with the back of a spoon to keep them submerged. Cut all fat from pork, and cut into thin slices. Stack slices, and cut into thin ribbons. Place pork in the slow cooker.

2. Remove mushrooms from water, and strain soaking liquid through a coffee filter or paper towel into the slow cooker. Discard stems, and slice mushrooms into thin slices. Add mushrooms to the slow cooker along with stock, tofu, water chestnuts, vinegar, soy sauce, sesame oil, and pepper.

3. Cook on Low for 6–8 hours or on High for 3–4 hours, or until pork is cooked through.

4. If cooking on Low, raise the heat to High. Combine cornstarch and water in a small cup. Stir cornstarch mixture into soup. Cook on High for 10–20 minutes, or until the liquid has thickened and is bubbly. Stir eggs into soup, and continue to stir so eggs form thin strands. Cover the slow cooker, and bring soup back to a simmer. Season to taste with salt and additional pepper, and ladle soup into bowls, sprinkling each serving with scallion slices.

If cooking conventionally: Follow the recipe to the end of Step 2, assembling the dish in a saucepan, and adding the additional $1/2$ cup stock to the ingredients. Bring to a boil, then reduce the heat to low and simmer soup, covered, for 20–30 minutes, or until pork is cooked. Combine cornstarch and water in a small cup. Stir cornstarch mixture into soup, and return soup to a boil. Simmer for 3 minutes, then stir eggs into soup, and continue to stir so eggs form thin strands. Season to taste with salt and additional pepper, and ladle soup into bowls, sprinkling each serving with scallion slices.

Note: Using either cooking method, the soup can be made up to 2 days in advance and refrigerated, tightly covered. Reheat it over low heat, covered.

Variations:
- To make the soup vegetarian, substitute vegetable stock for the chicken stock, omit the pork, and increase the amount of tofu to $1/4$ pounds.
- Substitute $3/4$ pound boneless, skinless chicken thighs, cut into $3/4$-inch dice, for the pork.

* Available in the Asian aisle of most supermarkets and in specialty markets.

Chunky Canadian Yellow Split Pea Soup with Ham

While green split pea soup is the norm, I prefer the lighter color of its first cousin made with equally inexpensive yellow split peas. This is the way the dish is traditionally made north of our border in Canada.

Yield: 4–6 servings | **Active time:** 15 minutes | **Start to finish (minimum time, slow cooker):** 3¼ hours in a medium slow cooker | **Start to finish (conventional):** 1 hour

SOUP

2 tablespoons vegetable oil

1 large onion, peeled and finely chopped

1 carrot, peeled and finely chopped

1 celery rib, rinsed, trimmed, and finely chopped

2 garlic cloves, peeled and minced

1 pound yellow split peas, rinsed

1 large russet potato peeled and cut into ¾-inch dice

½ pound baked ham, trimmed of fat and cut into ½-inch dice

5½ cups Chicken Stock (recipe on page 84) or purchased stock (*6 cups if cooking conventionally*)

3 tablespoons chopped fresh parsley

1 teaspoon dried thyme

1 bay leaf

Salt and freshly ground black pepper to taste

GARNISH

4 (¾-inch-thick) slices French or Italian bread

2 tablespoons olive oil

4–6 tablespoons chopped ham

2 tablespoons chopped fresh parsley

1. Heat oil in a medium skillet over medium-high heat. Add onion, carrot, celery, and garlic. Cook, stirring frequently, for 3 minutes, or until onion is translucent. Scrape mixture into the slow cooker.
2. Add split peas, potato, ham, stock, parsley, thyme, and bay leaf to the slow cooker. Stir well.
3. Cook on Low for 6–8 hours or on High for 3–4 hours, or until split peas have disintegrated. Remove and discard bay leaf, season to taste with salt and pepper.

4. While soup simmers, prepare garnish. Preheat oven to 370°F, and line a baking sheet with foil. Cut bread into ½-inch cubes, and toss with olive oil. Bake cubes for 6–8 minutes, or until browned. Remove cubes from oven, and set aside.

5. To serve, ladle soup into bowls, and top each serving with croutons and 1 tablespoon chopped ham. Sprinkle each serving with parsley, and serve immediately

If cooking conventionally: Follow the recipe to the end of Step 2, assembling the dish in a saucepan, and adding the additional ½ cup stock to the ingredients. Bring to a boil, then reduce the heat to low and simmer soup, covered, for 40–50 minutes, or until split peas have disintegrated. Remove and discard bay leaf, and season to taste with salt and pepper. Prepare croutons as described in Step 4. To serve, ladle soup into bowls, and top each serving with croutons and 1 tablespoon chopped ham. Sprinkle each serving with parsley, and serve immediately.

Note: Using either cooking method, the soup can be made up to 2 days in advance and refrigerated, tightly covered. Reheat it over low heat, covered.

Variation:
- For a vegetarian version, omit the ham, substitute vegetable stock for the chicken stock, and double the amount of parsley and thyme to boost the flavor.

While I don't give a recipe for ham stock, should you have a ham bone from a baked ham, save it and follow the recipe for chicken stock on page 84. Another option to add a smoky nuance is to throw a few smoked pork hocks into the chicken stock.

Spicy Thai Pork Soup

Main course soups are part of most Asian cuisines, and this one made with woodsy dried shiitake mushrooms is especially yummy. The broth is a pleasing green tone from the cilantro in its base, and a stir-fried cabbage salad goes nicely with it.

Yield: 4-6 servings | **Active time:** 20 minutes | **Start to finish (minimum time, slow cooker):** 4 hours in a medium slow cooker | **Start to finish (conventional):** 55 minutes

½ cup dried shiitake mushrooms
1 cup boiling water
1 (1-ounce) package cellophane noodles
¾ pound boneless pork loin
1 cup firmly packed fresh cilantro leaves
1 tablespoon grated fresh ginger
3 garlic cloves, peeled and minced
1 jalapeño or serrano chile, seeds and ribs removed, and chopped
2 tablespoons fish sauce *(nam pla)* *
1 tablespoon firmly packed light brown sugar
6 cups Chicken Stock (recipe on page 84) or purchased stock (6½
   cups *if cooking conventionally)*
1 large carrot, peeled and thinly sliced
2 celery ribs, rinsed, trimmed, and sliced
Salt and freshly ground black pepper to taste
4 scallions, white parts and 4 inches of green tops, rinsed,
   trimmed, and sliced

1. Combine shiitake mushrooms and boiling water, pushing mushrooms down into the water with the back of a spoon. Soak for 10 minutes, then drain mushrooms, reserving soaking liquid. Discard stems, and chop mushrooms. Set aside. Strain soaking liquid through a sieve lined with a paper coffee filter or a paper towel. While mushrooms soak, follow package directions to soak cellophane noodles. Drain, and cut noodles into 2-inch lengths with sharp scissors.

2. Cut all fat from pork, and cut into thin slices. Stack slices, and cut into thin ribbons.

3. Combine cilantro, ginger, garlic, chile, fish sauce, and brown sugar in a food processor fitted with the steel blade or in a blender. Puree until smooth. Scrape mixture into the slow cooker, and stir in chicken

stock and reserved mushroom soaking liquid. Add carrot, celery, mushrooms, and pork slivers.

4. Cook on Low for 6–8 hours or on High for 3–4 hours, or until pork is cooked through. If cooking on Low, raise the heat to High. Add cellophane noodles and cook for 10–20 minutes to heat. Season to taste with salt and pepper, and ladle soup into bowls, sprinkling each serving with scallions.

If cooking conventionally: Follow the recipe to the end of Step 3, assembling the dish in a saucepan, and adding the additional ½ cup stock to the ingredients. Bring to a boil, then reduce the heat to low and simmer soup, covered, for 30–35 minutes. Add cellophane noodles and cook for 2 minutes to heat. Season to taste with salt and pepper, and ladle soup into bowls, sprinkling each serving with scallions.

Note: Using either cooking method, the soup can be made up to 2 days in advance and refrigerated, tightly covered. Reheat it over low heat, covered.

Variations:

- Substitute boneless, skinless chicken thighs for the pork.
- To add more protein, add 1 cup of diced extra-firm tofu to the broth.
- Add sliced bok choy to the soup 1 hour before the end of cooking to increase the vegetable content without diluting the flavor.

* Available in the Asian aisle of most supermarkets and in specialty markets.

Chicken Stock

You'll be amazed at the difference in flavor homemade chicken stock makes to all your dishes. And you'll notice a change in your grocery bill when you can stop buying it!

Yield: 4 quarts | **Active time:** 10 minutes | **Start to finish:** 4 hours

   6 quarts water
   5 pounds chicken bones, skin, and trimmings
   4 celery ribs, rinsed and cut into thick slices
   2 onions, trimmed and quartered
   2 carrots, trimmed, scrubbed, and cut into thick slices
   2 tablespoons whole black peppercorns
   6 garlic cloves, peeled
   4 sprigs parsley
   1 teaspoon dried thyme
   2 bay leaves

1. Place water and chicken in a large stockpot, and bring to a boil over high heat. Reduce the heat to low, and skim off foam that rises during the first 10–15 minutes of simmering. Simmer stock, uncovered, for 1 hour, then add celery, onions, carrots, peppercorns, garlic, parsley, thyme, and bay leaves. Simmer for 2½ hours.

2. Strain stock through a fine-meshed sieve, pushing with the back of a spoon to extract as much liquid as possible. Discard solids, spoon stock into smaller containers, and refrigerate. Remove and discard fat from surface of stock.

Note: The stock can be refrigerated and used within 3 days, or it can be frozen for up to 6 months.

Variation:
   • For turkey stock, use the same amount of turkey giblets and necks as chicken pieces.

Beef Stock

While beef stock is not specified as often as chicken stock in recipes, it is the backbone to certain soups and the gravy for stews and roasts.

Yield: 2 quarts | **Active time:** 15 minutes | **Start to finish:** 3½ hours

2 pounds beef trimmings (bones, fat) or inexpensive beef shank
3 quarts water
1 carrot, trimmed, scrubbed, and cut into thick slices
1 medium onion, peeled and sliced
1 celery rib, trimmed and sliced
1 tablespoon whole black peppercorns
3 sprigs fresh parsley
1 teaspoon dried thyme
2 garlic cloves, peeled
2 bay leaves

1. Preheat the oven broiler, and line a broiler pan with heavy-duty aluminum foil. Broil beef for 3 minutes per side, or until browned. Transfer beef to a large stockpot, and add water. Bring to a boil over high heat. Reduce the heat to low, and skim off foam that rises during the first 10–15 minutes of simmering. Simmer for 1 hour, uncovered, then add carrot, onion, celery, peppercorns, parsley, thyme, garlic, and bay leaves. Simmer for 3 hours.

2. Strain stock through a fine-meshed sieve, pushing with the back of a spoon to extract as much liquid as possible. Discard solids, and spoon stock into smaller containers, and refrigerate. Remove and discard fat from surface of stock.

Note: The stock can be refrigerated and used within 3 days, or it can be frozen for up to 6 months.

Vegetable Stock

You may think it's not necessary to use vegetable stock if making a vegetarian dish that includes the same vegetables, but that's not the case. Using stock creates a much more richly flavored dish that can't be replicated by increasing the quantity of vegetables cooked in it.

Yield: 2 quarts | **Active time:** 10 minutes | **Start to finish:** 1 hour

    2 quarts water
    2 carrots, scrubbed, trimmed, and thinly sliced
    2 celery ribs, trimmed and sliced
    2 leeks, white part only, trimmed, rinsed, and thinly sliced
    1 small onion, peeled and thinly sliced
    1 tablespoon whole black peppercorns
    3 sprigs fresh parsley
    1 teaspoon dried thyme
    2 garlic cloves, peeled
    1 bay leaf

1. Pour water into a stockpot, and add carrots, celery, leeks, onion, peppercorns, parsley, thyme, garlic, and bay leaf. Bring to a boil over high heat, then reduce the heat to low and simmer stock, uncovered, for 1 hour.

2. Strain stock through a fine-meshed sieve, pushing with the back of a spoon to extract as much liquid as possible. Discard solids, and allow stock to cool to room temperature. Spoon stock into smaller containers, and refrigerate.

Note: The stock can be refrigerated and used within 3 days, or it can be frozen for up to 6 months.

Seafood Stock

Seafood stock is a great reason to make friends with the head of the fish department of your supermarket. You can arrange in advance to have them save you bodies if the store cooks lobster meat, or purchase them at minimal cost. The same is true with fish bones, if a store actually fillets the fish on site.

Yield: 2 quarts | **Active time:** 15 minutes | **Start to finish:** $1^3/_4$ hours

> 3 lobster bodies (whole lobsters from which the tail and claw meat has been removed), shells from 3 pounds raw shrimp, or 2 pounds bones and skin from firm-fleshed white fish such as halibut, cod, or sole
> 3 quarts water
> 1 cup dry white wine
> 1 carrot, scrubbed, trimmed, and cut into 1-inch chunks
> 1 medium onion, peeled and sliced
> 1 celery rib, rinsed, trimmed, and sliced
> 1 tablespoon whole black peppercorns
> 3 sprigs fresh parsley
> 1 teaspoon dried thyme
> 2 garlic cloves, peeled
> 1 bay leaf

1. If using lobster shells, pull top shell off 1 lobster body. Scrape off and discard feathery gills, then break body into small pieces. Place pieces into a stockpot, and repeat with remaining lobster bodies. If using shrimp shells or fish bones, rinse and place in the stockpot.
2. Add water, wine, carrot, onion, celery, peppercorns, parsley, thyme, garlic, and bay leaf. Bring to a boil over high heat, then reduce the heat to low and simmer stock, uncovered, for $1^1/_2$ hours.
3. Strain stock through a fine-meshed sieve, pushing with the back of a spoon to extract as much liquid as possible. Discard solids, and allow stock to cool to room temperature. Spoon stock into smaller containers, and refrigerate.

Note: The stock can be refrigerated and used within 3 days, or it can be frozen for up to 6 months.

Seafood stock is perhaps the hardest to make if you don't live near the coast. A good substitute is bottled clam juice. Use it in place of the water, and simmer it with vegetables and wine to intensify its flavor.

Chapter 5:

From the Seas and Lakes: Fish Dishes from Lean to Luscious

While fish is usually higher in price than most meats, there is no waste to a fish fillet, and with its low fat content it doesn't shrink the way that meats do. So the price per edible ounce of fish is really about the same as for other forms of protein like a chuck roast or pork loin, if still more expensive than chicken.

What makes these dishes different from those in other chapters of this book is that the seafood is cooked for a very brief time at the end of the cooking cycle. Unlike meats, which can take a whole workday to cook in the slow cooker, fish and seafood need only a fraction of that time.

In fact, overcooking fish is more of a risk than undercooking. It's the finale rather than the overture. The trick is to cook the background ingredients, such as the vegetables and sauces, for hours so the vegetables are tender and sauces are deeply flavored. Then the fish gets added and usually cooks for no more than 30 minutes. The exact cooking time depends on how much fish you are using, and whether other ingredients are added at the same time.

The timing of these recipes takes into account the cooking time for the fish used in the recipe. If you fear that the carrots might not be tender when the fish is added, they will be by the time the fish is done.

If you use the Low setting for the majority of the cooking, you'll be instructed to increase the temperature to High before adding the seafood. The seafood should cook quickly once the dish is ready to have it added.

You will notice that in very rare occasions have I listed a specific species. That is because fish basically falls into families, and almost all the recipes in this chapter can be done with any member of the thin white fish fillet family—which includes flounder, tilapia, snapper, trout, or even catfish—and the thick white fish fillet family—such as cod, halibut, or sea bass.

It's more important to use the freshest fish—and one that is reasonably priced—than any specific fish. So judge accordingly when you go to the fish store.

FISH FACTS

Fish is high in protein and low to moderate in fat, cholesterol, and sodium. A 3-ounce portion of fish has between 47 and 170 calories depending on the species. Fish is an excellent source of B vitamins, iodine, phosphorus, potassium, iron, and calcium.

The most important nutrient in fish may be the Omega-3 fatty acids. These are the primary polyunsaturated fatty acids found in the fat and oils of fish. They have been found to lower the levels of low-density lipoproteins (LDL), the "bad" cholesterol, and raise the levels of high-density lipoproteins (HDL), the "good" cholesterol. Fatty fish that live in cold water, such as mackerel and salmon, seem to have the most Omega-3 fatty acids, although all fish have some.

HANDLING THE AQUATICS

Most supermarkets still display fish on chipped ice in a case rather than pre-packaging it, and they should. Fish should be kept at an even lower temperature than meats. Fish fillets or steaks should look bright, lustrous, and moist, with no signs of discoloration or drying.

When making your fish selection, keep a few simple guidelines in mind: above all, do not buy any fish that actually smells fishy, indicating that it is no longer fresh or hasn't been cut or stored properly. Fresh fish has the mild, clean scent of the sea—nothing more. Look for bright, shiny colors in the fish scales, because as a fish sits, its skin becomes more pale and dull looking. Then peer into the eyes; they should be black and beady. If they're milky or sunken, the fish has been dead too long. And if the fish isn't behind glass, gently poke its flesh. If the indentation remains, the fish is old.

Rinse all fish under cold running water before cutting or cooking. With fillets, run your fingers in every direction along the top of the fillet before cooking, and feel for any pesky little bones.

You can remove bones easily in two ways. Larger bones will come out if they're stroked with a vegetable peeler, and you can pull out smaller bones with tweezers. This is not a long process, but it's a gesture that will be greatly appreciated by all who eat the fish.

TALKING TUNA

There are a dizzying array of cans, and now pouches, on supermarket shelves, but they essentially fall into four categories. These categories are solid white tuna packed in water, solid white tuna packed in oil, light tuna packed in water, and light tuna packed in oil. Water-packed tuna is a relative newcomer to the market, following decades of oil-packed tuna. While the process does trim the fat from the fish, it also trims much of the flavor since it tends to be less moist.

There are health concerns as well as cost reasons for specifying light tuna rather than white tuna, sometimes called albacore tuna, in these recipes. White tuna has been found to be much higher in mercury than light tuna, so light tuna is better on both scores. Feel free in any of the recipes containing canned tuna to substitute canned salmon. Almost all canned salmon is packaged complete with bones and skin, however, so some preparatory work is needed before using it in recipes.

There are thousands of species that fit the definitions of thick and thin. Here are some of the most common:

- Thin fillets: flounder, sole, perch, red snapper, trout, tilapia, ocean perch, catfish, striped bass, turbot, and whitefish.

- Thick fillets: halibut, scrod, grouper, sea bass, mahi-mahi, pompano, yellowtail, and swordfish.

Basic Poached Fish

Poaching fish in an aromatic liquid, called a *court bouillon* in classic French cooking, produces delicious fish that is still moist and tender. It can be served hot or cold, and takes to countless sauces.

Yield: 4-6 servings | **Active time:** 10 minutes | **Start to finish (minimum time, slow cooker):** 3 hours in a medium slow cooker | **Start to finish (conventional):** 40 minutes

> 2 cups Seafood Stock (recipe on page 87) or bottled clam juice
>   (2¹/₂ *cups if cooking conventionally*)
> 1 cup dry white wine
> 1 medium onion, peeled and thinly sliced
> ¹/₂ lemon, thinly sliced
> 3 parsley sprigs
> 1 teaspoon dried thyme
> 1 bay leaf
> Salt and freshly ground black pepper to taste
> 4-6 (4-ounce) thick white fish fillets or salmon fillets

1. Combine stock, wine, onion, lemon, parsley, thyme, bay leaf, salt, and pepper in the slow cooker.
2. Cook on Low for 5-7 hours or on High for 2¹/₂-3 hours, or until onion is tender.
3. If cooking on Low, raise the heat to High. Gently add fish, and cook for 20-40 minutes, or until fish is cooked through and flakes easily. Season to taste with salt and pepper, and serve hot, at room temperature, or chilled.

If cooking conventionally: Follow the recipe to the end of Step 1, assembling the dish in a large skillet, and adding the additional ¹/₂ cup stock to the ingredients. Bring to a boil over high heat, and simmer, covered, over low heat, for 20 minutes, or until onion is tender. Add fish, and cook an additional 10 minutes per inch of thickness, or until fish is cooked through. Season to taste with salt and pepper, and serve hot, at room temperature, or chilled.

Note: Using either cooking method, the dish can be made up to 1 day in advance and refrigerated, tightly covered. Reheat it, covered, over low heat if serving it hot.

Spicy Mexican Fish

People seem to lose sight of the fact that most of Mexico is bounded by coastline because so much of our beloved Tex-Mex food is based on dishes from landlocked Sonora province. This delicate fish in a spicy tomato sauce is wonderful served either over rice or with corn tortillas.

Yield: 4-6 servings | **Active time:** 15 minutes | **Start to finish (minimum time, slow cooker):** 3 hours in a medium slow cooker | **Start to finish (conventional):** 40 minutes

>   2 tablespoons olive oil
>   2 medium onions, peeled and thinly sliced
>   4 garlic cloves, peeled and minced
>   1 jalapeño or serrano chile, seeds and ribs removed, and finely chopped
>   2 tablespoons chili powder
>   2 teaspoons dried oregano
>   1 (14.5-ounce) can diced tomatoes, undrained
>   1 cup Seafood Stock (recipe on page 87) or bottled clam juice (*1½ cups if cooking conventionally*)
>   2 tablespoons lime juice
>   2 tablespoons tomato paste
>   ⅓ cup sliced pimiento-stuffed green olives
>   1½ pounds thick white fish fillets, cut into serving pieces
>   Salt and freshly ground black pepper to taste

1. Heat oil in a medium skillet over medium-high heat. Add onion, garlic, and chile, and cook, stirring frequently, for 3 minutes, or until onion is translucent. Stir in chili powder and oregano. Cook for 1 minute, stirring constantly. Scrape mixture into the slow cooker.
2. Add tomatoes, stock, lime juice, tomato paste, and olives to the slow cooker. Stir well.
3. Cook on Low for 4-6 hours or on High for 2-3 hours, or until vegetables are crisp-tender.
4. If cooking on Low, raise the heat to High. Gently add fish, and cook for 20-40 minutes, or until fish is cooked through and flakes easily. Season to taste with salt and pepper, and serve immediately.

If cooking conventionally: Follow the recipe to the end of Step 2, assembling the dish in a large skillet, and adding the additional ½ cup stock to the ingredients. Bring to a boil over high heat, and simmer, covered, over low heat, for 20 minutes, or until vegetables are crisp-tender. Add fish, and cook an additional 5 minutes, or until fish is cooked through. Season to taste with salt and pepper, and serve immediately.

Note: Using either cooking method, the dish can be made up to 2 days in advance and refrigerated, tightly covered. Reheat it, covered, over low heat.

Variations:
- Substitute vegetable stock for the seafood stock, and substitute thin slices of firm tofu for the fish.
- Substitute chicken stock for the seafood stock, and substitute 4-6 boneless, skinless chicken thighs, cut into $1/2$-dice dice, for the fish. Add the chicken at the start of the cooking time, and add 1 hour if cooking on Low or 30 minutes if cooking on High.

There are various ways to remove tiny bones from fish fillets. Run your fingers over the surface of the fish, and then either pull out the bones with tweezers or use a vegetable peeler.

Cajun Fish Gumbo

Gumbo is a Louisiana culinary classic that dates back to the French and Spanish settlers and the African slaves who served them. Although it can contain fish, meats, or poultry, the constant that gives it its name is okra. Okra is what thickens the dish, and the word *gumbo* comes from the African word *gombo,* which means okra. Serve it over rice with a bowl of crunchy coleslaw.

Yield: 4-6 servings | **Active time:** 20 minutes | **Start to finish (minimum time, slow cooker):** 4 hours in a medium slow cooker | **Start to finish (conventional):** 1¼ hours

> ⅓ cup vegetable oil, divided
> ¼ cup all-purpose flour
> 4 cups Seafood Stock (recipe on page 87) or bottled clam juice, divided (*4½ cups if cooking conventionally*)
> 3 medium onions, peeled and diced
> 1 green bell pepper, seeds and ribs removed, and diced
> 2 celery ribs, rinsed, trimmed, and sliced
> 4 garlic cloves, peeled and minced
> 1 (14.5-ounce) can diced tomatoes, undrained
> 1 teaspoon dried thyme
> 1 teaspoon dried oregano
> 2 bay leaves
> 1 pound frozen sliced okra, thawed
> 1 pound thick white fish fillets, cut into 1-inch cubes
> Salt and cayenne to taste

1. Heat ¼ cup oil in a small saucepan over medium-high heat. Whisk in flour, and reduce the heat to medium. Whisk flour constantly for 5-7 minutes, or until mixture is walnut brown. Whisk in 1 cup stock, and whisk until mixture is thick and smooth. Scrape mixture into the slow cooker.

2. Heat remaining oil in a medium skillet over medium-high heat. Add onion, green bell pepper, celery, and garlic. Cook, stirring frequently, for 3 minutes, or until onion is translucent. Scrape mixture into the slow cooker, and add tomatoes, remaining stock, thyme, oregano, and bay leaves.

3. Cook on Low for 5-6 hours or on High for 2½-3 hours, or until vegetables are almost tender.

4. If cooking on Low, raise the heat to High. Add okra, and cook for 30 minutes. Add fish, and cook for 15–30 minutes, or until fish is cooked through. Remove and discard bay leaves, and season to taste with salt and cayenne. Serve immediately.

If cooking conventionally: Follow the recipe to the end of Step 2, assembling the dish in a saucepan, and adding the additional ½ cup stock to the ingredients. Bring to a boil, and cook over low heat, covered, for 25–30 minutes, or until vegetables are almost tender. Add okra, and cook an additional 15 minutes. Add fish, and cook an additional 5 minutes, or until fish is cooked through. Remove and discard bay leaves, and season to taste with salt and cayenne. Serve immediately.

Note: Using either cooking method, the gumbo can be prepared up to 1 day in advance and refrigerated, tightly covered. Reheat it, covered, over low heat until hot.

Variations:
- Substitute chicken stock for the seafood stock, and substitute 4–6 boneless, skinless chicken thighs, cut into ³/₄-inch dice, for the fish. Add the chicken at the start of the cooking time, and add 1 hour if cooking on Low and 30 minutes if cooking on High.
- Substitute chicken stock for the seafood stock, and substitute ³/₄ pound andouille sausage, sautéed until browned, for the fish. Add the sausage at the same time as the okra.
- Substitute vegetable stock for the seafood stock, and substitute 1 pound zucchini, rinsed, trimmed, and cut into ½-inch dice, for the fish. Add zucchini at the same time as the okra.

Chinese Sweet and Sour Fish Stew

This healthful and vibrant dish proves that the slow cooker can create food with appealing crisp texture, because that's the way the vegetables remain. Everything you need for dinner, except for some cooked rice, is in the stew.

Yield: 4-6 servings | **Active time:** 20 minutes | **Start to finish (minimum time, slow cooker):** 3¾ hours in a medium slow cooker | **Start to finish (conventional):** 50 minutes

2 tablespoons Asian sesame oil *

1 large onion, peeled, halved, and sliced

4 garlic cloves, peeled and minced

2 tablespoons grated fresh ginger

1½ cups Seafood Stock (recipe on page 87) or bottled clam juice
  (*2 cups if cooking conventionally*)

¼ cup cider vinegar

¼ cup firmly packed dark brown sugar

2 tablespoons soy sauce

1 teaspoon Chinese chile paste with garlic *

2 celery ribs, rinsed, trimmed, and sliced

2 carrots, peeled and thinly sliced

2 cups firmly packed sliced green cabbage

1¼ pounds thick white fish fillet, cut into 1-inch cubes

1 cup frozen green beans, thawed

1 tablespoon cornstarch

2 tablespoons cold water

Salt and crushed red pepper flakes to taste

1. Heat oil in a medium skillet over medium-high heat. Add onion, garlic, and ginger. Cook, stirring frequently, for 3 minutes, or until onion is translucent. Scrape mixture into the slow cooker.

2. Add stock, vinegar, brown sugar, soy sauce, and chile paste to the slow cooker. Stir well. Add celery, carrots, and cabbage.

3. Cook on Low for 5-7 hours or on High for 2½-3 hours, or until vegetables are crisp-tender.

4. If cooking on Low, raise the heat to High. Add fish and green beans to the slow cooker. Cook for 30-45 minutes, or until fish is cooked through. Mix cornstarch with water, and stir cornstarch mixture into the slow cooker. Cook for an additional 10-20 minutes, or until juices

are bubbling and slightly thickened. Season to taste with salt and red pepper flakes, and serve immediately.

If cooking conventionally: Follow the recipe to the end of Step 2, assembling the dish in a saucepan, and adding the additional ½ cup stock to the ingredients. Bring to a boil over high heat, and simmer, covered, over low heat, for 15 minutes, or until vegetables are crisp-tender. Add fish and green beans, and cook an additional 5 minutes, or until fish is cooked through. Mix cornstarch with water, and stir cornstarch mixture into the pan. Cook on top of the stove for 3–5 minutes, or until slightly thickened. Season to taste with salt and red pepper flakes, and serve immediately.

Note: Using either cooking method, the dish can be made up to 2 days in advance and refrigerated, tightly covered. Reheat it, covered, over low heat.

Variations:
- Substitute vegetable stock for the seafood stock, and substitute ³/₄ pound firm tofu, thinly sliced, for the fish.
- Substitute chicken stock for the seafood stock, and substitute ³/₄ pound boneless, skinless chicken thighs for the fish. Add the chicken at the same time as the vegetables to the slow cooker or saucepan.

* Available in the Asian aisle of most supermarkets and in specialty markets.

Greek Fish Stew with Potatoes

The delectable combination of lemon, garlic, and oregano is one of the hallmarks of Greek cuisine, and those are the flavors you'll find in this light and flavorful fish stew. A Greek salad made with sharp feta cheese is a good choice to complete the meal.

Yield: 4-6 servings | **Active time:** 15 minutes | **Start to finish (minimum time, slow cooker):** 4 hours in a medium slow cooker | **Start to finish (conventional):** 50 minutes

3 tablespoons olive oil

1 medium onion, peeled and diced

3 garlic cloves, peeled and minced

2 celery ribs, rinsed, trimmed, and sliced

$\frac{1}{4}$ cup chopped fresh parsley

2 tablespoons dried oregano

1 bay leaf

2 cups Seafood Stock (recipe on page 87) or bottled clam juice
 ($2\frac{1}{2}$ cups if cooking conventionally)

$\frac{3}{4}$ cup dry white wine

$\frac{1}{4}$ cup lemon juice

1 pound redskin potatoes, scrubbed and cut into 1-inch dice

2 small zucchini, trimmed, halved lengthwise, and thinly sliced

$1\frac{1}{4}$ pounds thick white fish fillet, rinsed and cut into 1-inch cubes

Salt and freshly ground black pepper to taste

1 tablespoon cornstarch

2 tablespoons cold water

1. Heat olive oil in a small skillet over medium-high heat. Add onion, garlic, and celery, and cook, stirring frequently, for 3 minutes, or until onion is translucent. Scrape mixture into the slow cooker.

2. Add parsley, oregano, bay leaf, stock, wine, lemon juice, and potatoes to the slow cooker. Stir well.

3. Cook on Low for 6-8 hours or on High for 3-4 hours, or until vegetables are almost soft.

4. If cooking on Low, raise the heat to High. Add zucchini and fish, and cook for 30-40 minutes, or until fish is cooked through. Remove and discard bay leaf, and season to taste with salt and pepper. Mix cornstarch with water, and stir cornstarch mixture into the slow cooker.

Cook for an additional 10–20 minutes, or until juices are bubbling and slightly thickened. Serve immediately.

If cooking conventionally: Follow the recipe to the end of Step 2, assembling the dish in a saucepan, and adding the additional ½ cup stock to the ingredients. Bring to a boil over high heat, and simmer, covered, over low heat, for 15 minutes, or until potatoes are almost tender. Add zucchini, and cook 5 minutes. Add fish, and cook an additional 5 minutes, or until fish is cooked through. Remove and discard bay leaf, and season to taste with salt and pepper. Mix cornstarch with water, and stir cornstarch mixture into the pan. Cook on top of the stove for 3–5 minutes, or until slightly thickened.

Note: Using either cooking method, the dish can be made up to 2 days in advance and refrigerated, tightly covered. Reheat it, covered, over low heat.

Variations:
- Substitute chicken stock for the seafood stock, and substitute 1 pound boneless, skinless chicken, cut into ³/₄-inch dice, for the fish. Add the chicken at the start of the cooking time.
- Substitute vegetable stock for the seafood stock, and substitute 1 pound firm tofu, drained and cut into 1-inch dice, for the fish.
- Substitute beef stock for the seafood stock, and substitute 1 pound lean stewing beef, cut into ½-inch cubes, for the fish. Add the beef at the start of the cooking time.

Creole Fish

Creole cuisine was born in the restaurants of New Orleans, as opposed to Cajun cooking, which originated in the rural bayous. Fish cooked in a spiced—but not spicy—tomato sauce is a classic dish. Serve it on top of rice with a salad or steamed green vegetable.

Yield: 4-6 servings | **Active time:** 20 minutes | **Start to finish (minimum time, slow cooker):** 3½ hours in a medium slow cooker | **Start to finish (conventional):** 45 minutes

> 3 tablespoons olive oil
> 1 large onion, peeled and diced
> 2 celery ribs, rinsed, trimmed, and sliced
> 1 green bell pepper, seeds and ribs removed, and diced
> 3 garlic cloves, peeled and minced
> 1 tablespoon dried oregano
> 1 tablespoon paprika
> 1 teaspoon ground cumin
> ½ teaspoon dried basil
> 1 (15-ounce) can tomato sauce
> ½ cup Seafood Stock (recipe on page 87) or bottled clam juice (*1 cup if cooking conventionally*)
> 2 bay leaves
> 1¼ pounds thick white fish fillets, cut into 1-inch cubes
> Salt and hot red pepper sauce to taste

1. Heat oil in a medium skillet over medium-high heat. Add onion, celery, green bell pepper, and garlic. Cook, stirring frequently, for 3 minutes, or until onion is translucent. Reduce the heat to low, and stir in oregano, paprika, cumin, and basil. Cook for 1 minute, stirring constantly. Scrape mixture into the slow cooker.
2. Stir tomato sauce, stock, and bay leaves into the slow cooker.
3. Cook on Low for to 6–8 hours or on High for 3–4 hours, or until vegetables are soft.
4. If cooking on Low, raise the heat to High. Remove and discard bay leaves, and stir in fish. Cook for 15–30 minutes, or until fish is cooked through. Season to taste with salt and red pepper sauce, and serve immediately.

If cooking conventionally: Follow the recipe to the end of Step 2, assembling the dish in a saucepan, and adding the additional ½ cup stock to the ingredients. Bring to a boil over high heat, and simmer, covered, over low heat, for 20 minutes, or until vegetables are tender. Add fish, and cook an additional 5 minutes, or until fish is cooked through. Remove and discard bay leaves, season to taste with salt and red pepper sauce, and serve immediately.

Note: Using either cooking method, the dish can be made up to 2 days in advance and refrigerated, tightly covered. Reheat it, covered, over low heat.

Variations:
- Substitute vegetable stock for the seafood stock, and add 1 pound zucchini or yellow squash, cut into 1-inch cubes, at the onset of the cooking time.
- Substitute chicken stock for the seafood stock, and add 1 pound boneless, skinless chicken thighs, cut into ¾-inch cubes, at the onset of the cooking time. Add 1 hour if cooking on Low and 30 minutes if cooking on High to the cooking time.
- Omit the basil, and add 2 tablespoons chili powder and 1 (4-ounce) can chopped mild green chiles to give the dish Southwestern flavor.

Nantucket Seafood Stew

There's a Portuguese influence on the cooking of Nantucket and Cape Cod from the era of the whaling trade, and the linguiça sausage in this recipe reflects that tradition. Except for a tossed salad, everything you need for dinner is in the stew.

Yield: 4–6 servings | **Active time:** 25 minutes | **Start to finish (minimum time, slow cooker):** 4 hours in a medium slow cooker | **Start to finish (conventional):** 50 minutes

¼ pound bacon, cut into 1-inch pieces
1 medium onion, peeled and diced
1 carrot, peeled and thinly sliced
1 celery rib, trimmed and thinly sliced
6 garlic cloves, peeled and minced, divided
½ pound mild linguiça or chorizo sausage, diced
1 (14.5-ounce) can diced tomatoes, undrained
3 cups Seafood Stock (recipe on page 87) or bottled clam juice
   (3½ cups if cooking conventionally)
½ cup orange juice
½ cup dry white wine
3 tablespoons chopped fresh parsley
1 teaspoon dried thyme
1 bay leaf
1 pound redskin potatoes, scrubbed and cut into ¾-inch dice
½ cup mayonnaise
¼ cup pimiento, drained
1 tablespoon lemon juice
Salt and freshly ground black pepper to taste
1¼ pounds thick white fish fillet, rinsed and cut into 1-inch cubes

1. Cook bacon in a heavy skillet over medium-high heat for 5–7 minutes, or until crisp. Remove bacon from the pan with a slotted spoon, and place it in the slow cooker. Discard all but 2 tablespoons fat from the skillet.

2. Add onion, carrot, celery, and 3 garlic cloves to the skillet. Cook, stirring frequently, for 3 minutes, or until onion is translucent. Add linguiça, and cook for 3 minutes more. Scrape mixture into the slow cooker.

3. Add tomatoes, stock, orange juice, wine, parsley, thyme, bay leaf, and potatoes to the slow cooker. Stir well.

4. Cook on Low for 6–8 hours or on High for 3–4 hours, or until vegetables are soft.

5. While stew base cooks, combine remaining garlic, mayonnaise, pimiento, and lemon juice in a blender. Puree until smooth. Scrape sauce into a serving bowl, and season to taste with salt and pepper. Refrigerate until ready to serve.

6. If cooking on Low, raise the heat to High. Add fish, and cook for 15–30 minutes, or until fish is cooked through. Remove and discard bay leaf, and season to taste with salt and pepper. Serve immediately, passing sauce separately.

If cooking conventionally: Follow the recipe to the end of Step 3, assembling the dish in a saucepan, and adding the additional $1/2$ cup stock to the ingredients. Bring to a boil over high heat, and simmer, covered, over low heat, for 20 minutes, or until vegetables are tender. Prepare the sauce as described in Step 5. Add fish, and cook an additional 5 minutes, or until fish is cooked through. Remove and discard bay leaf, and season to taste with salt and pepper. Serve immediately, passing sauce separately.

Note: Using either cooking method, the dish can be made up to 2 days in advance and refrigerated, tightly covered. Reheat it, covered, over low heat.

Variation:
- To make this a vegetarian dish, substitute vegetable stock for the seafood stock, omit both the bacon and the linguiça, and add 2 chipotle chiles, finely chopped, to the broth.

Caponata Tuna Sauce

Caponata is a traditional Italian vegetable dish, and in this case, canned tuna transforms a vegetable side dish into a vibrant pasta sauce flecked with olives. Use whatever pasta you like, and serve a tossed salad.

Yield: 4–6 servings | **Active time:** 20 minutes | **Start to finish (minimum time, slow cooker):** 3½ hours in a medium slow cooker | **Start to finish (conventional):** 1 hour

> 1 (¾-pound) eggplant, peeled and cut into ½-inch cubes
> Salt and freshly ground black pepper
> ¼ cup olive oil
> 1 medium onion, peeled and diced
> 2 celery ribs, rinsed, trimmed, and diced
> ½ green bell pepper, seeds and ribs removed, and diced
> 4 garlic cloves, peeled and minced
> ¼ cup red wine vinegar
> 2 tablespoons granulated sugar
> 1 (14.5-ounce) can diced tomatoes, undrained
> 1 (15-ounce) can tomato sauce
> ½ cup sliced pitted green or black olives
> 2 (6-ounce) cans light tuna, drained and broken into chunks

> *If cooking conventionally:*
> ½ cup water

1. Place eggplant in a colander, and sprinkle cubes liberally with salt. Place a plate on top of eggplant cubes, and weight the plate with some cans. Place the colander in the sink or on a plate, and allow eggplant to drain for 30 minutes. Rinse eggplant cubes, and squeeze hard to remove water. Wring out remaining water with a cloth tea towel.

2. Heat ½ cup olive oil in large skillet over medium-high heat. Add onion, celery, green bell pepper, and garlic, and cook, stirring frequently, for 3 minutes, or until onion is translucent. Scrape mixture into the slow cooker.

3. Return the pan to the stove, and heat remaining olive oil over medium-high heat. Add eggplant cubes and cook, stirring frequently, for 3 minutes, or until cubes are lightly browned. Scrape eggplant into the slow cooker, and stir in vinegar, sugar, tomatoes, tomato sauce, and olives.

4. Cook on Low for 5-6 hours or on High for 2½-3 hours, or until vegetables are almost soft.
5. If cooking on Low, raise the heat to High. Add tuna, and cook for 20-30 minutes, or until vegetables are tender. Season to taste with salt and pepper, and serve immediately over cooked pasta.

If cooking conventionally: Follow the recipe to the end of Step 3, assembling the dish in a saucepan, and adding ½ cup water to the ingredients. Bring to a boil, and cook over low heat, covered, for 15-20 minutes, stirring occasionally, or until vegetables are tender. Add tuna, and cook an additional 5 minutes. Season to taste with salt and pepper, and serve immediately over cooked pasta.

Note: Using either cooking method, the dish can be prepared up to 2 days in advance and refrigerated, tightly covered. Reheat it, covered, over low heat until hot.

Eggplants have male and female gender, and the males are preferable since they have fewer seeds and are less bitter. To tell a male from a female, look at the stem end. The male is rounded and has a more even hole; the female hole is indented.

Southwest Tuna and Cheese Casserole

This easy-to-make casserole is held together with an egg custard, and it includes spicy cheese for creaminess and corn tortillas to replicate enchiladas. Some sautéed zucchini provides a good textural contrast.

Yield: 4-6 servings | **Active time:** 15 minutes | **Start to finish (minimum time, slow cooker):** N/A | **Start to finish (conventional):** 50 minutes

 2 tablespoons unsalted butter
 1 medium onion, peeled and diced
 2 garlic cloves, peeled and minced
 1 poblano chile, seeds and ribs removed, and chopped
 1 1/2 teaspoons dried oregano
 1 teaspoon ground cumin
 6 (6-inch) corn tortillas, cut into 1/2-inch strips
 1 cup grated jalapeño Jack cheese
 2 (6-ounce) cans light tuna, drained and broken into chunks
 3 large eggs
 1 cup whole milk
 1/4 cup chopped fresh cilantro
 Salt and freshly ground black pepper to taste

1. Preheat the oven to 350°F, and grease a 9 x 13-inch baking pan.
2. Heat butter in a small skillet over medium-high heat. Add onion, garlic, and chile. Cook, stirring frequently, for 3 minutes, or until onion is translucent. Add oregano and cumin, and cook for 1 minute, stirring constantly.
3. Place 1/2 of tortilla strips in the prepared pan, and top with 1/2 of cheese, 1/2 of tuna, and 1/2 of onion mixture. Repeat with second layer. Whisk eggs with milk and cilantro, and season to taste with salt and pepper. Pour egg mixture into pan.
4. Cover the pan with aluminum foil, and bake for 15 minutes. Remove foil, and bake for an additional 20–25 minutes, or until top is brown and a toothpick inserted in the center comes out clean. Allow to sit for 5 minutes before serving.

Note: The dish can be prepared for baking up to 1 day in advance and refrigerated, tightly covered. Add 10 minutes to covered baking time if chilled.

Variation:

- For a milder dish, substitute Monterey Jack cheese for the jalapeño Jack, and use a small green bell pepper instead of the poblano chile.

Poblano chiles are dark green and about 4 inches long; they have a tapered shape and are only slightly spicy. If you can't find one, substitute an Anaheim chile, or even a green bell pepper. If using a green bell pepper, increase the spicing of the dish in another way; use some hot red pepper sauce or crushed red pepper flakes.

Overnight Italian Tuna Bake

This casserole is entirely prepared in advance, and allowed to sit overnight so that the pasta softens and absorbs flavors from the sauce. Or, make it in the morning, and bake it when you come in after work; it can bake while you make a salad.

Yield: 4–6 servings | **Active time:** 15 minutes | **Start to finish (minimum time, slow cooker):** N/A | **Start to finish (conventional):** 9¼ hours, including 8 hours to chill

3 tablespoons unsalted butter
1 small onion, peeled and chopped
2 garlic cloves, peeled and minced
¼ cup all-purpose flour
2 cups whole milk
1 cup grated whole milk mozzarella cheese
½ cup freshly grated Parmesan cheese
2 tablespoons chopped fresh parsley
2 teaspoons Italian seasoning
Salt and freshly ground black pepper to taste
1 (10-ounce) package frozen leaf spinach, thawed and squeezed dry
2 cups small shells or other small pasta
2 (6-ounce) cans light tuna, drained and broken into chunks

1. Grease a 9 x 13-inch baking pan. Melt butter in a saucepan over medium-high heat. Add onion and garlic, and cook, stirring frequently, for 3 minutes, or until onion is translucent. Reduce the heat to low, stir in flour, and cook, stirring constantly, for 2 minutes. Whisk in milk, raise the heat to medium-high, and bring to a boil. Reduce the heat to low, and simmer sauce 2 minutes. Stir in mozzarella and Parmesan cheeses and Italian seasoning, and season to taste with salt and pepper.

2. Pour sauce into the prepared pan, and stir in spinach, pasta shells, and tuna. Cover pan tightly, and refrigerate at least 8 hours, or overnight.

3. Preheat the oven to 350°F. Cover the pan with aluminum foil, and bake for 50 minutes, or until pasta is tender. Serve immediately.

Note: The dish can be prepared for baking up to 1 day in advance.

Variations:

- For a different flavor profile, substitute Swiss cheese for the mozzarella, and use herbes de Provence instead of Italian seasoning.
- Substitute 1 (10-ounce) package frozen chopped broccoli, cooked according to package instructions, for the spinach.

You can use this technique with many pasta dishes, and it means that you don't have to dirty a pan cooking the pasta separately! Always use a small pasta, like shells or macaroni, and use the same proportion of sauce to pasta found in this recipe.

Greek Tuna Balls

Tomatoes and kalamata olives enliven the sauce topping these "meat-balls" made with canned tuna. Serve the dish on top of orzo, or another small pasta, along with a tossed salad.

Yield: 4–6 servings | **Active time:** 20 minutes | **Start to finish (minimum time, slow cooker):** N/A | **Start to finish (conventional):** 50 minutes

Vegetable oil spray
2 tablespoons mayonnaise
1 large egg
½ cup Italian breadcrumbs
¼ cup freshly grated Parmesan cheese
Salt and freshly ground black pepper to taste
3 (6-ounce) cans light tuna, drained and flaked
2 tablespoons olive oil
1 small onion, peeled and chopped
3 garlic cloves, peeled and minced
1 celery rib, rinsed, trimmed, and chopped
1 (28-ounce) can crushed tomatoes in tomato puree
½ cup dry white wine
¾ cup chopped pitted kalamata olives
¼ cup chopped fresh parsley
1 tablespoon dried oregano
1 bay leaf

1. Preheat the oven to 425°F, line a rimmed baking sheet with heavy-duty aluminum foil, and spray the foil with vegetable oil spray.
2. Combine mayonnaise and egg in a mixing bowl, and whisk well. Stir in breadcrumbs and cheese, season to taste with salt and pepper, and gently fold in tuna.
3. Make mixture into 1½-inch balls, and arrange tuna balls on the pre-pared pan. Spray tops of tuna balls with vegetable oil spray. Bake tuna balls for 8–10 minutes, or until lightly browned.
4. While tuna balls bake, heat oil in a large skillet over medium-high heat. Add onion, garlic, and celery. Cook, stirring frequently, for 3 minutes, or until onion is translucent. Add tomatoes, wine, olives, parsley, oregano, and bay leaf. Bring to a boil, reduce the heat to medium, and simmer sauce, uncovered, for 15 minutes.

5. Remove the pan from the oven, and add tuna balls to sauce. Bring to a boil and simmer, uncovered, for 10 minutes. Remove and discard bay leaf, season to taste with salt and pepper, and serve immediately.

Note: The dish can be cooked up to 2 days in advance and refrigerated, tightly covered. Reheat, covered, over low heat until hot.

Variation:
- Substitute 1½ cups finely chopped cooked chicken for the tuna.

The slightly higher per-ounce cost of pitted olives is well worth the money considering how labor intensive it is to pit them yourself. But should a few olives with pits end up in your container, here's how to pit them: Hit them with the bottom of a small skillet, and they will split apart, at which time you can quickly discard the pits.

Overnight Fish and Broccoli Bake

Soaking the uncooked pasta in liquid softens it so that it cooks easily in the sauce, and absorbs the flavor from it. The combination of the fish with cheese and broccoli is homey and delicious.

Yield: 4–6 servings | **Active time:** 10 minutes | **Start to finish (minimum time, slow cooker):** N/A | **Start to finish (conventional):** 9 hours, including 8 hours to chill

3 tablespoons unsalted butter

3 tablespoons all-purpose flour

1 cup Seafood Stock (recipe on page 87) or bottled clam juice

¾ cup whole milk

1 cup grated sharp cheddar cheese

½ teaspoon dried thyme

Salt and freshly ground black pepper to taste

2 cups elbow macaroni

1 (10-ounce) package frozen chopped broccoli, thawed and drained

1¼ pounds thick white fish fillet, rinsed and cut into 1-inch cubes

1. Grease a 9 x 13-inch baking pan. Melt butter in a small saucepan over low heat. Stir in flour, and cook, stirring constantly, for 2 minutes. Whisk in stock and milk, raise the heat to medium-high, and bring to a boil. Reduce the heat to low, and simmer sauce 2 minutes. Stir in cheddar cheese and thyme, and season to taste with salt and pepper.

2. Pour sauce into the prepared pan, and stir in macaroni. Cover pan tightly, and refrigerate at least 8 hours, or overnight.

3. Preheat the oven to 350°F. Remove the pan from the refrigerator, and stir in broccoli and fish. Cover the pan with aluminum foil, and bake for 50 minutes, or until pasta is tender. Serve immediately.

Note: The dish can be prepared for baking up to 1 day in advance; however, do not add the fish cubes until just prior to baking.

Variations:
- Substitute Swiss cheese for the cheddar.
- Substitute frozen chopped spinach for the broccoli.

Chapter 6:

From the Coops: Chicken and Turkey Entrees

What would our lives be without poultry? These foods are the blank canvases of the culinary world, and they present a great price/value relationship in these difficult financial times.

However, the very popular boneless, skinless chicken breast remains expensive—unless on sale—and is really not the best choice for the slow cooker. The chicken dishes that the slow cooker renders succulent and luscious are whole pieces cooked on the bone.

I've written these recipes for whole, cut-up chickens; there are instructions below on how to accomplish this easy task yourself to save even more money. However, if you have certain pieces you like more than others, feel free to substitute. With the low heat of the slow cooker, all pieces are cooked in the amount of time listed.

That's assuming, however, that the pieces have bones, even if the skin has been removed. Boneless meat cooks more rapidly, and should not be substituted in these recipes.

SAFETY FIRST

Always rinse poultry under cold running water after taking it out of the package. If it's going to be pre-browned in the oven or in a skillet on the stove, pat the pieces dry with paper towels, and then wash your hands. Chicken often contains salmonella, a naturally occurring bacteria that is killed by cooking, but you don't want to transfer this bacteria to other foods.

For the sake of food safety, it's best not to cook a whole chicken in the slow cooker, because the low heat might keep the meat of a whole bird in the bacterial danger zone for more than two hours.

CUTTING WITH CUNNING

Just look at the range of prices for chicken in the supermarket. The least-processed piece—the whole chicken—is always the lowest in cost per pound. Then there are the legs and thighs or leg quarters, which can sometimes be even less expensive than a whole bird because the white meat removed from the whole chicken is more in demand.

It is far more economical to purchase a whole chicken, and cut it up yourself, rather than buying one already cut. There are also times that your choice of chicken pieces, such as thighs, aren't available, and you can always cut up a few chickens to glean the parts for that meal, and freeze what's left; another benefit is that you can save the scraps and freeze them to keep you "stocked up" for soups and sauces; see the recipe for chicken stock on page 84.

Cutting up a whole chicken is very easy. Start by breaking back the wings until the joints snap; then use a boning knife to cut through the ball joints and detach the wings. When holding the chicken on its side, you will see a natural curve outlining the boundary between the breast and the leg/thigh quarters. Use sharp kitchen shears to cut along this line. Cut the breast in half by scraping away the meat from the breastbone, and using a small paring knife to remove the wishbone. Cut away the breastbone using shears, and save it for stock. Divide the thigh and leg quarters by turning the pieces over and finding the joint joining them. Cut through the joint and sever the leg from the thigh.

LUSCIOUS LEFTOVERS

One of the reasons I adopted the approach of including conventional recipes in with those intended for the slow cooker is to present myriad ways to utilize leftover chicken and turkey; you'll find them at the end of this chapter in a section titled "The Second Time Around."

While some of these recipes are written for chicken and others for turkey, the different birds can be used interchangeably. If you have leftovers, and don't plan to use them within a few days, cut them up and freeze them. It's very quick to defrost cut up cooked poultry in a microwave oven, or you can toss the contents of the freezer bag into a dish, still frozen, if there's a sauce simmering in which it can thaw.

While the recipes in this chapter are designed for cooked poultry that is a neutral ingredient, if you have poultry that was cooked in a sauce, such as any of the other recipes in this chapter, they can still earn a second life. Remove all of the skin, and use meat that is clearly flavored by the sauce for another dish or as a snack. Then use the pristine meat for one of the variations of leftovers.

You'll notice that some recipes utilizing cooked poultry specify shredded while others call for the meat to be diced. The reason for this is that certain sauces and forms of dishes are better for one than the other, although if you have cooked poultry diced in your freezer, go ahead and use it for a recipe calling for shredded.

Chicken with Bacon and Vegetables

We tend to overlook the lettuce family when thinking about vegetables to cook, but it adds a delicate flavor to balance the hearty, salty bacon in this sauce. Because potatoes are included, this dish is a complete meal.

Yield: 4-6 servings | **Active time:** 15 minutes | **Start to finish (minimum time, slow cooker):** 3¼ hours in a medium slow cooker | **Start to finish (conventional):** 1¼ hours

> 1 (3½–4-pound) frying chicken, cut into serving pieces
> ¼ pound bacon, cut into 1-inch pieces
> 1 small onion, peeled and diced
> 2 garlic cloves, peeled and minced
> 1 pound redskin potatoes, scrubbed and cut into 1½-inch cubes
> 1½ cups Chicken Stock (recipe on page 84) or purchased stock (*2 cups if cooking conventionally*)
> 2 tablespoons chopped fresh parsley
> 1 tablespoon dried rosemary, crumbled
> 1 teaspoon dried thyme
> 2 (10-ounce) packages frozen pearl onions and peas, thawed
> 2 cups firmly packed leaf or Boston lettuce, rinsed and cut into 3-inch sections
> 1 tablespoon cornstarch
> 2 tablespoons cold water
> Salt and freshly ground black pepper to taste

1. Preheat the oven broiler, and line a broiler pan with heavy-duty aluminum foil. Rinse chicken and pat dry with paper towels. Broil chicken pieces for 3–5 minutes, or until browned. Turn pieces, and brown the other side. Arrange chicken in the slow cooker.

2. While chicken browns, place bacon in a heavy skillet over medium-high heat. Cook, stirring often, for 5–7 minutes, or until bacon is crisp. Remove bacon from the pan with a slotted spoon, and set aside. Discard all but 2 tablespoons bacon fat from the skillet, and add onion and garlic. Cook, stirring often, for 3 minutes, or until onion is translucent. Scrape mixture into the slow cooker. Add potatoes, chicken stock, parsley, rosemary, and thyme. Stir well.

3. Cook chicken on Low for 5–7 hours or on High for 2½–3 hours.

4. If cooking on Low, raise the heat to High. Add pearl onions and peas and lettuce, and cook for an additional 45 minutes, or until chicken is cooked through and no longer pink. Mix cornstarch and cold water in a small cup. Stir mixture into the slow cooker, and cook for an additional 10–20 minutes, or until the liquid is bubbling and has slightly thickened. Season to taste with salt and pepper, and serve immediately.

If cooking conventionally: Preheat the oven to 375°F after chicken browns, and follow the recipe to the end of Step 2, assembling the dish in a Dutch oven, and adding the additional ½ cup stock to the ingredients. Cook chicken, covered, for 30 minutes, then add pearl onions and peas and lettuce. Bake for an additional 15–25 minutes, or until chicken is cooked through and no longer pink. Add cornstarch mixture, and cook on top of the stove for 3–5 minutes, or until slightly thickened.

Note: Using either cooking method, the chicken can be prepared up to 2 days in advance and refrigerated, tightly covered. Reheat it, covered, in a 350°F oven for 20–25 minutes, or until hot.

Variations:
- Substitute 2 (10-ounce) packages of mixed vegetables for the onions and peas for more variety and color in the dish.
- Substitute escarole for the lettuce for a more assertive flavor.

Chicken Provençal

The French cuisine in the sun-drenched region of Provence is known for its bright flavors and healthful ingredients. This chicken dish, made with colorful vegetables as well as olives, epitomizes this style of cooking.

Yield: 4–6 servings | **Active time:** 20 minutes | **Start to finish (minimum time, slow cooker):** 3½ hours in a medium slow cooker | **Start to finish (conventional oven):** 1¼ hours

  1 (3½–4-pound) frying chicken, cut into serving pieces
  ¼ cup olive oil
  1 large onion, peeled and diced
  2 garlic cloves, peeled and minced
  1 green bell pepper, seeds and ribs removed, and diced
  2 celery ribs, rinsed, trimmed, and sliced
  ½ cup orange juice
  ½ cup dry white wine
  1 (14.5-ounce) can diced tomatoes, undrained
  2 tablespoons chopped fresh parsley
  2 teaspoons herbes de Provence
  ½ cup pitted oil-cured black olives
  If cooking conventionally: ½ cup Chicken Stock (see recipe page 84) or purchased stock
  1 tablespoon cornstarch
  2 tablespoons cold water
  Salt and freshly ground black pepper to taste

1. Preheat the oven broiler, and line a broiler pan with heavy-duty aluminum foil. Rinse chicken and pat dry with paper towels. Broil chicken pieces for 3–5 minutes, or until browned. Turn pieces, and brown the other side. Arrange chicken in the slow cooker.
2. While chicken browns, heat oil in a large skillet over medium-high heat. Add onion, garlic, green bell pepper, and celery. Cook, stirring frequently, for 3 minutes, or until onion is translucent. Scrape mixture into the slow cooker. Add orange juice, wine, tomatoes, parsley, herbes de Provence, and olives. Stir well.
3. Cook chicken on Low for 6–8 hours or on High for 3–4 hours, or until chicken is cooked through and no longer pink.

4. If cooking on Low, raise the heat to High. Mix cornstarch and cold water in a small cup. Stir mixture into the slow cooker, and cook for an additional 10–20 minutes, or until the liquid is bubbling and has slightly thickened. Season to taste with salt and pepper, and serve immediately.

If cooking conventionally: Preheat the oven to 375°F after chicken browns, and follow the recipe to the end of Step 2, assembling the dish in a Dutch oven, and adding the additional 1/2 cup stock to the ingredients. Cook chicken, covered, for 45 minutes–1 hour, or until chicken is cooked through and no longer pink. Add cornstarch mixture, and cook on top of the stove for 3–5 minutes, or until slightly thickened. Season to taste with salt and pepper, and serve immediately.

Note: Using either cooking method, the chicken can be prepared up to 2 days in advance and refrigerated, tightly covered. Reheat it, covered, in a 350°F oven for 20–25 minutes, or until hot.

Herbes de Provence, like Italian seasoning, is a blend of many herbs, so you don't have to own them all to achieve a complex flavor. If you don't have it, use a combination of oregano, thyme, and rosemary.

Hungarian Chicken

Paprika and sour cream are two hallmarks of this traditional Hungarian dish, which can be made with many different meats, too. Serve it with buttered egg noodles to enjoy the sauce.

Yield: 4-6 servings | **Active time:** 20 minutes | **Start to finish (minimum time, slow cooker):** 3½ hours in a medium slow cooker | **Start to finish (conventional oven):** 1¼ hours

1 (3½-4-pound) frying chicken, cut into serving pieces
2 tablespoons unsalted butter
1 large onion, peeled and diced
1 garlic clove, peeled and minced
2 tablespoons sweet paprika
1 teaspoon dried thyme
1¼ cups Chicken Stock (recipe on page 84) or purchased stock
  (1¾ cups if cooking conventionally)
2 tablespoons chopped fresh parsley
1 tablespoon cornstarch
2 tablespoons cold water
½ cup sour cream
Salt and freshly ground black pepper to taste

1. Preheat the oven broiler, and line a broiler pan with heavy-duty aluminum foil. Rinse chicken and pat dry with paper towels. Broil chicken pieces for 3-5 minutes, or until browned. Turn pieces, and brown the other side. Arrange chicken in the slow cooker.

2. While chicken browns, heat butter in a large skillet over medium-high heat. Add onion and garlic, and cook, stirring frequently, for 3 minutes, or until onion is translucent. Stir in paprika and thyme, and cook, stirring constantly, for 1 minute. Add chicken stock and parsley to the skillet, and stir well. Scrape mixture into the slow cooker.

3. Cook chicken on Low for 6-8 hours or on High for 3-4 hours, or until chicken is cooked through and no longer pink.

4. If cooking on Low, raise the heat to High. Mix cornstarch and cold water in a small cup. Stir mixture into the slow cooker, and cook for an additional 10-20 minutes, or until the liquid is bubbling and has slightly thickened. Stir in sour cream, and season to taste with salt and pepper. Do not allow mixture to boil, or sauce will curdle.

If cooking conventionally: Preheat the oven to 375°F after chicken browns, and follow the recipe to the end of Step 2, assembling the dish in a Dutch oven, and adding the additional ½ cup stock to the ingredients. Cook chicken, covered, for 45 minutes–1 hour, or until chicken is cooked through and no longer pink. Add cornstarch mixture, and cook on top of the stove for 3–5 minutes, or until slightly thickened. Then stir in sour cream, and season with salt and pepper. Do not allow mixture to boil, or sauce will curdle.

Note: Using either cooking method, the chicken can be prepared up to 2 days in advance and refrigerated, tightly covered. Reheat it, covered, in a 350°F oven for 20–25 minutes, or until hot.

Variations:
- Substitute 1½ pounds of pork loin or beef chuck, cut into 1-inch cubes, for the chicken. Add 2 hours if cooking on Low, 1 hour if cooking on High, or 30 minutes if cooking conventionally.
- Substitute plain nonfat yogurt for the sour cream to reduce the fat in the dish.

> You'll see many types of paprika in the supermarket, all of which are made from grinding dried red bell peppers. Spanish paprika tends to have some bite to it, so don't use it in a dish calling for sweet paprika.

Country Captain

Country Captain is a chicken dish that dates back to Colonial times. Some food historians say it originated in Savannah, Georgia, a major port for the spice trade. There's a hint of curry as well as raisins and vegetables in the sauce that give it vibrant flavor.

Yield: 4–6 servings | **Active time:** 15 minutes | **Start to finish (minimum time, slow cooker):** 3½ hours in a medium slow cooker | **Start to finish (conventional):** 1¼ hours

1 (3½–4-pound) frying chicken, cut into serving pieces
2 tablespoons vegetable oil
1 large onion, peeled and diced
3 garlic cloves, peeled and minced
1 green bell pepper, seeds and ribs removed, and diced
2 tablespoons curry powder
1 teaspoon ground ginger
1 teaspoon dried thyme
1 cup Chicken Stock (see recipe page 84) or purchased stock (1½ cups if cooking conventionally)
1 (14.5-ounce) can diced tomatoes, undrained
¼ cup dry sherry
2 tablespoons chopped fresh parsley
⅔ cup raisins
1 tablespoon cornstarch
2 tablespoons cold water
Salt and freshly ground black pepper to taste

1. Preheat the oven broiler, and line a broiler pan with heavy-duty aluminum foil. Rinse chicken and pat dry with paper towels. Broil chicken pieces for 3–5 minutes, or until browned. Turn pieces, and brown the other side. Arrange chicken in the slow cooker.

2. While chicken browns, heat oil in a skillet over medium-high heat. Add onion, garlic, and green bell pepper. Cook, stirring frequently, for 3 minutes, or until onion is translucent. Stir in curry powder, ginger, and thyme, and cook, stirring constantly, for 1 minute. Scrape mixture into the slow cooker, and add chicken stock, tomatoes, sherry, parsley, and raisins.

3. Cook chicken on Low for 6–8 hours or on High for 3–4 hours, or until chicken is cooked through and no longer pink.

4. If cooking on Low, raise the heat to High. Mix cornstarch and cold water in a small cup. Stir mixture into the slow cooker, and cook for an additional 10–20 minutes, or until the liquid is bubbling and has slightly thickened. Season to taste with salt and pepper, and serve immediately.

If cooking conventionally: Preheat the oven to 375°F after chicken browns, and follow the recipe to the end of Step 2, assembling the dish in a Dutch oven, and adding the additional 1/2 cup stock to the ingredients. Cook chicken, covered, for 45 minutes–1 hour, or until chicken is cooked through and no longer pink. Add cornstarch mixture, and cook on top of the stove for 3–5 minutes, or until slightly thickened. Season to taste with salt and pepper.

Note: Using either cooking method, the chicken can be prepared up to 2 days in advance and refrigerated, tightly covered. Reheat it, covered, in a 350°F oven for 20–25 minutes, or until hot.

Variations:
- Substitute dried cranberries or chopped dried apricots for the raisins, and the fruit flavor will be more pronounced.
- Substitute 1 1/4 pounds boneless country pork ribs or pork loin, cut into 1-inch cubes, for the chicken. Add 2 hours if cooking on Low, 1 hour if cooking on High, or 30 minutes if cooking conventionally.

Indian Chicken with Toasted Cashews

This dish just explodes with exotic flavors; the chicken is first marinated in yogurt and spices, and then the marinade is used as part of the cooking liquid. The sauce is thickened with ground nuts, which increases the protein content, too. Serve it over rice, preferably aromatic basmati rice.

Yield: 4-6 servings | **Active time:** 15 minutes | **Start to finish (minimum time, slow cooker):** 9½ hours in a medium slow cooker, including 6 hours to marinate | **Start to finish (conventional):** 7½ hours, including 6 hours to marinate

1 (8-ounce) container plain yogurt
4 garlic cloves, peeled and minced
2 tablespoons grated fresh ginger
2 tablespoons curry powder
½ teaspoon ground cinnamon
¼–½ teaspoon cayenne
Salt and freshly ground black pepper to taste
1 (3½–4-pound) frying chicken, cut into serving pieces
1 cup roasted cashew nuts, divided
¾ cup Chicken Stock (recipe on page 84) or purchased stock (1¼ cups if cooking conventionally), divided
3 tablespoons vegetable oil
1 large onion, peeled and chopped
1 carrot, peeled and sliced
1 (10-ounce) package frozen green beans, thawed
Salt and freshly ground black pepper to taste

1. Combine yogurt, garlic, ginger, curry powder, cinnamon, cayenne, salt, and pepper in heavy resealable plastic bag, and mix well. Rinse chicken and pat dry with paper towels. Add chicken pieces, and turn the bag to coat pieces evenly. Marinate chicken, refrigerated, for a minimum of 6 hours, preferably overnight.
2. Preheat the oven broiler, and line a broiler pan with heavy-duty aluminum foil. Remove chicken from marinade, scrape off marinade, and reserve marinade. Broil chicken pieces for 3–5 minutes, or until browned. Turn pieces, and brown the other side. Arrange chicken in the slow cooker.

3. Grind ¾ cup cashews with ¼ cup chicken stock in a food processor fitted with a steel blade or in a blender. Set aside. Coarsely chop remaining cashews, and set aside.

4. Heat oil in large skillet over medium-high heat. Add onion, and cook, stirring frequently, for 3 minutes, or until onion is translucent. Add carrot to pan, along with nut puree, remaining chicken stock, and reserved marinade, and bring to a boil. Pour mixture into the slow cooker.

5. Cook chicken on Low for 6–8 hours or on High for 3–4 hours, or until chicken is cooked through and no longer pink.

6. If cooking on Low, raise the heat to High. Add green beans, and cook for an additional 15–20 minutes, or until green beans are cooked. Season to taste with salt and pepper, and serve immediately, sprinkled with remaining cashews.

If cooking conventionally: Preheat the oven to 375°F after chicken browns, and follow the recipe to the end of Step 4, assembling the dish in a Dutch oven, and adding the additional ½ cup stock to the ingredients. Cook chicken, covered, for 45 minutes–1 hour, or until chicken is cooked through and no longer pink. Add green beans, and cook for an additional 5 minutes, or until green beans are cooked. Season to taste with salt and pepper, and serve immediately, sprinkled with remaining cashews.

Note: Using either cooking method, the chicken can be prepared up to 2 days in advance and refrigerated, tightly covered. Reheat it, covered, in a 350°F oven for 20–25 minutes, or until hot.

Variation:
- Substitute 1¼ pounds of beef chuck, cut into 1-inch cubes, for the chicken pieces. Add 2 hours if cooking on Low, 1 hour if cooking on High, or 30 minutes if cooking conventionally.

Mexican Chicken in Jalapeño-Beer Sauce

Beer is used in a lot of cooking around the world, and the lusty yeasty flavor of dark beer is wonderful in the spicy sauce for this chicken. Serve it with some Mexican rice and a tossed salad.

Yield: 4–6 servings | **Active time:** 20 minutes | **Start to finish (minimum time, slow cooker):** 3¾ hours | **Start to finish (conventional):** 1¼ hours

> 1 (3½–4-pound) frying chicken, cut into serving pieces
> 2 tablespoons olive oil
> 1 large onion, peeled and diced
> 3 garlic cloves, peeled and minced
> 1 green bell pepper, seeds and ribs removed, and diced
> 2 jalapeño or serrano chiles, seeds and ribs removed, and finely chopped
> 1 tablespoon dried oregano
> 2 teaspoons ground cumin
> 1 (14.5-ounce) can diced tomatoes, drained
> 1 cup dark beer, preferably Mexican
> ½ cup Chicken Stock (recipe on page 84) or purchased stock (*1 cup if cooking conventionally*)
> 1 (15-ounce) can kidney beans, drained and rinsed
> Salt and freshly ground black pepper to taste

1. Preheat the oven broiler, and line a broiler pan with heavy-duty aluminum foil. Rinse chicken and pat dry with paper towels. Broil chicken pieces for 3–5 minutes, or until browned. Turn pieces, and brown the other side. Arrange chicken in the slow cooker.
2. While chicken browns, heat oil in a medium skillet over medium-high heat. Add onion, garlic, green bell pepper, and chiles, and cook, stirring frequently, for 3 minutes, or until onion is translucent. Add oregano and cumin, and cook for 1 minute, stirring constantly. Scrape mixture into the slow cooker.
3. Add tomatoes, beer, stock, and beans to the slow cooker. Stir well.
4. Cook chicken on Low for 6–8 hours or on High for 3–4 hours, or until chicken is cooked through and no longer pink. Season to taste with salt and pepper.

If cooking conventionally: Preheat the oven to 375°F after chicken browns, and follow the recipe to the end of Step 3, assembling the dish in a Dutch oven, and adding the additional ½ cup stock to the ingredients. Cook chicken, covered, for 45 minutes–1 hour, or until chicken is cooked through and no longer pink. Season to taste with salt and pepper.

Note: Using either cooking method, the chicken can be prepared up to 2 days in advance and refrigerated, tightly covered. Reheat it, covered, in a 350°F oven for 20–25 minutes, or until hot.

Variation:
- Substitute ¼ pound boneless country pork ribs or pork loin, cut into 1-inch cubes, for the chicken. Add 2 hours if cooking on Low, 1 hour if cooking on High, or 30 minutes if cooking conventionally

When cooking with beer, wine, or any form of alcohol, almost all the alcohol evaporates during a long cooking process such as this one.

Moroccan Sweet and Sour Chicken

A combination of aromatic herbs and spices, salty olives, and succulent dried fruits give this dish a deliciously vibrant flavor. Serve it over couscous, the traditional North African granular pasta.

Yield: 4-6 servings | **Active time:** 15 minutes | **Start to finish (minimum time, slow cooker):** 3½ hours | **Start to finish (conventional):** 1¼ hours

1 (3½-4-pound) frying chicken, cut into serving pieces
2 tablespoons olive oil
1 large red onion, peeled and diced
4 garlic cloves, peeled and minced
2 carrots, peeled and sliced
2 tablespoons dried oregano
1 tablespoon ground cumin
2 teaspoons ground coriander
¾ cup dry white wine
¾ cup Chicken Stock (recipe on page 84) or purchased stock (1¼ cups if cooking conventionally)
¼ cup cider vinegar
¼ pound dried apricots, finely chopped
½ cup sliced pimiento-stuffed green olives
¼ cup firmly packed dark brown sugar
1 tablespoon cornstarch
2 tablespoons cold water
Salt and freshly ground black pepper to taste

1. Preheat the oven broiler, and line a broiler pan with heavy-duty aluminum foil. Rinse chicken and pat dry with paper towels. Broil chicken pieces for 3-5 minutes, or until browned. Turn pieces, and brown the other side. Arrange chicken in the slow cooker.

2. Heat oil in a medium skillet over medium-high heat. Add onion, garlic, and carrots, and cook, stirring frequently, for 3 minutes, or until onion is translucent. Add oregano, cumin, and coriander, and cook for 1 minute, stirring constantly. Scrape mixture into the slow cooker. Add wine, stock, vinegar, dried apricots, olives, and brown sugar to the slow cooker. Stir well.

3. Cook on Low for 6-8 hours or on High for 3-4 hours, or until chicken is cooked through and no longer pink.

4. If cooking on Low, raise the heat to High. Mix cornstarch and cold water in a small cup. Stir mixture into the slow cooker, and cook for an additional 10–20 minutes, or until the liquid is bubbling and has slightly thickened. Season to taste with salt and pepper, and serve immediately.

If cooking conventionally: Preheat the oven to 375°F after chicken browns, and follow the recipe to the end of Step 2, assembling the dish in a Dutch oven, and adding the additional $1/2$ cup stock to the ingredients. Cook chicken, covered, for 45 minutes–1 hour, or until chicken is cooked through and no longer pink. Add cornstarch mixture, and cook on top of the stove for 3–5 minutes, or until slightly thickened. Season to taste with salt and pepper.

Note: Using either cooking method, the chicken can be prepared up to 2 days in advance and refrigerated, tightly covered. Reheat it, covered, in a 350°F oven for 20–25 minutes, or until hot.

Variation:

- Substitute $1^1/_4$ pounds boneless country pork ribs or pork loin, cut into 1-inch cubes, for the chicken. Add 2 hours if cooking on Low, 1 hour if cooking on High, or 30 minutes if cooking conventionally.

The combination of sweet dried fruit with salty olives is characteristic of Moroccan cooking, as it is across the Mediterranean Sea in Sicily.

Chinese Chicken Curry

While we associate curry with Indian food, the spice is also used in the Caribbean, and has a role in Chinese-American food. Even cooking in the slow cooker, the vegetables remain crisp, and the sauce should be enjoyed with rice.

Yield: 4-6 servings | **Active time:** 20 minutes | **Start to finish (minimum time, slow cooker):** 3½ hours in a medium slow cooker | **Start to finish (conventional):** 1¼ hours

1 (3½–4-pound) frying chicken, cut into serving pieces
3 tablespoons Asian sesame oil *
4 scallions, white parts and 3 inches of green tops, rinsed, trimmed, and chopped
4 garlic cloves, peeled and minced
2 tablespoons grated fresh ginger
1 jalapeño or serrano chile, seeds and ribs removed, and finely chopped
2 tablespoons curry powder
½ teaspoon Chinese five-spice powder *
1 cup Chicken Stock (recipe on page 84) or purchased stock (*1½ cups if cooking conventionally*)
1 cup light coconut milk
2 tablespoons rice vinegar
2 tablespoons firmly packed dark brown sugar
2 tablespoons soy sauce
2 tablespoons vegetable oil
1 large onion, peeled, halved, and cut into ¼-inch slices
1 carrot, peeled and cut into ¼-inch slices
1 green bell pepper, seeds and ribs removed, and diced
2 celery ribs, rinsed, trimmed and cut into ¼-inch slices
1 tablespoon cornstarch
2 tablespoons cold water
Salt and freshly ground black pepper to taste

1. Preheat the oven broiler, and line a broiler pan with heavy-duty aluminum foil. Rinse chicken and pat dry with paper towels. Broil chicken pieces for 3–5 minutes, or until browned. Turn pieces, and brown the other side. Arrange chicken in the slow cooker.

2. While chicken browns, heat sesame oil in a medium skillet over medium-high heat. Add scallions, garlic, ginger, and chile, and cook, stirring frequently, for 3 minutes, or until scallions are translucent. Add curry powder and five-spice powder, and cook for 1 minute, stirring constantly. Scrape mixture into the slow cooker. Add stock, coconut milk, vinegar, brown sugar, and soy sauce to the slow cooker. Stir well.
3. Cook on Low for 6–7 hours or on High for $2\frac{1}{2}$–3 hours, or until chicken is almost cooked through.
4. While chicken cooks, heat vegetable oil in a large skillet over medium-high heat. Add onion, carrot, bell pepper, and celery. Cook, stirring frequently, for 3 minutes, or until onion is translucent.
5. If cooking on Low, raise the heat to High. Add vegetables to the slow cooker, and cook for 20–30 minutes, or until vegetables are crisp-tender and chicken is no longer pink. Mix cornstarch and cold water in a small cup. Stir mixture into the slow cooker, and cook for an additional 10–20 minutes, or until the liquid is bubbling and has slightly thickened. Season to taste with salt and pepper, and serve immediately.

If cooking conventionally: Preheat the oven to 375°F after chicken browns, and follow the recipe to the end of Step 2, assembling the dish in a Dutch oven, and adding the additional $\frac{1}{2}$ cup stock to the ingredients. Cook chicken, covered, for 30 minutes. Follow Step 4 above, and add vegetables to the Dutch oven. Bake for an additional 15–20 minutes, or until vegetables are crisp-tender and chicken is cooked through and no longer pink. Add cornstarch mixture, and cook on top of the stove for 3–5 minutes, or until slightly thickened. Season to taste with salt and pepper, and serve immediately.

Note: Using either cooking method, the chicken can be prepared up to 2 days in advance and refrigerated, tightly covered. Reheat it, covered, in a 350°F oven for 20–25 minutes, or until hot.

Variation:
- Substitute $1\frac{1}{4}$ pounds boneless country pork ribs or pork loin, cut into 1-inch cubes, for the chicken. Add 1 hour to the cooking time on Low, 30 minutes on High, or 15 minutes if cooking conventionally.

* Available in the Asian aisle of most supermarkets and in specialty markets.

North African Chicken with Garbanzo Beans

Garbanzo beans have the nuttiest flavor and meatiest texture of the legumes, and they are used extensively in Mediterranean cuisines. They are joined in this chicken dish by colorful green beans and a number of spices. Serve this dish with couscous to enjoy the sauce.

Yield: 4-6 servings | **Active time:** 20 minutes | **Start to finish (minimum time, slow cooker):** 3½ hours | **Start to finish (conventional):** 1¼ hours

1 (3½-4-pound) frying chicken, cut into serving pieces
2 tablespoons olive oil
1 large onion, peeled and diced
3 garlic cloves, peeled and minced
2 carrots, peeled and sliced
3 tablespoons paprika
2 tablespoons ground cumin
1 tablespoon ground coriander
2 cups Chicken Stock (recipe on page 84) or purchased stock (2½ cups if cooking conventionally)
¼ cup balsamic vinegar
1 (15-ounce) can garbanzo beans, drained and rinsed
1 (10-ounce) package frozen cut green beans, thawed
Salt and freshly ground black pepper to taste

1. Preheat the oven broiler, and line a broiler pan with heavy-duty aluminum foil. Rinse chicken and pat dry with paper towels. Broil chicken pieces for 3-5 minutes, or until browned. Turn pieces, and brown the other side. Arrange chicken in the slow cooker.

2. While chicken browns, heat oil in a medium skillet over medium-high heat. Add onion, garlic, and carrots, and cook, stirring frequently, for 3 minutes, or until onion is translucent. Add paprika, cumin, and coriander, and cook for 1 minute, stirring constantly. Scrape mixture into the slow cooker. Add stock, vinegar, and garbanzo beans to the slow cooker. Stir well.

3. Cook on Low for 6-8 hours or on High for 3-4 hours, or until chicken is cooked through and no longer pink.

4. If cooking on Low, raise the heat to High. Add green beans, and cook for an additional 15-20 minutes, or until green beans are cooked. Season to taste with salt and pepper, and serve immediately.

If cooking conventionally: Preheat the oven to 375°F after chicken browns, and follow the recipe to the end of Step 2, assembling the dish in a Dutch oven, and adding the additional ½ cup stock to the ingredients. Cook chicken, covered, for 45 minutes–1 hour, or until chicken is cooked through and no longer pink. Add green beans after 35 minutes. Season to taste with salt and pepper, and serve immediately.

Note: Using either cooking method, the chicken can be prepared up to 2 days in advance and refrigerated, tightly covered. Reheat it, covered, in a 350°F oven for 20–25 minutes, or until hot.

Variations:
- Substitute 1¼ pounds boneless country pork ribs or pork loin, cut into 1-inch cubes, for the chicken. Add 2 hours if cooking on Low, 1 hour if cooking on High, or 30 minutes if cooking conventionally.
- Substitute chili powder for the paprika, omit the ground coriander, and add 1 teaspoon dried oregano to give this dish Southwestern flavors.

New England Turkey Meatloaf

The slow cooker produces wonderfully moist meatloaf, which is especially important when cooking with lean ground turkey. This version is topped with cranberry sauce, and flavored with the same herbs I use on a roast turkey. Serve it with mashed potatoes and some succotash.

Yield: 4-6 servings | **Active time:** 15 minutes | **Start to finish (minimum time, slow cooker):** 3¼ hours | **Start to finish (conventional):** 1¼ hours

  2 tablespoons vegetable oil
  1 large onion, peeled and chopped
  2 garlic cloves, peeled and minced
  1 celery rib, rinsed, trimmed, and chopped
  1 pound ground turkey
  2 large eggs, lightly beaten
  ½ cup plain breadcrumbs
  2 tablespoons chopped fresh parsley
  1 teaspoon dried sage
  1 teaspoon dried thyme
  Salt and freshly ground black pepper to taste
  ½ cup canned whole-berry cranberry sauce
  Vegetable oil spray

1. Heat oil in a medium skillet over medium-high heat. Add onion, garlic, and celery. Cook, stirring frequently, for 5 minutes, or until onion softens. Scrape mixture into a mixing bowl. Add turkey, eggs, breadcrumbs, parsley, sage, thyme, salt, and pepper. Mix well to combine.
2. Grease the inside of the slow cooker insert liberally with vegetable oil spray. Fold a sheet of heavy-duty aluminum foil in half, and place it in the bottom of the slow cooker with the sides of the foil extending up the sides of the slow cooker. Form meat mixture into an oval or round, depending on the shape of your slow cooker, and place it into the slow cooker on top of the foil. Spread cranberry sauce on top of meat.
3. Cook meatloaf on Low for 6-8 hours or on High for 3-4 hours, or until an instant-read thermometer inserted into the center of meat registers 165°F.
4. Remove meatloaf from the slow cooker by pulling it up by the sides of the foil. Drain off any grease from the foil, and slide meatloaf onto a serving platter. Serve immediately.

If cooking conventionally: Preheat the oven to 375°F, and follow the recipe through the end of Step 2. Line a rimmed baking sheet with heavy-duty aluminum foil, and grease the foil with vegetable oil spray. Form the mixture into a loaf. Spread the top with cranberry sauce, and bake for 1 hour, or until an instant-read thermometer inserted into the center of the loaf registers 165°F. Serve immediately.

Note: Using either cooking method, the meatloaf can be made up to 2 days in advance and refrigerated, tightly covered. Reheat it in a 350°F oven, covered with foil, for 20–30 minutes, or until hot.

Variations:
- Try this recipe with ground pork or a combination of pork and veal. The cooking time will not change.
- Using the method outlined above, substitute Italian breadcrumbs for the plain, and 2 teaspoons Italian seasoning for the thyme and sage. Add ¼ cup freshly grated Parmesan cheese to the turkey mixture, and top the meatloaf with chunky marinara sauce instead of cranberry sauce.
- To "sneak" more vegetables into your children, add 1 grated carrot to the turkey mixture.

Turkey Chili

Turkey chili has become increasingly popular with good reason; it has all the great flavor of its beef prototype with fewer calories and less fat. Serve this with all the usual chili garnishes of onion, cheddar, and sour cream or plain yogurt.

Yield: 4–6 servings | **Active time:** 15 minutes | **Start to finish (minimum time, slow cooker):** 3¼ hours in a medium slow cooker | **Start to finish (conventional):** 45 minutes

3 tablespoons olive oil
1 large onion, peeled and chopped
1 green bell pepper, seeds and ribs removed, and chopped
3 garlic cloves, peeled and minced
3 tablespoons chili powder
2 tablespoons ground cumin
1 tablespoon paprika
2 teaspoons dried oregano
1 pound ground turkey
2 (14.5-ounce) cans diced tomatoes, drained (*undrained if cooking conventionally*)
1 (8-ounce) can tomato sauce
2 (15-ounce) cans red kidney beans, drained and rinsed
Salt and cayenne to taste

1. Heat oil in a large skillet over medium-high heat. Add onion, green bell pepper, and garlic, and cook, stirring frequently, for 3 minutes, or until onion is translucent. Add chili powder, cumin, paprika, and oregano, and cook for 1 minute, stirring constantly. Scrape mixture into the slow cooker. Add turkey, tomatoes, tomato sauce, and beans to the slow cooker. Stir well.

2. Cook on Low for 6–8 hours or on High for 3–4 hours, or until vegetables are soft. Season to taste with salt and cayenne, and serve immediately.

If cooking conventionally: Follow the recipe to the end of Step 1, assembling the dish in a saucepan, and adding the liquid from the tomatoes to the ingredients. Bring to a boil over medium-high heat, stirring occasionally. Reduce the heat to low and simmer chili, partially covered, for

30 minutes, stirring occasionally. Season to taste with salt and cayenne, and serve immediately.

Note: Using either cooking method, the chili can be prepared up to 2 days in advance and refrigerated, tightly covered. Reheat it, covered, over low heat, stirring frequently, until hot.

Variations:
- Substitute 1 pound of ground beef for the ground turkey, and brown it in a skillet over medium-high heat before adding it to the slow cooker.
- For either turkey or beef picadillo, add ½ teaspoon ground cinnamon, ½ cup raisins, and 2 tablespoons cider vinegar to the recipe.

The reason to cook the herbs and spices in this and many other recipes is that the initial cooking releases much more flavor than if the spices were merely added to the slow cooker.

Basic Roast Chicken

While we credit President Herbert Hoover with the expression "a chicken in every pot," the phrase praising this luxury actually dates back to the kings of seventeenth-century France. There are few foods as wonderful, and there's so much you can do with the leftovers.

Yield: 6-8 servings | **Active time:** 15 minutes | **Start to finish (minimum time, slow cooker):** N/A | **Start to finish:** 2 hours

> 1 (5-7-pound) roasting chicken
> 4 sprigs fresh parsley, divided
> 4 sprigs fresh rosemary, divided
> 6 garlic cloves, peeled and minced, divided
> 2 sprigs fresh thyme
> Salt and freshly ground black pepper to taste
> 4 tablespoons (½ stick) unsalted butter, softened
> 1 large onion, peeled and roughly chopped
> 1 carrot, peeled and thickly sliced
> 1 celery rib, rinsed, trimmed, and sliced
> 1 cup Chicken Stock (recipe on page 84) or purchased stock

1. Preheat the oven to 425°F. Rinse chicken, and pat dry with paper towels. Place 2 sprigs parsley, 2 sprigs rosemary, 4 garlic cloves, and thyme in cavity of chicken. Sprinkle salt and pepper inside cavity, and close it with skewers and string.

2. Chop remaining parsley, rosemary, and garlic. Mix with butter, and season to taste with salt and pepper. Gently stuff mixture under the skin of breast meat. Rub skin with salt and pepper. Place chicken on a rack in a roasting pan, breast side up.

3. Bake for 30 minutes, reduce the oven temperature to 350°F, and add onion, carrot, and celery to the roasting pan. Cook an additional 1-1½ hours, or until chicken is cooked through and no longer pink, and white meat registers 160°F and dark meat registers 165°F on an instant-read thermometer. Remove chicken from the oven, and allow it to rest on a heated platter for 10 minutes.

4. Spoon grease out of the pan, and add the chicken stock. Stir over medium-high heat until the liquid is reduced to a syrupy consistency. Strain sauce into a sauce boat, and add to it any liquid that accumulates on the platter when the chicken is carved. Serve immediately.

Note: The chicken can be roasted up to 3 hours in advance and kept at room temperature, covered with aluminum foil.

Variations:
While the method remains the same, here are some other seasoning blends to flavor the chicken:

- Use 3 tablespoons smoked Spanish paprika, 1 tablespoon ground cumin, 1 tablespoon dried thyme, and 3 minced garlic cloves.
- Use 3 tablespoons Italian seasoning, 3 tablespoons chopped fresh parsley, and 3 garlic cloves.
- Use 3 tablespoons dried oregano and 5 garlic cloves, and add 1 sliced lemon to the cavity.
- Rather than chicken stock, deglaze the pan with white wine.

Here's how to carve a roast chicken or turkey: To add a flourish to carving that also assures crisp skin for all, first "unwrap" the breast. Use a well-sharpened knife and fork. Carve and serve one side at a time. From neck, cut just through skin down middle of breast and around side. Hook fork on skin at tail and roll skin back to neck. Holding bird with fork, remove leg by severing hip joint. Separate drumstick from thigh and serve. Cut thin slices of breast at slight angle and add a small piece of rolled skin to each serving. Repeat all steps for other side. Remove wings last.

Basic Roast Turkey

There are two schools of thought to roasting a turkey—either relatively low heat or high heat—and I prefer the latter. Using this roasting method, the turkey basically steams; the meat remains moist since it is being cooked by a moist rather than dry heat method.

Yield: 8–10 servings, plus enough for leftovers | **Active time:** 15 minutes | **Start to finish (minimum time, slow cooker):** N/A | **Start to finish (conventional):** at least 2 hours, but varies by the weight of the turkey

> 1 (12–16-pound) turkey
> 6 tablespoons (³/₄ stick) unsalted butter, softened and divided
> 3 garlic cloves, peeled and minced
> 3 tablespoons smoked Spanish paprika
> 1 tablespoon dried thyme
> Salt and freshly ground black pepper to taste
> 1 large onion, peeled and diced
> 1 ½ cups Chicken Stock (recipe on page 84) or purchased stock
> 1 tablespoon cornstarch
> 2 tablespoons cold water

1. Preheat the oven to 450°F. Rinse turkey inside and out under cold running water, and place it in a large roasting pan.

2. Combine 3 tablespoons butter, garlic, paprika, thyme, salt, and pepper in a small bowl, and mix well. Rub mixture over skin of turkey and inside cavity. Place onion and stock in the roasting pan, and place turkey on top of it. Create a tent with two sheets of heavy-duty aluminum foil, crimping foil around the edges of the roasting pan, and joining the two sheets in the center by crimping.

3. Place turkey in the oven, and roast for 12–15 minutes per pound. After 2 hours, remove the foil, and remove liquid from the roasting pan with a bulb baster and reserve for making gravy. Return turkey to the oven, covered as before.

4. Reduce the oven temperature to 350°F, and uncover turkey for the last 1 hour of roasting so skin browns. Rub skin with remaining butter after removing the foil. Turkey is done when it is cooked through and no longer pink, and dark meat registers 165°F on an instant-read thermometer. Remove turkey from the oven, and allow it to rest on a heated platter for 10–15 minutes, lightly covered with foil.

5. While turkey rests, prepare gravy. Pour all juices and flavoring ingredients from the roasting pan into a saucepan. Add 1 cup of turkey or chicken stock to the roasting pan. Stir over medium heat, scraping brown bits from bottom of pan. Add liquid to the saucepan. In a small bowl, mix cornstarch and water, and set aside. Remove as much fat as possible from the surface of juices in the saucepan with a soup ladle, and then reduce liquid by at least $\frac{1}{4}$ to concentrate flavor. Stir cornstarch mixture into the pan, and cook for 3–5 minutes, or until liquid boils and slightly thickens. Season gravy to taste with salt and pepper.

6. To serve, carve turkey, and pass gravy separately.

Note: The turkey can be left at room temperature for up to 1 hour after removing it from the oven; keep it lightly tented with aluminum foil.

Variations:

While the method remains the same, here are some other seasoning blends to flavor the turkey:

- Use 2 tablespoons herbes de Provence or Italian seasoning along with 3 garlic cloves.
- Use $\frac{1}{4}$ cup chopped fresh rosemary, 1 tablespoon grated lemon zest, and 3 garlic cloves.

An easy way to soften butter quickly is to grate it through the large holes of a box grater.

Turkey and Pasta with Spicy Tomato Sauce

This sauce is hearty and spicy, made with red wine and olives as well as other seasonings. The sauce enlivens the mild flavors of the turkey, beans, and vegetables. All you need to complete the meal is a tossed salad; the pasta is right in the dish.

Yield: 4–6 servings | **Active time:** 20 minutes | **Start to finish (minimum time, slow cooker):** N/A | **Start to finish (conventional):** 50 minutes

½ pound penne, or similar sized pasta

¼ cup olive oil, divided

1 large onion, peeled and diced

4 garlic cloves, peeled and minced

1 (28-ounce) can crushed tomatoes in tomato puree

¼ cup dry red wine

½ cup chopped pitted kalamata olives

2 tablespoons chopped fresh parsley

2 teaspoons Italian seasoning

Salt and crushed red pepper flakes to taste

2 small summer squash, rinsed, trimmed, and thinly sliced

1 green bell pepper, seeds and ribs removed, and thinly sliced

3 cups shredded cooked turkey

1 (15-ounce) can canellini beans, drained and rinsed

½ cup freshly grated Parmesan cheese

¾ cup Italian breadcrumbs

1. Preheat the oven to 350°F, and grease a 9 x 13-inch baking pan. Bring a large pot of salted water to a boil, and cook penne according to package directions until al dente. Drain, and place penne in the prepared pan.

2. While water heats, heat 2 tablespoons olive oil in a saucepan over medium-high heat. Add onion and garlic, and cook, stirring occasionally, for 3 minutes, or until onion is translucent. Stir in tomatoes, wine, olives, parsley, and Italian seasoning. Season to taste with salt and red pepper flakes. Bring to a boil, reduce the heat to medium, and simmer sauce, uncovered, for 10 minutes, stirring occasionally.

3. While sauce simmers, heat remaining olive oil in a large skillet over medium heat. Add squash and green bell pepper, and cook, stirring frequently, for 5–10 minutes, or until vegetables are soft.

4. Add sauce, cooked vegetables, turkey, and beans to pasta in pan, and stir well. Cover pan with aluminum foil, and bake for 10 minutes. Remove foil, and sprinkle top with Parmesan cheese and breadcrumbs. Bake for an additional 15 minutes, or until bubbly. Serve immediately.

Note: The dish can be prepared for baking up to 2 days in advance and refrigerated, tightly covered. Add 10 minutes to covered bake time if chilled.

Variation:
- Substitute 3 (6-ounce) cans light tuna, drained, for the turkey.

Casseroles containing cooked poultry can be assembled in advance, but do not assemble dishes with raw poultry. Those must be thoroughly cooked to avert foodborne illness.

Turkey, Broccoli, and Cheddar Noodle Pudding

This is one of my favorite ways to use up cooked poultry; the creamy ricotta adds richness to the dish with very little fat, and the noodles make it homey. Serve the pudding with a tossed salad and your meal is complete.

Yield: 4-6 servings | **Active time:** 15 minutes | **Start to finish (minimum time, slow cooker):** N/A | **Start to finish (conventional):** 50 minutes

½ pound medium-width egg noodles

2 tablespoons unsalted butter

4 scallions, white parts and 3 inches of green tops, rinsed, trimmed, and thinly sliced

3 cups shredded cooked turkey

1 (10-ounce) package frozen chopped broccoli, thawed

1 (15-ounce) container low-fat ricotta cheese

½ cup whole milk

1 teaspoon dried thyme

1 cup grated sharp cheddar cheese

Salt and freshly ground black pepper to taste

1. Preheat the oven to 375°F, and grease a 9 x 13-inch baking pan. Bring a large pot of salted water to a boil, and cook egg noodles according to package directions until al dente. Drain and place noodles in the prepared pan.

2. Heat butter in small skillet over medium heat. Add scallions and cook, stirring frequently, for 3 minutes, or until scallions are translucent. Scrape scallions into the pan, along with turkey, broccoli, ricotta, milk, thyme, and cheddar. Season to taste with salt and pepper, and stir well.

3. Cover the pan with aluminum foil, and bake for 15 minutes. Uncover the pan, and bake an additional 20 minutes, or until bubbly. Serve immediately.

Note: The dish can be prepared for baking up to 2 days in advance and refrigerated, tightly covered. Add 10 minutes to covered bake time if chilled.

Variations:
- Substitute 1 (10-ounce) package frozen chopped spinach, thawed and squeezed dry, for the broccoli.
- Substitute Swiss or Gruyère cheese for the cheddar.

Ricotta means "re-cooked" in Italian, because this mildly flavored cheese is made from the whey resulting from making fresh mozzarella cheese. Farmer's cheese is a good substitute.

Spicy Turkey Jambalaya

Jambalaya is part of the Cajun tradition of Louisiana; it's a first cousin to the Spanish *paella* on which it is based. The addition of andouille sausage adds bold flavor, and vegetables add color. All you need is a green salad, and perhaps one of the bread pudding recipes in Chapter 9 as a treat for dessert.

Yield: 4-6 servings | **Active time:** 15 minutes | **Start to finish (minimum time, slow cooker):** N/A | **Start to finish (conventional):** 50 minutes

   2 tablespoons olive oil
   1 large onion, peeled and diced
   2 garlic cloves, peeled and minced
   1 green bell pepper, seeds and ribs removed, and diced
   2 celery ribs, rinsed, trimmed, and sliced
   1/2 pound andouille or other spicy sausage, sliced
   1½ cups long-grain rice
   2 cups Chicken Stock (recipe on page 84) or purchased stock
   1 (14.5-ounce) can diced tomatoes, drained
   2 tablespoons chopped fresh parsley
   1 teaspoon dried thyme
   1 bay leaf
   Cajun seasoning to taste
   3 cups bite-sized pieces cooked turkey
   1 cup frozen peas, thawed

1. Preheat the oven to 350°F, and grease a 9 x 13-inch baking pan.
2. Heat olive oil in a large saucepan over medium-high heat. Add onion, garlic, green bell pepper, celery, and andouille to the pan. Cook, stirring frequently, for 5 minutes, or until vegetables begin to soften. Add rice, and cook for 2 minutes, stirring frequently. Add stock, tomatoes, parsley, thyme, and bay leaf to the pan, and season to taste with Cajun seasoning.
3. Bring to a boil, cover the pan, and cook over low heat for 15–18 minutes, or until rice is tender and liquid is absorbed. Remove and discard bay leaf, stir in turkey and peas, and season to taste with additional Cajun seasoning, if needed.
4. Scrape mixture into the prepared pan, and bake for 10 minutes. Serve immediately.

Note: The dish can be prepared up to 2 days in advance and refrigerated, tightly covered. Reheat it, covered, in a 350°F oven for 20–25 minutes, or until hot.

Variations:
- Omit the sausage, and add ½ pound cooked fish.
- Substitute cooked pork for the turkey.

Most food historians agree that jambalaya got its name from the Spanish word for ham, *jamón*. The dish has been part of the Cajun tradition since the eighteenth century, and recipes for it date back to before the Civil War.

Turkey and Spinach Enchilada Bake

While making individual enchiladas is time-consuming, creating one casserole with all of the component parts of an enchilada is relatively quick, and the results are just as delicious. The dish features a creamy turkey filling with a spicy tomato sauce as the topping.

Yield: 4–6 servings | **Active time:** 15 minutes | **Start to finish (minimum time, slow cooker):** N/A | **Start to finish (conventional):** 50 minutes

1 (28-ounce) can diced tomatoes, drained
1 medium onion, peeled and diced
3 garlic cloves, peeled and minced
2 jalapeño or serrano chiles, seeds and ribs removed, and diced
¼ cup firmly packed fresh cilantro leaves
1 tablespoon ground cumin
2 teaspoons dried oregano
½ cup Chicken Stock (recipe on page 84) or purchased stock
3 tablespoons olive oil
Salt and freshly ground black pepper to taste
2 tablespoons unsalted butter
4 scallions, white parts and 3 inches of green tops, rinsed, trimmed, and sliced
3 cups shredded cooked turkey
1 (10-ounce) package frozen leaf spinach, thawed and well drained
1 (3-ounce) package cream cheese, softened
12 (6-inch) corn tortillas
1½ cups grated Monterey Jack cheese
½ cup freshly grated Parmesan cheese

1. Preheat the oven to 350°F, and grease a 9 x 13-inch baking pan.
2. Combine tomatoes, onion, garlic, chiles, cilantro, cumin, oregano, and stock in a food processor fitted with a steel blade or in a blender. Puree until smooth. Heat oil in a medium saucepan over medium-high heat. Add tomato puree, and cook over medium heat for 5 minutes, stirring occasionally. Season to taste with salt and pepper, and set aside.
3. Heat butter in a small skillet over medium-high heat. Add scallions, and cook, stirring frequently, for 3 minutes, or until scallions are translucent. Scrape mixture into a mixing bowl, and add turkey, spinach, and cream cheese. Mix well.

4. To assemble the dish, spoon ½ cup tomato sauce into the bottom of the prepared pan. Arrange 4 tortillas on top of sauce, and spread tortillas with ½ of turkey mixture and top with ½ of Monterey Jack cheese and ½ cup sauce. Cover with 4 more tortillas, and continue layering with remaining turkey mixture, Monterey Jack, and ½ cup sauce. Top with remaining 4 tortillas, and pour remaining sauce over all. Sprinkle with Parmesan.

5. Cover the pan with aluminum foil, and bake for 15 minutes. Remove foil, and bake, uncovered, for an additional 10–15 minutes, or until cheese is bubbling. Allow to rest for 5 minutes, then serve.

Note: The dish can be prepared up to 2 days in advance and refrigerated, tightly covered. Reheat it, covered, in a 350°F oven for 20–25 minutes, or until hot.

Variations:
- For a spicier dish, substitute jalapeño Jack cheese for the Monterey Jack.
- For a more colorful dish, substitute 1 (10-ounce) package frozen mixed vegetables, cooked according to package directions, for the spinach.
- For a vegetarian dish, substitute 3 cups canned kidney beans, drained and rinsed, for the turkey, and substitute vegetable stock for the chicken stock.

Turkey Shepherd's Pie

Shepherd's pie is a classic that dates back to the eighteenth century, served at pubs in Great Britain as a way to utilize leftover leg of lamb. If you happen to have leftover mashed potatoes as well as the necessary turkey, the dish can be created in merely minutes.

Yield: 4–6 servings | **Active time:** 20 minutes | **Start to finish (minimum time, slow cooker):** N/A | **Start to finish (conventional):** 45 minutes

TOPPING:

1½ pounds redskin potatoes, scrubbed and cut into ¾-inch dice
¾ cup heavy cream
3 tablespoons unsalted butter, cut into small pieces
Salt and freshly ground black pepper to taste
¼ cup freshly grated Parmesan cheese

FILLING:

3 tablespoons unsalted butter
1 small onion, peeled and chopped
1 cup turkey gravy
¾ cup heavy cream
2 teaspoons dried sage
½ teaspoon dried thyme
3 cups chopped cooked turkey
1 (10-ounce) package frozen mixed vegetables, thawed
Salt and freshly ground black pepper to taste

1. Preheat the oven to 400°F, and grease a 9 x 13-inch baking pan. Cover potatoes with salted water in a saucepan, and bring to a boil over high heat. Reduce the heat to medium, and cook potatoes for 12–15 minutes, or until very tender when pierced with the tip of a paring knife. Drain potatoes, shaking the colander briskly. Return potatoes to the saucepan, and add cream and butter. Mash with a potato masher until consistency you like is reached. Season to taste with salt and pepper, and set aside.

2. While potatoes cook, prepare filling. Heat butter in a saucepan over medium-high heat. Add onion and cook, stirring frequently, for 3 minutes, or until onion is translucent. Stir in turkey gravy, cream, sage, and thyme. Bring to a boil, whisking often. Reduce the heat to low,

and simmer sauce, uncovered, for 5 minutes. Stir in turkey and vegetables, season to taste with salt and pepper, and transfer filling to the prepared pan.

3. Spread potatoes evenly on top of filling, and sprinkle with Parmesan cheese. Bake for 20 minutes, or until bubbly and the top is browned. Allow to sit for 5 minutes, then serve.

Note: The dish can be prepared up to 2 days in advance and refrigerated, tightly covered. Reheat it, covered, in a 350°F oven for 20–25 minutes, or until hot.

Variations:

- Substitute ½ cup grated sharp cheddar cheese or ½ cup grated Swiss cheese for ½ cup of the heavy cream in the topping, and omit the Parmesan cheese.
- Substitute cooked meatloaf, crumbled, for the turkey, and use beef gravy for a mix for the turkey gravy.
- Substitute sweet potatoes for the redskin potatoes.

Cheddar Biscuit-Topped Chicken Pot Pie

Biscuits are to the American South what a baguette is to France; it wouldn't be a day without them. In this case, they're flavored with cheddar cheese, and used to top a pot pie made with lots of vegetables in a creamy sauce.

Yield: 4–6 servings | **Active time:** 20 minutes | **Start to finish (minimum time, slow cooker):** N/A | **Start to finish (conventional):** 50 minutes

FILLING:

4 tablespoons (½ stick) unsalted butter, divided
1 small onion, peeled and chopped
1 cup Chicken Stock (recipe on page 84) or purchased stock
1 large carrot, peeled and thinly sliced
2 celery ribs, rinsed, trimmed and thinly sliced
1 large Russet potato, peeled and cut into ½-inch dice
2 tablespoons chopped fresh parsley
1 teaspoon dried thyme
1 bay leaf
1 cup frozen peas, thawed
3 tablespoons all-purpose flour
1 cup half-and-half
3 cups bite-sized pieces cooked chicken
Salt and freshly ground black pepper to taste

BISCUITS:

1 ½ cups all-purpose flour
2 teaspoons baking powder
½ teaspoon baking soda
½ teaspoon salt
Freshly ground black pepper to taste
2 tablespoons cold unsalted butter, cut into bits
1 cup grated sharp cheddar cheese
1 cup sour cream

1. Preheat the oven to 400°F, and grease a 9 x 13-inch baking pan. Heat 2 tablespoons butter in a medium skillet over medium-high heat. Add onion, and cook, stirring frequently, for 3 minutes, or until onion is translucent.

2. Add stock, carrot, celery, potato, parsley, thyme, and bay leaf to the skillet. Bring to a boil, reduce the heat to low, and simmer, partially covered, for 8–10 minutes, or until potato is tender. Add peas to the skillet, and cook 1 minute. Strain mixture, reserving stock. Remove and discard bay leaf, and transfer vegetables to the prepared baking pan.

3. Heat remaining butter in a saucepan over low heat. Stir in flour, and cook, stirring constantly, for 2 minutes. Whisk in reserved stock, and bring to a boil over medium-high heat, whisking constantly. Add half-and-half, and simmer 2 minutes. Season to taste with salt and pepper. Add chicken to the pan with vegetables, and stir in sauce.

4. While vegetables simmer, prepare biscuits. Sift flour, baking powder, baking soda, salt, and pepper together into a mixing bowl. Cut in butter using a pastry blender, two knives, or your fingertips until mixture resembles coarse meal. Add cheddar and sour cream, and stir until a soft but not sticky dough forms. Knead dough gently on a lightly floured surface, roll or pat it out 1/2 inch thick, and cut out 8–12 rounds with a floured cookie cutter. Arrange biscuits on top of filling, and bake for 30–40 minutes, or until biscuits are brown and filling is bubbling. Allow to stand for 5 minutes, then serve.

Note: The chicken mixture can be prepared up to 2 days in advance and refrigerated, tightly covered. Reheat mixture in a saucepan or in the microwave oven before topping with biscuits, and do not make biscuit dough until just prior to baking.

Variations:
- Substitute diced ham for the chicken.
- Substitute Swiss cheese for the cheddar cheese.
- For a Southwestern pot pie, substitute cilantro for the parsley and 2 tablespoons chili powder for the thyme. Add 1 (4-ounce) can chopped mild green chiles, drained, to the filling, and substitute jalapeño Jack cheese for the cheddar.

Skillet Chicken and Dumplings

Dumplings are basically biscuits that are steamed rather than baked, which makes this a great dish for warm weather because you don't have to turn on the oven and add heat to the kitchen. The creamy filling is flavored with herbs, and the dumplings are light and fluffy.

Yield: 4–6 servings | **Active time:** 20 minutes | **Start to finish (minimum time, slow cooker):** N/A | **Start to finish (conventional):** 40 minutes

CHICKEN:

4 tablespoons (½ stick) unsalted butter, divided
1 large onion, peeled and chopped
2 garlic cloves, peeled and minced
2 carrots, peeled and thinly sliced
2 celery ribs, rinsed, trimmed, and thinly sliced
¼ cup dry white wine
3 tablespoons all-purpose flour
1 cup Chicken Stock (recipe on page 84) or purchased stock
1 cup half-and-half
2 tablespoons chopped fresh parsley
2 teaspoons dried rosemary, crumbled
1 teaspoon rubbed dried sage
½ teaspoon dried thyme
Salt and freshly ground black pepper to taste
3 cups bite-sized pieces cooked chicken
1 cup frozen cut green beans, thawed

DUMPLINGS:

1 cup all-purpose flour
1½ teaspoons baking powder
Pinch of salt
½ teaspoon dried thyme
½ teaspoon dried rosemary
3 tablespoons unsalted butter, cut into small bits
⅓ cup whole milk

1. For chicken, melt 2 tablespoons butter in a large covered skillet over medium-high heat. Add onion, garlic, carrots, and celery, and cook,

stirring frequently, for 3 minutes, or until onion is translucent. Add wine, and cook for 3 minutes, stirring occasionally, or until wine is almost evaporated. Set aside.

2. Heat remaining butter in a small saucepan over low heat. Stir in flour, and cook, stirring constantly, for 2 minutes. Whisk in stock, and bring to a boil over medium-high heat, whisking constantly. Add sauce to skillet, and cook vegetables for 5 minutes. Stir in half-and-half, parsley, rosemary, sage, and thyme. Simmer 2 minutes, season to taste with salt and pepper, and stir in chicken.

3. While vegetable mixture simmers, prepare dumpling dough. Combine flour, baking powder, salt, thyme, and rosemary in mixing bowl. Cut in butter using a pastry blender, two knives, or your fingertips until mixture resembles coarse crumbs. Add milk, and stir to blend. Knead dough lightly on lightly floured counter, then divide dough into 12 parts and roll each into a ball. Pat each ball into a patty ½ inch thick.

4. Stir green beans into chicken mixture, and place dough on top of chicken. Cover the skillet, and cook over medium-low heat for 15–20 minutes, or until dumplings are puffed and cooked through. Do not uncover the pan while dumplings are steaming. Serve immediately.

Note: The chicken mixture can be prepared up to 2 days in advance and refrigerated, tightly covered. Reheat mixture in the skillet before topping with dumplings, and do not make dumpling dough until just prior to cooking.

Variation:
- For Cajun flavor, substitute Cajun seasoning for the salt and pepper.

Chapter 7:

From the Farms and Plains: Beef and Pork Dishes with International Flavors

If you are like me, and almost everyone I know, then the first dish you cooked in a slow cooker was a pot roast or beef stew. Tenderizing inexpensive cuts of beef was touted as the miracle use of this simple appliance, and indeed the perception is correct.

When picking beef for the slow cooker, price is a good guideline, but there are others. Anything that says "chuck," "rump," or "shank" is a good slow cooker choice.

The shape of your slow cooker should be factored into the decision of what to buy. If your slow cooker is round, a rump roast is your best bet. If it's oval, go with a chuck roast or a brisket. If you're cooking a stew, it doesn't matter.

The two best cuts of pork for the slow cooker are boneless country ribs and boneless loin. Very often whole loins—usually about 10 pounds—are on sale for a very low price, so it is worth it to buy one and freeze most for future meals. Boneless country ribs, on the other hand, are the pork equivalent of a chuck roast; they have great flavor and become meltingly tender.

You'll notice that vegetables are placed in the slow cooker prior to meat in most cases. That's because it actually take longer to cook vegetables in a slow cooker than it does meat; the meat contains more fat, which heats to a higher temperature than the water in vegetables. There are more heating coils at the bottom of the slow cooker than at the top, so that is where you want your vegetables to be. The same is not true, however, if cooking conventionally.

Regardless of how you cook these dishes, it's best to cook them in advance and chill them, if possible. That way all the saturated fat rises to the top and becomes a hard layer once the food chills. It can then be removed in its entirety, and very easily at that. An alternative to removing the fat, if you're serving the dish the same day, is to tilt the slow cooker insert or Dutch oven by setting one side about 2 inches higher than the other. That way the fat will create a pool on the low side, and you can ladle it off with a soup ladle.

CREATIVE CUTTING

Compared to the precision needed to cut a whole chicken into its component parts, boning and cutting meat for the recipes in this chapter is a free-for-all. The bones should be removed, however. Not only do they take up space needed for vegetables in the slow cooker, but the bones slow down the cooking process, too, because they absorb the heat generated by the coils that should go to cooking the meat and vegetables. But do save any beef bones for making beef stock (recipe on page 85); unfortunately, pork bones do not make a good stock.

The first step of boning is to cut away the bones. Then cut away any large areas of fat that can be easily discarded. The last step is to decide how the remaining boneless meat should be cut. The rule is to cut across the grain rather than with the grain. If you're not sure which way the grain runs, make a test slice. You should see the ends of fibers if you cut across the grain. The reason for this is that meat becomes more tender if the ends of the fibers are exposed to the liquid and heat.

You notice that I discuss beef and pork, but not lamb and veal. The reason is simple—those meats are far more expensive. If you hit upon a sale, most likely it will be for lamb shanks; they can be cooked for the same amount of time as a beef pot roast.

Moroccan Beef Stew with Apricots and Prunes

Aromatic spices are balanced by the sweetness of succulent dried fruits in this recipe hailing from the southern coast of the Mediterranean Sea. Serve it over couscous to enjoy all the sauce.

Yield: 4–6 servings | **Active time:** 20 minutes | **Start to finish (minimum time, slow cooker):** 4½ hours in a medium slow cooker | **Start to finish (conventional):** 3 hours

> 1 (2-pound) chuck roast, trimmed and cut into 1-inch cubes (or 1½ pounds stewing beef)
>
> 2 carrots, peeled and cut into 1-inch sections
>
> 2 parsnips, peeled and cut into 1-inch sections
>
> 1 small celery root, peeled and cut into 1-inch dice
>
> 2 tablespoons olive oil
>
> 1 large onion, peeled and diced
>
> 3 garlic cloves, peeled and minced
>
> 1 large jalapeño or serrano chile, seeds and ribs removed, and finely chopped
>
> 2 tablespoons grated fresh ginger
>
> 2 tablespoons ground coriander
>
> 1 tablespoon ground cumin
>
> 2½ cups Beef Stock (recipe on page 85) or purchased stock (3 cups if cooking conventionally)
>
> ¾ cup pitted prunes
>
> ¾ cup dried apricots
>
> 1 tablespoon cornstarch
>
> 2 tablespoons cold water
>
> Salt and freshly ground black pepper to taste
>
> ¾ cup slivered blanched almonds

1. Preheat the oven broiler, and line a broiler pan with heavy-duty aluminum foil. Broil beef for 3 minutes per side, or until browned, and set aside.
2. Arrange carrots, parsnips, and celery root in the bottom of the slow cooker. Transfer beef to the slow cooker, and pour in any juices that have collected in the pan.
3. Heat oil in a medium skillet over medium heat. Add onion, garlic, chile, and ginger. Cook, stirring frequently, for 3 minutes, or until onion is translucent. Add coriander and cumin and cook over low

heat, stirring constantly, for 1 minute. Scrape mixture into the slow cooker. Add stock, prunes, and apricots, and stir well.

4. Cook on Low for 8–10 hours or on High for 4–5 hours, or until beef and vegetables are tender.

5. If cooking on Low, raise the heat to High. Mix cornstarch with water, and stir cornstarch mixture into the slow cooker. Cook for an additional 10–20 minutes, or until juices are bubbling and slightly thickened. Season to taste with salt and pepper, and serve immediately, sprinkling each serving with almonds.

If cooking conventionally: Preheat the oven to 350°F after beef browns, and follow the recipe to the end of Step 3, assembling the dish in a Dutch oven, and adding the additional ½ cup stock to the ingredients. However, do not add the carrots, parsnips, and celery root. Bring to a boil on top of the stove, and then bake, covered, for 1 hour. Add vegetables, and bake for an additional 1½ hours, or until beef and vegetables are tender. Add cornstarch mixture, and cook on top of the stove for an additional 2–3 minutes, or until slightly thickened. Season to taste with salt and pepper, and serve immediately, sprinkling each serving with almonds.

Note: Using either cooking method, the beef can be made up to 2 days in advance and refrigerated, tightly covered. Reheat it over low heat or in a 350°F oven for 30 minutes, or until hot.

Variations:
- Substitute pork loin for the beef, and substitute chicken stock for the beef stock. Reduce the cooking time by 2 hours on Low, 1 hour on High, or 30 minutes if cooking conventionally.
- Add 1 (15-ounce) can garbanzo beans, drained and rinsed, to the stew.

Beef Braised in Red Wine with Potatoes and Vegetables (*Boeuf Bourguignon*)

While cooking with wine is more expensive than cooking with stock, a cooking wine hardly needs to be of high quality; forget the old adage that "you never cook with a wine you wouldn't drink." This hearty stew is perfect for a fall or winter night.

Yield: 4–6 servings | **Active time:** 20 minutes | **Start to finish (minimum time, slow cooker):** 4½ hours in a medium slow cooker | **Start to finish (conventional):** 3 hours

1 (2-pound) chuck roast, trimmed and cut into 1-inch cubes (or 1½ pounds stewing beef)

2 carrots, peeled and cut into 1-inch chunks

1 pound redskin potatoes, scrubbed and cut into 1-inch dice

¼ cup olive oil

1 large onion, peeled and diced

3 garlic cloves, peeled and minced

½ pound small mushrooms, wiped with a damp paper towel, trimmed, and halved if large

1¾ cups dry red wine

½ cup Beef Stock (recipe on page 85) or purchased stock (*1 cup if cooking conventionally*)

2 tablespoons tomato paste

2 tablespoons chopped fresh parsley

2 teaspoons herbes de Provence

1 bay leaf

Salt and freshly ground black pepper to taste

1. Preheat the oven broiler, and line a broiler pan with heavy-duty aluminum foil. Broil beef for 3 minutes per side, or until browned. Arrange carrots and potatoes in the slow cooker, transfer beef to the slow cooker, and pour in any juices that have collected in the pan.

2. Heat olive oil in a medium skillet over medium heat. Add onion, garlic, and mushrooms. Cook, stirring frequently, for 4–5 minutes, or until onion is translucent and mushrooms soften. Scrape mixture into the slow cooker.

3. Combine wine, stock, tomato paste, parsley, herbes de Provence, and bay leaf in a mixing bowl. Stir well to dissolve tomato paste. Pour mixture into the slow cooker.

4. Cook on Low for 8-10 hours or on High for 4-5 hours, or until beef and vegetables are tender. Remove and discard bay leaf, season to taste with salt and pepper, and serve immediately.

If cooking conventionally: Preheat the oven to 350°F after beef browns, and follow the recipe to the end of Step 3, assembling the dish in a Dutch oven, and adding the additional ½ cup stock to the ingredients. However, do not add carrots and potatoes. Bring to a boil on top of the stove, and then bake, covered, for 1 hour. Add carrots and potatoes, and bake for an additional 1½ hours, or until beef and vegetables are tender. Remove and discard bay leaf, season to taste with salt and pepper, and serve immediately.

Note: Using either cooking method, the beef can be made up to 2 days in advance and refrigerated, tightly covered. Reheat it over low heat or in a 350°F oven for 30 minutes, or until hot.

Buy one of the new 3-liter boxes of wine on the market to use as cooking wine. Because the wine is in a plastic bag that deflates as it's used, the wine is not exposed to air, so it lasts for months.

Greek Beef Stew

Many cuisines around the world, including Greek, use cinnamon as a savory spice as well as an addition to sweet baked goods. This stew has a hint of cinnamon, as well as a slight sweet and sour flavor. Serve it over orzo, or some other small pasta, along with a tossed salad.

Yield: 4–6 servings | **Active time:** 25 minutes | **Start to finish (minimum time, slow cooker):** 5 hours in a medium slow cooker | **Start to finish (conventional):** 3½ hours

- 1 (1-pound) eggplant, trimmed and cut into ¾-inch dice
- Salt
- 1 (2-pound) chuck roast, trimmed and cut into 1-inch cubes (or 1½ pounds stewing beef)
- ⅓ cup olive oil, divided
- 1 medium onion, peeled and chopped
- 3 garlic cloves, peeled and minced
- 1 green bell pepper, seeds and ribs removed, and thinly sliced
- 1 teaspoon dried oregano
- 1 teaspoon ground cumin
- 1¼ cups dry red wine
- 2 tablespoons balsamic vinegar
- 2 tablespoons firmly packed light brown sugar
- 1 (6-ounce) can tomato paste
- 3 tablespoons chopped fresh parsley
- 2 bay leaves
- 2 (2-inch) cinnamon sticks
- ½ cup raisins
- If cooking conventionally, ½ cup Beef Stock (recipe on page 85) or purchased stock
- 1 tablespoon cornstarch
- 2 tablespoons cold water
- Freshly ground black pepper to taste

1. Place eggplant in a colander, and sprinkle cubes liberally with salt. Place a plate on top of eggplant cubes, and weight the plate with some cans. Place the colander in the sink or on a plate, and allow eggplant to drain for 30 minutes. Rinse eggplant cubes, and squeeze hard to remove water. Wring out remaining water with a cloth tea towel.

2. While eggplant sits, preheat the oven broiler, and line a broiler pan with heavy-duty aluminum foil. Broil beef for 3 minutes per side, or until browned. Transfer beef to the slow cooker, and pour in any juices that have collected in the pan.
3. Heat half of the oil in a medium skillet over medium heat. Add onion, garlic, and green bell pepper. Cook, stirring frequently, for 3 minutes, or until onion is translucent. Add oregano and cumin, and cook over low heat, stirring constantly, for 1 minute. Scrape mixture into the slow cooker.
4. Heat remaining olive oil in a large skillet over medium-high heat. Add eggplant cubes, and cook, stirring frequently, for 3 minutes, or until eggplant begins to soften. Transfer eggplant to the slow cooker.
5. Combine wine, vinegar, brown sugar, tomato paste, and parsley in a mixing bowl. Stir well to dissolve tomato paste. Pour mixture into the slow cooker, and add bay leaves, cinnamon sticks, and raisins.
6. Cook on Low for 8–10 hours or on High for 4–5 hours, or until beef and vegetables are tender.
7. If cooking on Low, raise the heat to High. Mix cornstarch and cold water in a small cup, and stir cornstarch mixture into beef. Cook for an additional 10–20 minutes, or until juices are bubbling and slightly thickened. Remove and discard bay leaves and cinnamon sticks. Season to taste with salt and pepper, and serve immediately.

If cooking conventionally: Preheat the oven to 350°F after beef browns, and follow the recipe to the end of Step 5, assembling the dish in a Dutch oven, and adding the additional ½ cup stock to the ingredients. Bring to a boil on top of the stove, and then bake, covered, for 2½ hours, or until beef and vegetables are tender. Add cornstarch mixture, and cook on top of the stove for an additional 2–3 minutes, or until slightly thickened. Remove and discard bay leaves and cinnamon sticks. Season to taste with salt and pepper, and serve immediately.

Note: Using either cooking method, the beef can be made up to 2 days in advance and refrigerated, tightly covered. Reheat it over low heat or in a 350°F oven for 30 minutes, or until hot.

Variation:
- Lamb shanks are about the most affordable version of that richly flavored meat, and they work wonderfully in this recipe. The cooking time does not change.

Caribbean Beef Stew

Coconut milk is used in tropical cuisines where coconuts grow, so it's found in the Caribbean as well as in Asian dishes. In this recipe, the creamy coconut milk blends wonderfully with the fiery chile and spices. Serve it over rice.

Yield: 4–6 servings | **Active time:** 20 minutes | **Start to finish (minimum time, slow cooker):** 4½ hours in a medium slow cooker | **Start to finish (conventional):** 3 hours

> 1 (2-pound) chuck roast, trimmed and cut into 1-inch cubes (or 1½ pounds stewing beef)
> 2 carrots, peeled and cut into 1-inch sections
> 2 parsnips, peeled and cut into 1-inch sections
> 1 celery root, peeled and cut into 1-inch dice
> 2 tablespoons vegetable oil
> 3 large onions, peeled and diced
> 4 garlic cloves, peeled and minced
> 1 large jalapeño or serrano chile, seeds and ribs removed, and finely chopped
> 3 tablespoons grated fresh ginger
> 2 tablespoons ground coriander
> 1 tablespoon ground cumin
> 1 (14-ounce) can light coconut milk
> 1½ cups Beef Stock (recipe on page 85) or purchased stock (*2 cups if cooking conventionally*)
> 1 tablespoon cornstarch
> 2 tablespoons cold water
> Salt and freshly ground black pepper to taste

1. Preheat the oven broiler, and line a broiler pan with heavy-duty aluminum foil. Broil beef for 3 minutes per side, or until browned, and set aside.
2. Arrange carrots, parsnips, and celery root in the bottom of the slow cooker. Transfer beef to the slow cooker, and pour in any juices that have collected in the pan.
3. Heat oil in a medium skillet over medium heat. Add onion, garlic, chile, and ginger. Cook, stirring frequently, for 3 minutes, or until onion is translucent. Add coriander and cumin and cook over low

heat, stirring constantly, for 1 minute. Scrape mixture into the slow cooker. Add coconut milk and stock, and stir well.

4. Cook on Low for 8–10 hours or on High for 4–5 hours, or until beef and vegetables are tender.

5. If cooking on Low, raise the heat to High. Mix cornstarch with water, and stir cornstarch mixture into the slow cooker. Cook for an additional 10–20 minutes, or until juices are bubbling and slightly thickened. Season to taste with salt and pepper, and serve immediately.

If cooking conventionally: Preheat the oven to 350°F after beef browns, and follow the recipe to the end of Step 3, assembling the dish in a Dutch oven, and adding the additional $1/2$ cup stock to the ingredients. However, do not add the carrots, parsnips, and celery root. Bring to a boil on top of the stove, and then bake, covered, for 1 hour. Add vegetables, and bake for an additional $11/2$ hours, or until beef and vegetables are tender. Add cornstarch mixture, and cook on top of the stove for an additional 2–3 minutes, or until slightly thickened. Season to taste with salt and pepper, and serve immediately.

Note: Using either cooking method, the beef can be made up to 2 days in advance and refrigerated, tightly covered. Reheat it over low heat or in a 350°F oven for 30 minutes, or until hot.

Variations:

- Substitute pork loin for the beef, and substitute chicken stock for the beef stock. Reduce the cooking time by 2 hours on Low, 1 hour on High, or 30 minutes if cooking conventionally.
- Add 1 (15-ounce) can black beans, drained and rinsed, to the stew.

Sauerbraten Stew

Sauerbraten is the classic German pot roast, but I like to make it as a stew because the wonderful ginger flavor permeates all through the meat. Serve it with buttered egg noodles and a steamed green vegetable.

Yield: 4-6 servings | **Active time:** 15 minutes | **Start to finish (minimum time, slow cooker):** 28½ hours in a medium slow cooker, including 24 hours to marinate meat | **Start to finish (conventional):** 26¾ hours, including 24 hours to marinate meat

   1 cup dry red wine
   1 cup Beef Stock (recipe on page 85) or purchased stock
   ½ cup red wine vinegar
   ¼ cup firmly packed dark brown sugar
   2 tablespoons tomato paste
   2 tablespoons Worcestershire sauce
   2 tablespoons Dijon mustard
   1 teaspoon ground ginger
   Salt and freshly ground black pepper to taste
   1 onion, peeled, halved, and thinly sliced
   3 garlic cloves, peeled and thinly sliced
   1 (2-pound) chuck roast, trimmed and cut into 1-inch cubes (or 1½
      pounds stewing beef)
   ⅔ cup crushed gingersnap cookies

   If cooking conventionally:
   ½ cup water

1. Combine wine, stock, vinegar, brown sugar, tomato paste, Worcestershire sauce, mustard, and ginger in a heavy resealable plastic bag. Season to taste with salt and pepper. Mix well, and add onion, garlic, and beef. Marinate, refrigerated, for at least 24 hours, and up to 48 hours, turning the bag occasionally.
2. Transfer beef and marinade to the slow cooker, and stir in gingersnap crumbs.
3. Cook on Low for 8–10 hours or on High for 4–5 hours, or until beef is very tender. Season to taste with salt and pepper, and serve immediately.

If cooking conventionally: Preheat the oven to 350°F, and follow the recipe to the end of Step 2, assembling the dish in a Dutch oven, and adding ½ cup water to the ingredients. Bring to a boil on top of the stove, and then bake, covered, for 2½ hours, or until beef is tender. Serve immediately.

Note: Using either cooking method, the beef can be made up to 2 days in advance and refrigerated, tightly covered. Reheat it over low heat or in a 350°F oven for 30 minutes, or until hot.

Several food historians credit the invention of sauerbraten, originally made with horse meat, to Charlemagne in the ninth century CE. Saint Albertus Magnus, also known as Saint Albert of Cologne, is also credited with popularizing the dish in the thirteenth century CE.

Curried Pot Roast

This dish is really a fusion recipe rather than authentically Indian; the curry flavor is balanced with chutney and ginger, and there are raisins in the sauce. Serve it over rice with a tossed salad, and some Indian bread like *naan*.

Yield: 4–6 servings | **Active time:** 15 minutes | **Start to finish (minimum time, slow cooker):** 6 hours in a medium slow cooker | **Start to finish (conventional):** 2¾ hours

> 1 (2–2½-pound) beef rump or boneless chuck roast
> 2 tablespoons Asian sesame oil *
> 1 large onion, peeled and diced
> 3 garlic cloves, peeled and minced
> 1 green bell pepper, seeds and ribs removed, and diced
> 2 tablespoons curry powder
> ½ teaspoon ground ginger
> ½ cup jarred mango chutney
> ⅓ cup raisins
> 1¾ cups Beef Stock (recipe on page 85) or purchased stock (2¼ cups *if cooking conventionally*)
> 2 carrots, peeled and cut into ⅓-inch slices on the diagonal
> 2 celery ribs, rinsed, trimmed, and cut into ⅓-inch slices on the diagonal
> 1 (8-ounce) can sliced water chestnuts, drained and rinsed
> 1 (10-ounce) package frozen cut green beans, thawed
> 1 tablespoon cornstarch
> 2 tablespoons cold water
> Salt and freshly ground black pepper to taste

1. Preheat the oven broiler, and line a broiler pan with heavy-duty aluminum foil. Broil beef for 3–5 minutes per side, or until browned. Place beef in the slow cooker.
2. While meat browns, heat oil in a large skillet over medium-high heat. Add onion, garlic, and green bell pepper. Cook, stirring frequently, for 3 minutes, or until onion is translucent. Add curry powder and ginger, and cook over low heat, stirring constantly, for 1 minute. Stir chutney, raisins, and beef stock into the skillet, and stir well. Pour mixture into the slow cooker, and stir in carrots, celery, and water chestnuts.

3. Cook for 9–11 hours on Low or 4½–5 hours on High, or until beef and vegetables are just tender.
4. If cooking on Low, raise the heat to High. Add green beans, and cook for an additional 20–30 minutes, or until beans are crisp-tender. Mix cornstarch with water, and stir cornstarch mixture into the slow cooker. Cook for an additional 10–20 minutes, or until juices are bubbling and slightly thickened. Season to taste with salt and pepper, and serve immediately.

If cooking conventionally: Preheat the oven to 350°F after beef browns, and follow the recipe to the end of Step 2, assembling the dish in a Dutch oven, and adding the additional ½ cup stock to the ingredients. Bring to a boil on top of the stove, and then bake, covered, for 2½ hours, or until beef and vegetables are tender. Add green beans 20 minutes before the end of the cooking time. Add cornstarch mixture, and cook on top of the stove for an additional 2–3 minutes, or until slightly thickened. Season to taste with salt and pepper, and serve immediately.

Note: Using either cooking method, the beef can be made up to 2 days in advance and refrigerated, tightly covered. Reheat it over low heat or in a 350°F oven for 30 minutes, or until hot.

Variation:
- Substitute chicken stock for the beef stock, and 1 (3½–4-pound) frying chicken, cut into serving pieces, for the beef. Reduce the cooking time to 5–7 hours on Low, 2½–3 hours on High, or 45 minutes if cooking conventionally.

* Available in the Asian aisle of most supermarkets and in specialty markets.

Classic American Pot Roast

Here's the Sunday dinner that Grandma used to make; it includes your veggies and potatoes, too. But Grandma might not have added the herbs, which enhance the flavor.

Yield: 4-6 servings | **Active time:** 15 minutes | **Start to finish (minimum time, slow cooker):** 5³/₄ hours in a medium slow cooker | **Start to finish (conventional):** 2¹/₂ hours

1 (2–2¹/₂-pound) boneless beef rump or boneless chuck roast

3 tablespoons vegetable oil

1 onion, peeled and diced

3 garlic cloves, peeled and minced

¹/₂ pound mushrooms, wiped with a damp paper towel, trimmed, and sliced

4 medium redskin potatoes, scrubbed and cut into ³/₄-inch cubes

2 carrots, peeled and cut into ¹/₂-inch slices

2 celery ribs, rinsed, trimmed, and cut into ¹/₂-inch slices

1 (14.5-ounce) can diced tomatoes, undrained

2 cups Beef Stock (recipe on page 85) or purchased stock (*2¹/₂ cups if cooking conventionally*)

3 tablespoons chopped fresh parsley

1 tablespoon dried rosemary, crumbled

1 teaspoon dried thyme

1 bay leaf

1 tablespoon cornstarch

2 tablespoons cold water

Salt and freshly ground black pepper to taste

1. Preheat the oven broiler, and line a broiler pan with heavy-duty aluminum foil. Broil beef for 3–5 minutes per side, or until browned. Set aside.

2. While meat browns, heat oil in a large skillet over medium-high heat. Add onion, garlic, and mushrooms. Cook, stirring frequently, for 3–5 minutes, or until onion is translucent and mushrooms are soft. Scrape mixture into the slow cooker.

3. Add potatoes, carrots, celery, tomatoes, stock, parsley, rosemary, thyme, and bay leaf to the slow cooker. Mix well, then place beef into the slow cooker, pushing it down into liquid.

4. Cook for 10–12 hours on Low or 5–6 hours on High, or until beef and vegetables are very tender.
5. If cooking on Low, raise the heat to High. Mix cornstarch with water, and stir cornstarch mixture into the slow cooker. Cook for an additional 10–20 minutes, or until juices are bubbling and slightly thickened. Remove and discard bay leaf, season to taste with salt and pepper, and carve into slices against the grain. Serve immediately.

If cooking conventionally: Preheat the oven to 350°F after beef browns, and assemble the recipe through the end of Step 3, adding the ½ cup of additional stock to the ingredients. Bring to a boil on top of the stove, and then bake, covered, for 2½ hours, or until beef and vegetables are tender. Add cornstarch mixture, and cook on top of the stove for an additional 2–3 minutes, or until bubbling and slightly thickened. Remove and discard bay leaf, season to taste with salt and pepper, and carve into slices against the grain. Serve immediately.

Note: Using either cooking method, the beef can be made up to 2 days in advance and refrigerated, tightly covered. Reheat it over low heat or in a 350°F oven for 30 minutes, or until hot.

Variations:
- Think of this recipe as a guideline. You can add any root vegetable you like—from parsnips and turnips to fennel or celery root—and it will not change the cooking time. You can also make this a stew instead of one large piece of meat; reduce the cooking time by 2 hours on Low, 1 hour on High, or 30 minutes conventionally.
- Substitute 1 cup of dry red wine for 1 cup of the beef stock.

Spicy Mexican Brisket

Here is a hearty and somewhat spicy beef dish with great Mexican flavors. Serve it over rice with a tossed salad, and any leftover meat can be used for burritos or nachos.

Yield: 4–6 servings | **Active time:** 15 minutes | **Start to finish (minimum time, slow cooker):** 5³/₄ hours in a medium slow cooker | **Start to finish (conventional):** 2³/₄ hours

> 1 (2-pound) beef brisket
> ¼ cup olive oil
> 1 large onion, peeled and diced
> 3 garlic cloves, peeled and minced
> 1 tablespoon chili powder
> 1 teaspoon ground cumin
> 1 teaspoon dried oregano
> 1–2 canned chipotle chiles in adobo sauce, finely chopped
> 1 tablespoon adobo sauce
> 1½ cups Beef Stock (recipe on page 85) or purchased stock (*2 cups if cooking conventionally*)
> 1 (14.5-ounce) can diced tomatoes, undrained
> 1 (15-ounce) can pinto beans, drained and rinsed
> 1 (10-ounce) package frozen corn, thawed
> Salt and freshly ground black pepper to taste

1. Preheat the oven broiler, and line a broiler pan with heavy-duty aluminum foil. Broil beef for 3–5 minutes per side, or until browned. Place beef in the slow cooker.

2. While meat browns, heat oil in a medium skillet over medium-high heat. Add onion and garlic, and cook, stirring frequently, for 3 minutes, or until onion is translucent. Add chili powder, cumin, and oregano, and cook over low heat, stirring constantly, for 1 minute. Scrape mixture into the slow cooker. Add chiles, adobo sauce, stock, tomatoes, and beans to the slow cooker.

3. Cook for 9–11 hours on Low or 4½–5 hours on High, or until beef is tender.

4. If cooking on Low, raise the heat to High. Add corn, and cook for an additional 20–30 minutes. Season to taste with salt and pepper, and carve into slices against the grain. Serve immediately.

If cooking conventionally: Preheat the oven to 350°F after beef browns, and follow the recipe to the end of Step 2, assembling the dish in a Dutch oven, and adding the additional ½ cup stock to the ingredients. Bring to a boil on top of the stove, and then bake, covered, for 2½ hours, or until beef is tender. Add corn 20 minutes before the end of the cooking time. Season to taste with salt and pepper, and carve into slices against the grain. Serve immediately.

Note: Using either cooking method, the beef can be made up to 2 days in advance and refrigerated, tightly covered. Reheat it over low heat or in a 350°F oven for 30 minutes, or until hot.

Variation:
- Omit the chipotle chiles and adobo sauce and add 1 (4-ounce) can chopped mild green chiles, drained, for a less spicy dish.

If you ever run out of chili powder, you can replicate the flavor by using a few tablespoons of paprika to which you add some cumin, oregano, and ground coriander.

Comfort Food Meatloaf

I've often wanted to do a whole book of various meatloaf recipes—that's how much I like it. This is my classic recipe, and the cheese in the meat mixture adds wonderful moisture as well as flavor. I serve meatloaf with mashed potatoes, and some sort of green vegetable.

Yield: 4–6 servings | **Active time:** 20 minutes | **Start to finish (minimum time, slow cooker):** 3½ hours in a medium slow cooker | **Start to finish (conventional):** 1½ hours

2 tablespoons olive oil

1 medium onion, peeled and chopped

1 small carrot, peeled and chopped

1 celery rib, rinsed, trimmed, and chopped

2 garlic cloves, peeled and minced

2 large eggs, lightly beaten

¼ cup whole milk

½ cup Italian breadcrumbs

½ cup grated mozzarella cheese

3 tablespoons chopped fresh parsley

1 teaspoon Italian seasoning

½ teaspoon dried thyme

Salt and freshly ground black pepper to taste

¾ pound lean ground beef

¾ pound ground pork

Vegetable oil spray

½ cup ketchup

1. Heat oil in a small skillet over medium-high heat. Add onion, carrot, celery, and garlic, and cook, stirring frequently, for 3 minutes, or until onion is translucent. Set aside.

2. Combine eggs, milk, breadcrumbs, cheese, parsley, Italian seasoning, thyme, salt, and pepper in a large mixing bowl, and stir well. Add beef, pork, and vegetable mixture, and mix well.

3. Grease the inside of the slow cooker insert liberally with vegetable oil spray. Fold a sheet of heavy-duty aluminum foil in half, and place it in the bottom of the slow cooker with the sides of the foil extending up the sides of the slow cooker. Form meat mixture into an oval or round, depending on the shape of your cooker, and place it into the cooker on top of the foil. Spread ketchup on top of meat.

4. Cook meatloaf on Low for 6–8 hours or on High for 3–4 hours, or until an instant-read thermometer inserted into the center of the loaf registers 165°F. Remove meatloaf from the slow cooker by pulling it up by the sides of the foil. Drain off any grease from the foil, and slide meatloaf onto a serving platter. Serve immediately.

If cooking conventionally: Preheat the oven to 375°F, and follow the recipe through the end of Step 2. Line a rimmed baking sheet with heavy-duty aluminum foil, spray the foil with vegetable oil spray, and form the mixture into a loaf. Spread the top with ketchup, and bake for 1 hour, or until an instant-read thermometer inserted into the center of the loaf registers 165°F. Serve immediately.

Note: Using either cooking method, the meatloaf can be made up to 2 days in advance and refrigerated, tightly covered. Reheat it in a 350°F oven, covered with foil, for 20–30 minutes, or until hot. Also the meatloaf mixture can be made up to 1 day in advance and refrigerated, tightly covered.

Variations:
- Substitute ground turkey for the beef and pork; the cooking time will remain the same.
- Place a row of hard-boiled eggs in the center of the meatloaf before cooking.
- Add ½ pound diced sautéed mushrooms.
- Add 1 cup frozen chopped spinach, thawed and squeezed dry.
- Substitute 1 tablespoon Cajun seasoning for the Italian seasoning, thyme, salt, and pepper. And substitute cheddar cheese for the mozzarella cheese.

Corned Beef and Cabbage

Corned beef remains a great supermarket bargain—especially around St. Patrick's Day. I like it as much for the leftovers it generates as for the meal itself, and cooking it in the slow cooker is so easy.

Yield: 4–6 servings | **Active time:** 15 minutes | **Start to finish (minimum time, slow cooker):** 5¼ hours in a medium slow cooker | **Start to finish (conventional):** 3 hours

> 1 (2½–3-pound) corned beef brisket
> 1 onion, peeled and sliced
> 1 celery rib, sliced
> 1 carrot, peeled and sliced
> 4 garlic cloves, peeled and minced
> 1 bay leaf
> Water
> ½ small green cabbage
> Freshly ground black pepper to taste

1. Cut off as much fat as possible from top of corned beef. Rinse and set aside. Place onion, celery, carrot, garlic, and bay leaf in the slow cooker. Place corned beef on top of vegetables. Add enough water to come halfway up the sides of corned beef.
2. Cut cabbage in half. Cut core from one half, and slice into wedges. Arrange wedges on top of corned beef. Cook on Low for 10–12 hours or on High for 5–6 hours, or until corned beef is tender. Remove as much grease as possible from the slow cooker with a soup ladle.
3. Remove and discard bay leaf, and thinly slice corned beef against the grain. Serve corned beef with cabbage and other vegetables, seasoning to taste with pepper.

If cooking conventionally: Follow the recipe to the end of Step 1, place the corned beef and vegetables in a stockpot or Dutch oven, and cover the corned beef with cold water by 6 inches. Bring to a boil over high heat, then reduce the heat to low, and simmer corned beef, covered, for 1½ hours. Add cabbage wedges, and cook for an additional 1 hour, or until corned beef is tender. Remove and discard bay leaf, and thinly slice corned beef against the grain. Serve corned beef with cabbage and other vegetables, seasoning to taste with pepper.

Note: Using either cooking method, the corned beef can be made up to 2 days in advance and refrigerated, tightly covered. Reheat it in a 350°F oven, covered, for 30 minutes, or until hot.

Variation:
- Corned beef and cabbage becomes New England Boiled Dinner if you use half wine and half chicken stock rather than water for the cooking. This modification is traditionally served with whole grain mustard on the side.

There are two basic cuts of corned beef—the flat cut and the point cut. The flat cut is more expensive because it contains less fat, both in the meat itself and as large pockets of fat forming layers in the beef. It's worth the extra money to buy the flat cut and get a leaner roast.

Corned Beef Hash

Corned beef hash is a wonderful dish that suffers because so many people only know its canned form that visually resembles cheap dog food, and most dogs wouldn't even eat. But *real* corned beef hash is a delight, and it's a great way to use up leftover corned beef.

Yield: 4–6 servings | **Active time:** 25 minutes | **Start to finish (minimum time, slow cooker):** N/A | **Start to finish (conventional):** 40 minutes

> Vegetable oil spray
> 1½ pounds redskin potatoes, scrubbed and cut into ½-inch dice
> 1 tablespoon unsalted butter
> 2 tablespoons vegetable oil
> 1 large sweet onion, such as Vidalia or Bermuda, peeled and diced
> 1 small green bell pepper, seeds and ribs removed, and chopped
> 2 garlic cloves, peeled and minced
> 1 pound cooked corned beef, coarsely chopped
> ½ teaspoon dried thyme
> Salt and freshly ground black pepper to taste

1. Preheat the oven to 375°F, and grease a 9 x 13-inch baking pan with vegetable oil spray. Place potato cubes in a large saucepan of salted water, and bring to a boil over high heat. Boil potatoes for 10–12 minutes, or until potatoes are very tender when tested with a knife. Drain potatoes and mash roughly with a potato masher. Set aside.

2. While potatoes cook, heat butter and oil in a large skillet over medium heat. Add onion, bell pepper, and garlic. Cook, stirring frequently, for 10 minutes or until vegetables are soft. Add corned beef, mashed potatoes, and thyme, and mix well. Season to taste with salt and pepper.

3. Spread hash in the prepared baking pan and bake for 12–15 minutes, or until hot. Serve immediately.

Note: The hash can be prepared up to 2 days in advance and refrigerated, tightly covered. Reheat hash, covered, in a 350°F oven until hot.

Variations:

- Substitute baked ham or leftover grilled chicken for the corned beef.
- For a brunch dish, create 4–6 indentations in top of hash, evenly spaced. Break 1 large egg into each indentation. Sprinkle eggs with salt and pepper, and bake for 12–15 minutes, or until whites are set.
- Top the hash with ⅔ cup grated cheddar cheese.

According to John Mariani in *The American Dictionary of Food and Drink*, the word *hash* entered the English language in the seventeenth century; it comes from the French word *hacher*, which means "to chop." The slang for cheap American restaurants in the nineteenth century was "hash house."

Reuben Sandwich Casserole

Although now defunct, Reuben's Delicatessen was a New York institution that opened in the late 1890s. Legend has it that the Reuben sandwich was invented in 1914 by owner Arthur Reuben for the cast of a Charlie Chaplin film. This easy casserole for a crowd contains all the requisite ingredients.

Yield: 4–6 servings | **Active time:** 10 minutes | **Start to finish (minimum time, slow cooker:** N/A | **Start to finish (conventional):** 45 minutes

.1 (2-pound) package sauerkraut

²/₃ cup mayonnaise

¹/₃ cup bottled chili sauce

2 tablespoons lemon juice

2 scallions, white parts and 3 inches of green tops, rinsed, trimmed, and chopped

2 tablespoons sweet pickle relish

2 tablespoons Dijon mustard

Salt and freshly ground black pepper to taste

2 cups grated Swiss cheese

1 pound thinly sliced cooked corned beef

6 slices seeded rye bread, cut horizontally into 1-inch strips

4 tablespoons (½ stick) unsalted butter, melted

1. Preheat oven to 375° F, and grease a 9 x 13-inch baking pan.
2. Place sauerkraut in a colander and press with back of a spoon to extract as much liquid as possible. Rinse sauerkraut under cold running water for 2 minutes. Then place sauerkraut in a large mixing bowl, and fill bowl with cold water. Soak for 5 minutes. Drain sauerkraut in colander again, pressing with back of a spoon to extract as much liquid as possible. Then wring out sauerkraut by handfuls, and place it in the prepared pan.
3. While sauerkraut soaks, prepare dressing. Combine mayonnaise, chili sauce, lemon juice, scallions, pickle relish, mustard, salt, and pepper in a mixing bowl. Whisk well.
4. Spread sauerkraut with ½ of cheese, ½ of dressing, and corned beef. Top corned beef with remaining dressing and cheese. Brush bread strips with melted butter. Place bread strips on top of pan.

5. Cover pan with aluminum foil, and bake for 10 minutes. Remove foil, and bake for an additional 25 minutes, or until bread is browned and cheese is melted. Serve immediately.

Note: The dish can be prepared for baking up to 1 day in advance and refrigerated, tightly covered.

Variation:
- Substitute sliced baked ham or roast turkey for the corned beef.

What many people object to about sauerkraut is the taste of the brine in which it's packed. Soaking the sauerkraut removes much of that flavor.

Szechwan Pork Ribs

Stews are called "sandpot cooking" in China, and this aromatic, spicy dish is an example. A benefit to this recipe is that the darkly colored sauce will transfer its hue to the meat, so there is no need to brown the meat. Serve it over rice, with some stir-fried vegetables on the side.

Yield: 4–6 servings | **Active time:** 10 minutes | **Start to finish (minimum time, slow cooker):** 3¼ hours in a medium slow cooker | **Start to finish (conventional):** 1¼ hours

> 1½ pounds boneless country pork ribs, cut into 2-inch cubes
> 1 cup water (*1½ cups if cooking conventionally*)
> 5 tablespoons Chinese fermented black beans, coarsely chopped *
> 10 garlic cloves, peeled and minced
> 2 tablespoons soy sauce
> 2 tablespoons Asian sesame oil *
> 1 tablespoon firmly packed dark brown sugar
> 1 tablespoon cornstarch
> 2 tablespoons cold water
> ½–1 teaspoon crushed red pepper flakes
> 4 scallions, white parts and 4 inches of green tops rinsed, trimmed, and thinly sliced

1. Arrange pork ribs in the slow cooker. Combine water, black beans, garlic, soy sauce, oil, and brown sugar in a small bowl, and stir well. Pour mixture over ribs.
2. Cook on Low for 6–8 hours or on High for 3–4 hours, or until meat is tender.
3. If cooking on Low, raise the heat to High. Mix cornstarch with cold water in a small cup, and stir cornstarch mixture into the slow cooker along with red pepper flakes. Cook for an additional 10–20 minutes, or until the sauce is bubbling and slightly thickened. Serve immediately, sprinkling each serving with scallions.

If cooking conventionally: Follow the recipe to the end of Step 1, assembling the dish in a Dutch oven, and adding an additional ½ cup water to the ingredients. Bring to a boil, and cook pork over low heat, covered, for 45 minutes–1 hour, or until pork is very tender. Add cornstarch mixture, and cook for an additional 2–3 minutes, or until slightly thickened. Serve immediately, sprinkling each serving with scallions.

Note: Using either cooking method, the pork can be prepared up to 2 days in advance and refrigerated, tightly covered. Reheat it, covered, in a 350°F oven for 20-25 minutes, or until hot.

Variation:

- Substitute beef chuck for the pork. Brown pork, and cook for a total of 8-10 hours on Low or 4-5 hours on High.

* Available in the Asian aisle of most supermarkets and in specialty markets.

Fermented black beans are small black soybeans with a pungent flavor that have been preserved in salt before being packed. They should be chopped and soaked in some sort of liquid to soften them and release their flavor prior to cooking. Because they are salted as a preservative, they last for up to 2 years if refrigerated once opened.

French Mixed Meats and Beans (*Cassoulet*)

Cassoulet goes back centuries and is one of the culinary triumphs of southwest France, with most authorities citing Castelnaudary in the province of Languedoc as its birthplace. Beans and a variety of meats are always part of the dish, but many versions exist.

Yield: 6–8 servings | **Active time:** 25 minutes | **Start to finish (minimum time, slow cooker):** 6½ hours in a large slow cooker, including 1 hour for beans to soak | **Start to finish (conventional):** 4½ hours, including 1 hour for beans to soak

> 1 pound dried small navy beans
>
> 2 tablespoons olive oil, divided
>
> 2 large onions, peeled and diced
>
> 5 garlic cloves, peeled and minced
>
> 1 large carrot, peeled and sliced
>
> 2 cups Chicken Stock (recipe on page 84) or purchased stock (*3 cups if cooking conventionally*)
>
> 1 cup dry white wine
>
> 1 (14.5-ounce) can diced tomatoes, undrained
>
> 3 tablespoons tomato paste
>
> 1 tablespoon herbes de Provence
>
> 1 bay leaf
>
> 1 pound boneless lamb shoulder, cut into 1-inch cubes, rinsed and patted dry with paper towels
>
> ½ pound boneless pork loin, cut into 1-inch cubes, rinsed and patted dry with paper towels
>
> ½ pound kielbasa, or other smoked sausage, cut into ½-inch slices
>
> Salt and freshly ground black pepper

1. Rinse beans in a colander and place them in a mixing bowl covered with cold water. Allow beans to soak overnight. Or place beans in a saucepan and bring to a boil over high heat. Boil 1 minute. Turn off the heat, cover the pan, and soak beans for 1 hour. With either soaking method, drain beans, discard soaking water, and begin cooking as soon as possible. Transfer beans to the slow cooker.

2. Heat oil in a medium skillet over medium-high heat. Add onions, garlic, and carrot, and cook, stirring frequently, for 3 minutes, or until onions are translucent. Scrape mixture into the slow cooker.

3. Add stock, wine, tomatoes, tomato paste, herbes de Provence, and bay leaf to the slow cooker. Cook bean mixture for 4 hours on Low or 2 hours on High.
4. Preheat the oven broiler, and line a broiler pan with heavy-duty aluminum foil. Broil lamb, pork, and kielbasa for 3 minutes per side, or until browned. Stir meats into the slow cooker along with any juices that have accumulated in the pan. Cook for 5–7 hours on Low or 3–4 hours on High, or until lamb is tender.
5. Remove and discard bay leaf, and season to taste with salt and pepper. Serve immediately.

If cooking conventionally: The dish can be assembled completely through the end of Step 4 in a Dutch oven; the beans do not need time to cook alone. Bring to a boil on top of the stove, and then bake in a 350°F oven for 2 hours, or until beans and lamb are tender.

Note: Using either cooking method, the dish can be prepared up to 2 days in advance and refrigerated, tightly covered. Reheat it, covered, in a 350°F oven for 20–25 minutes, or until hot.

Variation:
- You can make cassoulet with any variety of meats, including beef, duck, and all sorts of sausages. The cooking times will not change.

Here's a tip from traditional Spanish cooking: Add a wine cork or two to a braised meat dish before cooking. The cork releases enzymes that help the meat become tender.

Alsatian Sauerkraut and Sausages (*Choucroute Garnie*)

Even if you shy away from sauerkraut in general, you'll love this dish. The sauerkraut is soaked, and then braised to render it sweet and silky—nothing like a pickle, I promise. You can use any combination of sausages and ham in place of those listed, and steamed potatoes are the traditional accompaniment.

Yield: 6–8 servings | **Active time:** 20 minutes | **Start to finish (minimum time, slow cooker):** 4½ hours in a large slow cooker | **Start to finish (conventional):** 2½ hours

> 1 (2-pound) package sauerkraut
> 2 tablespoons unsalted butter
> 1 large onion, peeled, halved, and thinly sliced
> 1 carrot, peeled and thinly sliced
> 1 cup dry white wine
> ¼ cup gin
> 1 cup Chicken Stock (recipe on page 84) or purchased stock (*1½ cups if cooking conventionally*)
> 3 tablespoons chopped fresh parsley
> 1 bay leaf
> 1 pound smoked pork butt, cut into 1-inch cubes
> ¾ pound kielbasa, or other smoked sausage, cut into ½-inch slices
> Salt and freshly ground black pepper
> For serving: ½ cup prepared mustard

1. Place sauerkraut in a colander and press with back of a spoon to extract as much liquid as possible. Rinse sauerkraut under cold running water for 2 minutes. Then place sauerkraut in a large mixing bowl, and fill bowl with cold water. Soak for 5 minutes. Repeat twice more, draining and soaking sauerkraut. Drain sauerkraut in colander again, pressing with back of a spoon to extract as much liquid as possible. Then wring out sauerkraut by handfuls, and place it in the slow cooker.

2. Heat butter in a large skillet over medium-high heat. Add onion and carrot, and cook, stirring frequently, for 3 minutes, or until onion is translucent. Scrape mixture into the slow cooker, and add wine, gin, stock, parsley, and bay leaf. Mix well. Add pork and kielbasa. Press meats down into sauerkraut.

3. Cook on Low for 8-10 hours or on High for 4-5 hours, or until meats are very tender. Remove and discard bay leaf, and season to taste with salt and pepper. Serve immediately, passing mustard separately.

If cooking conventionally: Preheat the oven to 350°F, and follow the recipe to the end of Step 2, assembling the dish in a Dutch oven. Bake, covered, for 2 hours, or until meats are very tender. Remove and discard bay leaf, and season to taste with salt and pepper. Serve immediately, passing mustard separately.

Note: Using either cooking method, the dish can be prepared up to 2 days in advance and refrigerated, tightly covered. Reheat it, covered, in a 350°F oven for 20-25 minutes, or until hot.

Choucroute (pronounced *shoe-crude*) means "dressed sauerkraut" in French, and it hails from the Alsace region of northeastern France. Every village has its version, and the only constants appear to be sauerkraut cooked in wine and some sort of meat. Brigitte Bardot's beehive hair style was referred to as *choucroute* because of its disorderly appearance.

Caribbean Pork with Yams

Yams play a role in Caribbean food, and they are wonderfully sauced in this pork dish with heady rum as well as spices and brown sugar. This is a homey dish, and I've discovered children love it.

Yield: 4–6 servings | **Active time:** 20 minutes | **Start to finish (minimum time, slow cooker):** 3½ hours in a medium slow cooker | **Start to finish (conventional):** 1¼ hours

1½ pounds boneless country pork ribs, cut into 2-inch cubes
1½ pounds yams or sweet potatoes, peeled and cut into 1-inch cubes
2 tablespoons vegetable oil
2 large onions, peeled and thinly sliced
3 garlic cloves, peeled and minced
3 tablespoons grated fresh ginger
¾ cup Chicken Stock (recipe on page 84) or purchased stock (1¼ cups if cooking conventionally)
⅓ cup balsamic vinegar
⅓ cup rum
⅓ cup firmly packed dark brown sugar
1 teaspoon dried thyme
¼ teaspoon ground cinnamon
Salt and freshly ground black pepper to taste

1. Preheat the oven broiler, and line a broiler pan with heavy-duty aluminum foil. Brown pork for 3–5 minutes per side, or until lightly browned. Place yam cubes in the bottom of the slow cooker. Transfer pork to the slow cooker, and pour in any juices that accumulated in the pan.

2. While pork browns, heat oil in a large skillet over medium-high heat. Add onion, garlic, and ginger. Cook, stirring frequently, for 3 minutes, or until onion is translucent. Arrange mixture on top of pork chops.

3. Combine stock, vinegar, rum, brown sugar, thyme, and cinnamon in a small bowl. Stir well to dissolve sugar. Pour liquid into the slow cooker.

4. Cook on Low for 6–8 hours or on High for 3–4 hours, or until pork is tender. Season to taste with salt and pepper, and serve immediately.

If cooking conventionally: Follow the recipe to the end of Step 3, assembling the dish in a Dutch oven, and adding the additional ½ cup stock to the ingredients. Bring to a boil, and cook pork over low heat, covered, for 45 minutes–1 hour, or until pork is very tender. Season to taste with salt and pepper, and serve immediately.

Note: Using either cooking method, the pork can be prepared up to 2 days in advance and refrigerated, tightly covered. Reheat it, covered, in a 350°F oven for 20–25 minutes, or until hot.

Variation:

- Substitute 1 (3½–4-pound) frying chicken, cut into serving pieces, for the pork. The cooking time will remain the same; cook the chicken until it is cooked through and no longer pink.

Gingered Pork with Napa Cabbage

This Asian-inspired dish is light and healthful, and the sections of cabbage remain crisp for a textural contrast. Serve this over rice, and your meal is complete.

Yield: 4–6 servings | **Active time:** 20 minutes | **Start to finish (minimum time, slow cooker):** 3³/₄ hours in a medium slow cooker | **Start to finish (conventional):** 1¹/₄ hours

> 4–6 (4-ounce) boneless pork chops, trimmed of fat
> 2 tablespoons Asian sesame oil *
> 1 bunch scallions, white parts and 4 inches of green tops, rinsed, trimmed, and sliced, divided
> 3 garlic cloves, peeled and minced
> 3 tablespoons grated fresh ginger
> 1 cup Chicken Stock (recipe on page 84) or purchased stock (*1¹/₂ cups if cooking conventionally*)
> ¹/₃ cup dry sherry
> ¹/₄ cup soy sauce
> 1 tablespoon firmly packed dark brown sugar
> ¹/₂ teaspoon Chinese five-spice powder *
> ¹/₂ head Napa cabbage, leaves rinsed and cut into 2-inch pieces
> 1 tablespoon cornstarch
> 2 tablespoons cold water
> Salt and freshly ground black pepper to taste

1. Preheat the oven broiler, and line a broiler pan with heavy-duty aluminum foil. Brown pork for 3–5 minutes per side, or until lightly browned. Transfer pork to the slow cooker, and pour in any juices that accumulated in the pan.

2. While pork browns, heat oil in a small skillet over medium-high heat. Add ¹/₂ of scallions, garlic, and ginger. Cook, stirring frequently, for 2 minutes, and scrape mixture into the slow cooker.

3. Combine stock, sherry, soy sauce, brown sugar, and five-spice powder in a small bowl. Stir well to dissolve sugar. Pour liquid into the slow cooker.

4. Cook on Low for 4–6 hours or on High for 2–3 hours, or until pork is almost tender.

5. If cooking on Low, raise the heat to High. Add cabbage to the slow cooker, and cook for 45 minutes–1 hour, or until cabbage is crisp-tender. Mix cornstarch with water in a small cup, and stir cornstarch mixture into the juices in the slow cooker. Cook for an additional 10–20 minutes, or until juices are bubbling and slightly thickened. Season to taste with salt and pepper, and serve immediately, sprinkled with remaining scallions.

If cooking conventionally: Follow the recipe to the end of Step 3, assembling the dish in a Dutch oven and adding the additional ½ cup stock to the ingredients. Bring to a boil, and cook pork over low heat, covered, for 35–45 minutes, or until pork is almost tender. Add cabbage and cook for an additional 10–15 minutes. Add cornstarch mixture, and cook for an additional 2–3 minutes, or until slightly thickened. Season to taste with salt and pepper, and serve immediately, sprinkled with remaining scallions.

Note: Using either cooking method, the pork can be prepared up to 2 days in advance and refrigerated, tightly covered. Reheat it, covered, in a 350°F oven for 20–25 minutes, or until hot.

Variation:
- Substitute 1 (3½–4-pound) frying chicken, cut into serving pieces, for the pork. The cooking time will remain the same, and cook the chicken until it is cooked through and no longer pink.

* Available in the Asian aisle of most supermarkets and in specialty markets.

Spanish Pork with Garbanzo Beans

Topping off this flavorful pork with a sprinkling of garlic-laced parsley adds a fresh accent to the long-simmered dish, and the smoked paprika adds its nuance to the sauce. Serve this on top of rice, with a tossed a salad to complete the meal.

Yield: 4–6 servings | **Active time:** 25 minutes | **Start to finish (minimum time, slow cooker):** 3½ hours in a medium slow cooker | **Start to finish (conventional):** 2 hours

1¼ pounds boneless pork loin, cut into 1-inch cubes
2 tablespoons olive oil
1 large onion, peeled and diced
6 garlic cloves, peeled and minced, divided
1 large carrot, peeled and sliced
1 celery rib, rinsed, trimmed, and sliced
3 tablespoons smoked Spanish paprika
1 tablespoon chili powder
2 teaspoons ground cumin
1 (14.5-ounce) can diced tomatoes, undrained
¾ cup Chicken Stock (recipe on page 84) or purchased stock (1¼ cups if cooking conventionally)
½ cup dry sherry
2 tablespoons tomato paste
2 (15-ounce) cans garbanzo beans, drained and rinsed
1 bay leaf
¼ cup chopped fresh parsley
Salt and freshly ground black pepper to taste

1. Preheat the oven broiler, and line a broiler pan with heavy-duty aluminum foil. Brown pork for 3–5 minutes per side, or until lightly browned. Transfer pork to the slow cooker, and pour in any juices that accumulated in the pan.
2. While pork browns, heat oil in a medium skillet over medium-high heat. Add onion, ½ of garlic, carrot, and celery. Cook, stirring frequently, for 3 minutes, or until onion is translucent. Add paprika, chili powder, and cumin, and cook for 1 minute, stirring constantly. Scrape mixture into the slow cooker.

3. Combine tomatoes, stock, sherry, and tomato paste in a mixing bowl. Stir well to dissolve tomato paste. Pour liquid into the slow cooker, and add beans and bay leaf.

4. Cook on Low for 6–8 hours or on High for 3–4 hours, or until meat is tender.

5. While pork cooks, combine remaining garlic and parsley in a small bowl, and set aside. Remove and discard bay leaf, season to taste with salt and pepper, and serve immediately, sprinkled with parsley mixture.

If cooking conventionally: Preheat the oven to 375°F after pork browns, and follow the recipe to the end of Step 3, assembling the dish in a Dutch oven, and adding the additional 1/2 cup stock to the ingredients. Bring to a boil on top of the stove, and then cook pork, covered, for 1–1¼ hours, or until tender. While pork cooks, combine remaining garlic and parsley in a small bowl, and set aside. Remove and discard bay leaf, season to taste with salt and pepper, and serve immediately, sprinkled with parsley mixture.

Note: Using either cooking method, the pork can be prepared up to 2 days in advance and refrigerated, tightly covered. Reheat it, covered, in a 350°F oven for 20–25 minutes, or until hot.

Variation:
- Substitute 1 (3½–4-pound) frying chicken, cut into serving pieces, for the pork. The cooking time will remain the same; cook the chicken until it is cooked through and no longer pink.

Chinese Pork with Vegetables

I like to serve this hearty and flavorful Asian dish over angel hair pasta, which transforms it into a lo mein preparation; but you can always just cook up some rice. Stir-fried vegetables are an excellent way to complete the meal.

Yield: 4–6 servings | **Active time:** 25 minutes | **Start to finish (minimum time, slow cooker):** 3½ hours in a medium slow cooker | **Start to finish (conventional):** 1½ hours

> 1½ pounds boneless country pork ribs, cut into 2-inch sections
> 2 tablespoons Asian sesame oil *
> 2 bunches scallions, white parts and 4 inches of green tops, rinsed, trimmed, and sliced, divided
> 2 tablespoons grated fresh ginger
> 1 cup Chicken Stock (recipe on page 84) or purchased stock (1½ cups if cooking conventionally)
> ¼ cup hoisin sauce *
> 2 tablespoons soy sauce
> ½ pound mushrooms, wiped with a damp paper towel, trimmed, and quartered
> 1 (10-ounce) package cut green beans, thawed
> 1 tablespoon cornstarch
> 2 tablespoons cold water
> Salt and freshly ground black pepper to taste

1. Preheat the oven broiler, and line a broiler pan with heavy-duty aluminum foil. Brown pork for 3–5 minutes per side, or until lightly browned. Transfer pork to the slow cooker, and pour in any juices that accumulated in the pan.

2. While pork browns, heat oil in a small skillet over medium-high heat. Add ½ of scallions and ginger, and cook for 2 minutes. Scrape mixture into the slow cooker. Combine stock, hoisin sauce, and soy sauce in a mixing bowl. Stir well to incorporate hoisin sauce. Pour liquid into the slow cooker, and add mushrooms.

3. Cook on Low for 5–7 hours or on High for 2½–3 hours, or until meat is almost tender.

4. If cooking on Low, raise the heat to High. Add green beans to the slow cooker, and cook for 30 minutes. Mix cornstarch with cold water in a small cup, and stir cornstarch mixture into the slow cooker. Cook

for an additional 10-20 minutes, or until the sauce is bubbling and slightly thickened. Season to taste with salt and pepper, and serve immediately, sprinkling pork with remaining scallions.

If cooking conventionally: Follow the recipe to the end of Step 2, assembling the dish in a Dutch oven, and adding the additional ½ cup stock to the ingredients. Bring to a boil, and cook pork over low heat, covered, for 45 minutes–1 hour, or until pork is tender, adding green beans for the last 5 minutes of cooking. Add cornstarch mixture, and cook for an additional 2-3 minutes, or until slightly thickened. Season to taste with salt and pepper, and serve immediately, sprinkling pork with remaining scallions.

Note: Using either cooking method, the pork can be prepared up to 2 days in advance and refrigerated, tightly covered. Reheat it, covered, in a 350°F oven for 20-25 minutes, or until hot.

Variation:
- Substitute 1 (3½-4-pound) frying chicken, cut into serving pieces, for the pork. The cooking time will remain the same; cook the chicken until it is cooked through and no longer pink.

* Available in the Asian aisle of most supermarkets and in specialty markets.

An easy way to grate ginger is to peel just the portion you plan to grate, and then hold on to the remainder as a handle.

Southern Barbecued Pork Sandwiches

This recipe makes true barbecue—the noun and not the verb. The meat is so tender it falls apart, and the sauce is somewhat hot. Once piled on the roll and topped with coleslaw, your meal is done.

Yield: 4–6 servings | **Active time:** 20 minutes | **Start to finish (minimum time, slow cooker):** 4³/₄ hours in a medium slow cooker | **Start to finish (conventional):** 2³/₄ hours

1½ pounds boneless country pork ribs, cut into 2-inch sections
3 tablespoons vegetable oil
1 large onion, peeled and chopped
1 green bell pepper, seeds and ribs removed, and chopped
3 garlic cloves, peeled and minced
2 tablespoons smoked Spanish paprika
1 tablespoon chili powder
2 teaspoons dry mustard powder
³/₄ cup ketchup
¹/₃ cup cider vinegar
¹/₃ cup firmly packed dark brown sugar
3 tablespoons Worcestershire sauce
¹/₂ teaspoon hot red pepper sauce, or to taste
Salt and freshly ground black pepper to taste
4–6 rolls of your choice, split and toasted
1–1 ¹/₂ cups coleslaw (your favorite recipe or purchased)

If cooking conventionally:
¹/₂ cup water

1. Preheat the oven broiler, and line a broiler pan with heavy-duty aluminum foil. Brown pork for 3–5 minutes per side, or until lightly browned. Transfer pork to the slow cooker, and pour in any juices that accumulated in the pan.
2. When pork browns, heat oil in a saucepan over medium-high heat. Add onion, green bell pepper, and garlic, and cook, stirring frequently, for 3 minutes, or until onion is translucent. Stir in paprika, chili powder, and mustard, and cook over low heat for 1 minute, stirring constantly. Add ketchup, vinegar, brown sugar, Worcestershire sauce, and hot red pepper sauce, and stir well. Bring to a boil over medium-high heat, stirring frequently. Pour mixture into the slow cooker.

3. Cook on Low for 8–10 hours or on High for 4–5 hours, or until meat is falling apart. Tear meat into shreds with 2 forks, and season to taste with salt and pepper. To serve, mound meat on rolls, and top with coleslaw.

If cooking conventionally: Preheat the oven to 350°F, and follow the recipe to the end of Step 2, assembling the dish in a Dutch oven, and adding ½ cup water to the ingredients. Bake, covered, for 2½ hours, or until pork is falling apart. Tear meat into shreds with 2 forks, and season to taste with salt and pepper. To serve, mound meat on rolls, and top with coleslaw.

Note: Using either cooking method, the pork can be prepared up to 2 days in advance and refrigerated, tightly covered. Reheat it, covered, in a 350°F oven for 20–25 minutes, or until hot.

Variation:
- Substitute 1½ pounds beef brisket for the pork, and add 2 hours to the cooking time if cooking on Low, 1 hour if cooking on High, or 30 minutes if cooking conventionally.

Smoked Spanish paprika adds a wonderful nuance to dishes, as if they were cooked on a grill. Unlike chemical liquid smoke, the flavor is natural because the red peppers are dehydrated by cold smoking.

Hoppin' John

No self-respecting Southerner would start the New Year without eating a bowl of black-eyed peas stewed with ham; it's the regional good luck charm. The dish probably came from Africa, and it is mentioned in literature long before the Civil War. Serve it on rice to complete the protein.

Yield: 4–6 servings | **Active time:** 15 minutes | **Start to finish (minimum time, slow cooker):** 4½ hours in a medium slow cooker, including 1 hour for beans to soak | **Start to finish (conventional):** 3 hours, including 1 hour for beans to soak

> 1½ cups dried black-eyed peas
> ¾ pound smoked pork butt or ham, trimmed of fat and cut into ½-inch dice
> 3 cups Chicken Stock (recipe on page 84) or purchased stock (3½ cups if cooking conventionally)
> 2 tablespoons chopped fresh parsley
> 1 teaspoon dried thyme
> 1 bay leaf
> Salt and freshly ground black pepper to taste

1. Rinse black-eyed peas in a colander and place them in a mixing bowl covered with cold water. Allow black-eyed peas to soak overnight. Or place black-eyed peas into a saucepan and bring to a boil over high heat. Boil 1 minute. Turn off the heat, cover the pan, and soak black-eyed peas for 1 hour. With either soaking method, drain peas, discard soaking water, and begin cooking as soon as possible. Transfer black-eyed peas to the slow cooker.

2. Add pork butt or ham, stock, parsley, thyme, and bay leaf to the slow cooker.

3. Cook on Low for 6–8 hours or on High for 3–4 hours, or until black-eyed peas are tender. Remove and discard bay leaf, and season to taste with salt and pepper. Serve immediately.

If cooking conventionally: Follow the recipe to the end of Step 2, assembling the dish in a saucepan, and adding the additional ½ cup stock to the ingredients. Bring to a boil, and cook beans over low heat, covered, for 1-1¼ hours, or until black-eyed peas are tender. Remove and discard bay leaf, and season to taste with salt and pepper. Serve immediately.

Note: Using either cooking method, the dish can be prepared up to 2 days in advance and refrigerated, tightly covered. Reheat it, covered, in a 350°F oven for 20–25 minutes, or until hot.

Variation:
- For a vegetarian version, substitute vegetable stock for the chicken stock, omit the ham, and add 1–2 finely chopped chipotle peppers to lend a smoky flavor.

People around the world have traditionally eaten legumes of all types with rice, centuries before we had scientific proof of their value. Neither legumes nor grains have all the essential amino acids, but if eaten together the protein is completed.

Braised Ham with Vegetables

Ham is a most underutilized meat, and to buy and roast a whole ham is always economical. Here is one way to use up some leftovers; serve it with some small shells or other small pasta and a salad.

Yield: 4–6 servings | **Active time:** 15 minutes | **Start to finish (minimum time, slow cooker):** 3¼ hours in a medium slow cooker | **Start to finish (conventional):** 1 hour

2 tablespoons olive oil
2 large onions, peeled and thinly sliced
3 garlic cloves, peeled and minced
1 green bell pepper, seeds and ribs removed, and thinly sliced
1½ pounds baked ham, cut into thick slices
1 (14.5-ounce) can crushed tomatoes in tomato puree
2 tablespoons chopped fresh parsley
1 tablespoon Italian seasoning
1 bay leaf
Salt and freshly ground black pepper to taste

If cooking conventionally:
½ cup water

1. Heat oil in a medium skillet over medium-high heat. Add onion, garlic, and green bell pepper, and cook, stirring frequently, for 3 minutes, or until onions are translucent. Scrape mixture into the slow cooker. Arrange ham slices over vegetables, and add tomatoes, parsley, Italian seasoning, and bay leaf.

2. Cook on Low for 6–8 hours or on High for 3–4 hours, or until vegetables are tender. Remove and discard bay leaf, and season to taste with salt and pepper.

If cooking conventionally: Preheat the oven to 350°F. Follow the recipe to the end of Step 1, assembling the dish in a Dutch oven, and adding ½ cup water to the ingredients. Bake for 45 minutes–1 hour, or until vegetables are tender. Remove and discard bay leaf, and season to taste with salt and pepper.

Note: Using either cooking method, the pork can be prepared up to 2 days in advance and refrigerated, tightly covered. Reheat it, covered, in a 350°F oven for 20–25 minutes, or until hot.

Chapter 8:
From the Vegetable Patch: Hearty Vegetarian Entrees

Even though the first dish I made in the slow cooker was a pot roast, I also recall that the second dish was a bean soup. Beans—which remain one of the most affordable foods in the supermarket—need to be gently simmered, and that's why the slow cooker is perfect for the task.

A slow cooker is far more patient than any pot you would place on the stove, and due to the indirect heat there's no need to worry that the beans on the bottom are going to scorch and ruin the dish—a common pitfall to cooking beans conventionally. It shouldn't be surprising; today's slow cookers evolved from old-fashioned bean pots.

You'll find a range of great recipes for all things bean in this chapter, but that's not all. There are other types of vegetarian dishes that are colorful as well as delicious.

BEANS 101

Beans are justly praised for their nutritional value as well as their availability and economy, and dried beans play a role in almost all the world's cuisines. Beans are a high source of fiber and protein, and they are low in fat and contain no cholesterol. They are also a good source of B vitamins, especially B6.

Before using beans, rinse them in a colander or sieve under cold running water, and pick through them to discard any broken beans or pebbles that might have found their way into the bag. Then there's a secondary step once the beans have been covered with water; discard any that float to the top.

Cook dried beans until they are no longer crunchy, but still have texture. If beans are going to be cooked and then cooked further in a dish, such as in a chili, then stop the initial cooking when they are still slightly crunchy. The other caveat of bean cookery is to make sure beans are cooked to the proper consistency before adding any acidic ingredient—such as tomatoes, vinegar, or lemon—because acid prevents the beans from becoming tender.

Cooking beans is common sense; the larger the bean the longer it will take to soften. But it's not necessary to presoak larger beans for a longer period of time than smaller beans. There's only so much softening that happens at no or low heat.

Once you've soaked the beans, always discard the soaking liquid-before placing them in the slow cooker. If using a recipe, the amount of liquid to add is included.

You can use your slow cooker any time you want to cook beans. Place them in the slow cooker, and cover them with hot water by at least 3 inches. Keep in mind that beans should always be covered with liquid at all times while they're cooking, so towards the end of the cooking process, take a look and add boiling water if the water seems almost evaporated.

You'll notice that there is a wide range in the timing of cooking beans. In addition to acidic ingredients retarding softening, if the beans are a few years old, they'll take longer to cook. Also, the minerals in your tap water can retard the softening and require a longer cooking time.

Slow Cooker Bean Times

Here's a chart to tell you how long different species of beans should cook in the slow cooker. The calculations in this chart are based on 2 cups of dried beans, which yields 6 cups of cooked beans:

Bean	Cooking Time on High
Black beans	3 hours
Black-eyed peas	3¼ hours
Fava beans	2¾ hours
Garbanzo beans	3½ hours
Great Northern beans	2¾ hours
Kidney beans	3 hours
Lentils	2 hours (no presoaking)
Lima beans	2½ hours for baby, 3½ for large
Navy beans	2½ hours
Split peas	2½ hours (no presoaking)
White beans	3 hours

Bean Substitution Chart

Bean recipes are very tolerant to substitutions, and the chart on cooking times is a good guide to which one can become a stand-in for another. But color, texture, and flavor are also criteria to consider. Use this chart for guidance.

Bean	What to Substitute
Black (also called turtle)	Kidney
Black-eyed peas	Kidney
Cannellini	Navy
Cranberry	Kidney
Fava (broad beans)	Large lima
Flageolet	Navy
Kidney (pink and red, pinto)	Navy
Lentils (red, brown, green)	Split peas
Split peas	Lentils

Traditional Hawaiian cooks add a few slices of fresh ginger into the pot in which beans are cooked. They say it alleviates having problems with gas after eating them.

Slow-Cooked Risotto

Traditional risotto requires constant attention and stirring to achieve the creamy results you'll get with either the slow cooker or oven-baked versions of this recipe. I've added a lot of variations, but feel free to experiment; the recipe is for your basic rice.

Yield: 4–6 servings | **Active time:** 15 minutes | **Start to finish (minimum time, slow cooker):** 2¼ hours in a medium slow cooker | **Start to finish (conventional):** 45 minutes

> 4 tablespoons (½ stick) unsalted butter
> 1 medium onion, peeled and finely chopped
> 1 garlic clove, peeled and minced
> 1½ cups Arborio rice
> ½ cup dry white wine
> 3½ cups Vegetable Stock (recipe on page 86) or purchased stock
>   (*4 cups if cooking conventionally*)
> ½ cup freshly grated Parmesan cheese
> Salt and freshly ground black pepper to taste

1. Heat butter in a large skillet over medium-high heat. Add onion and garlic, and cook, stirring frequently, for 3 minutes, or until onion is translucent. Stir in rice, and cook, stirring constantly, for 2 minutes, or until rice is opaque.
2. Add wine to the skillet, raise the heat to high, and cook, stirring constantly, for 2 minutes, or until wine is almost evaporated. Scrape mixture into the slow cooker, and stir in stock.
3. Cook on High for 2–2½ hours, or until liquid is absorbed and rice is tender. Stir in Parmesan, and season to taste with salt and pepper.

If cooking conventionally: Preheat the oven to 400°F, and grease a 9 x 13-inch baking pan. Follow the recipe to the end of Step 2, adding the additional ½ cup stock to the ingredients. Add stock directly into the skillet to heat, and then transfer mixture to the prepared pan. Cover the pan with foil, and bake for 25–30 minutes, until liquid is absorbed and rice is tender. Stir in Parmesan, and season to taste with salt and pepper.

Note: Using either cooking method, the dish can be prepared up to 2 days in advance and refrigerated, tightly covered. Reheat it, covered, in a 350°F oven for 20–25 minutes, or until hot.

Variations:

- Add 1 (10-ounce) package frozen chopped broccoli, thawed, along with the stock.
- Add 1 (10-ounce) package frozen chopped spinach, thawed and drained well, along with the stock.
- Cook ½ pound mushrooms, wiped with a damp paper towel, trimmed, and sliced, to the skillet along with the onion and garlic.
- For a Mexican-style rice, substitute tomato juice for the Vegetable Stock, add 2 tablespoons tomato paste and 2 tablespoons chili powder to the recipe.
- Substitute seafood stock for the vegetable stock, and add 1 pound thick white fish fillet, cut into 1-inch cubes, to the rice.

The most famous risotto in Italy is associated with the city of Milan, and there are recipes dating to the sixteenth century. The Milanese version is made with saffron, which is the world's most expensive food, ounce for ounce.

Italian Vegetable Stew

This delicious combination of vegetables and beans cooked in an herbed tomato sauce is homey comfort food, and extremely low in calories! Serve it over whole-wheat pasta for a truly healthful meal.

Yield: 4–6 servings | **Active time:** 20 minutes | **Start to finish (minimum time, slow cooker):** 3 hours in a medium slow cooker | **Start to finish (conventional):** 1 hour

1 (1-pound) eggplant

Salt

⅓ cup olive oil, divided

1 large onion, peeled and diced

3 garlic cloves, peeled and minced

2 green bell peppers, seeds and ribs removed, and cut into ¾-inch dice

3 small summer squash, trimmed and cut into ¾-inch cubes

1 (15-ounce) can cannellini beans, drained and rinsed

1 (14.5-ounce) can crushed tomatoes, undrained

¾ cup Vegetable Stock (recipe on page 86) or purchased stock
   (*1 ¼ cups if cooking conventionally*)

1 (8-ounce) can tomato sauce

1 tablespoon Italian seasoning

½ cup freshly grated Parmesan cheese

Freshly ground black pepper to taste

1. Place eggplant in a colander, and sprinkle cubes liberally with salt. Place a plate on top of eggplant cubes, and weight the plate with some cans. Place the colander in the sink or on a plate, and allow eggplant to drain for 30 minutes. Rinse eggplant cubes, and squeeze hard to remove water. Wring out remaining water with a cloth tea towel.

2. Heat half of the oil in a medium skillet over medium-high heat. Add onion, garlic, and green bell peppers. Cook, stirring frequently, for 3 minutes, or until onion is translucent. Scrape mixture into the slow cooker. Add remaining oil to the skillet, and add eggplant cubes. Cook, stirring frequently, for 3 minutes, or until eggplant begins to soften. Scrape eggplant into the slow cooker.

3. Add summer squash, beans, tomatoes, stock, tomato sauce, and Italian seasoning to the slow cooker. Stir well.

4. Cook on Low for 5–7 hours or on High for 2½–3½ hours, or until vegetables are tender. Stir in Parmesan cheese, and season to taste with salt and pepper. Serve immediately over pasta.

If cooking conventionally: Follow the recipe to the end of Step 3, assembling the dish in a saucepan, and adding the additional ½ cup stock to the ingredients.

Bring to a boil and cook over medium heat, stirring occasionally, for 25–30 minutes, or until vegetables are tender. Stir in Parmesan cheese, and season to taste with salt and pepper. Serve immediately over pasta.

Note: Using either cooking method, the dish can be cooked up to 2 days in advance; reheat it in a 350°F oven, covered, for 20–25 minutes, or until hot.

Variations:
- For Mexican flavors, substitute kidney beans for the cannellini beans, 1 tablespoon chili powder, 1 teaspoon ground cumin, and 1 teaspoon dried oregano for the Italian seasoning, and jalapeño Jack cheese for the Parmesan.
- For a more French flavor, substitute herbes de Provence for the Italian seasoning, and Gruyère for the Parmesan cheese.

Southern Vegetable Stew with Cornmeal Dumplings

This is one of my favorite vegetarian dishes; the combination of vegetables is vibrantly seasoned, and the fluffy dumplings are delicious. It's all you need for dinner!

Yield: 4–6 servings | **Active time:** 20 minutes | **Start to finish (minimum time, slow cooker):** 4 hours in a medium slow cooker | **Start to finish (conventional):** 1 hour

STEW:

2 tablespoons vegetable oil

1 large onion, peeled and diced

3 garlic cloves, peeled and minced

2 celery ribs, rinsed, trimmed, and sliced

1 green bell pepper, seeds and ribs removed, and sliced

2 tablespoons Creole seasoning

1 teaspoon dried thyme

2 teaspoons dried oregano

2 bay leaves

3/4 pound butternut or acorn squash, peeled and cut into 1/2-inch cubes

2 (14.5-ounce) cans diced tomatoes, undrained

2 cups Vegetable Stock (recipe on page 86) or purchased stock (*2 1/2 cups if cooking conventionally*)

3 tablespoons chopped fresh parsley

1 (10-ounce) package frozen black-eyed peas, thawed

1 cup fresh corn or frozen corn, thawed

1 cup frozen sliced okra, thawed

Salt and freshly ground black pepper to taste

DUMPLINGS:

1/2 cup all-purpose flour

1/3 cup cornmeal

2 tablespoons chopped fresh parsley

1 teaspoon baking powder

1/4 teaspoon salt

1 large egg

2 tablespoons whole milk

2 tablespoons unsalted butter, melted

1. Heat oil in a medium skillet over medium-high heat. Add onion, garlic, celery, and green bell pepper, and cook, stirring frequently, for 3 minutes, or until onion is translucent. Reduce the heat to low, and add Creole seasoning, thyme, oregano, and bay leaves. Cook, stirring constantly, for 1 minute. Scrape mixture into the slow cooker.
2. Add butternut squash, tomatoes, and stock to the slow cooker. Stir well.
3. Cook on Low for 5–7 hours or on High for 2½–3 hours, or until squash is almost tender.
4. While stew cooks, prepare dumpling batter. In a medium bowl, stir together flour, cornmeal, parsley, baking powder, and salt. In a small bowl, whisk together egg, milk, and melted butter. Add liquids to flour mixture, and stir with a fork just until combined.
5. If cooking on Low, raise the heat to High. Add parsley, black-eyed peas, corn, and okra to the slow cooker. Remove and discard bay leaves, and season to taste with salt and pepper.
6. Drop dumpling batter into 8–12 mounds on top of stew. Cook for an additional 45–50 minutes, or until dumplings are puffed and cooked through. Do not lift the lid while dumplings steam. Serve immediately.

If cooking conventionally: Follow the recipe to the end of Step 2, assembling the dish in a saucepan or deep skillet, and adding the additional ½ cup stock to the ingredients. Bring to a boil and cook over medium heat, covered, stirring occasionally, for 25–30 minutes, or until squash is almost tender. Make dumpling batter as described in Step 4, and then follow Step 5. Drop dumpling batter into 8–12 mounds on top of stew. Cook for an additional 12–15 minutes, or until dumplings are puffed and cooked through. Do not lift the lid while dumplings steam. Serve immediately.

Note: Using either cooking method, the stew can be cooked up to 2 days in advance. Reheat it over low heat, and cook dumplings as detailed in the conventional instructions above.

Variation:
- I've also made this as a chicken dish. Substitute chicken stock for the vegetable stock, and add 1 pound boneless, skinless chicken, cut into ½-inch dice, at the start of the cooking time.

Southwestern Pinto Bean Stew

This is one of the most vibrant vegetable stews you'll ever eat; it zings with spices that enliven both the beans and zucchini. Serve it over rice with a bowl of guacamole and chips on the side.

Yield: 4–6 servings | **Active time:** 15 minutes | **Start to finish (minimum time, slow cooker):** 2¼ hours in a medium slow cooker | **Start to finish (conventional):** 40 minutes

> 3 tablespoons olive oil
> 1 large onion, peeled and diced
> 3 garlic cloves, peeled and minced
> 1 green bell pepper, seeds and ribs removed, and finely chopped
> 2 jalapeño or serrano chiles, seeds and ribs removed, and finely chopped
> 2 tablespoons chili powder
> 2 teaspoons ground cumin
> 2 teaspoons dried oregano
> 1 (15-ounce) can tomato sauce
> 1 (14.5-ounce) can diced tomatoes, drained (*do not drain tomatoes if cooking conventionally*)
> 2 medium zucchini, rinsed, trimmed and cut into ¾-inch dice
> 2 (15-ounce) cans pinto beans, drained and rinsed
> Salt and freshly ground black pepper to taste

1. Heat oil in a medium skillet over medium-high heat. Add onion, garlic, green bell pepper, and chiles, and cook, stirring frequently, for 3 minutes, or until onion is translucent. Stir in chili powder, cumin, and oregano. Cook for 1 minute, stirring constantly. Scrape mixture into the slow cooker.
2. Stir in tomato sauce, tomatoes, zucchini, and pinto beans.
3. Cook on Low for 3–5 hours or on High for 1½–2 hours, or until zucchini is tender. Season to taste with salt and pepper, and serve immediately.

If cooking conventionally: Follow the recipe to the end of Step 2, assembling the dish in a saucepan, and adding the liquid from the tomatoes to the ingredients.

Bring to a boil and cook over low heat, covered, stirring occasionally, for 25–30 minutes, or until vegetables are tender. Season to taste with salt and pepper, and serve immediately.

Note: Using either cooking method, the dish can be cooked up to 2 days in advance. Reheat it over low heat, covered, for 5–7 minutes, or until hot.

Variation:
- Substitute 1 (4-ounce) can chopped mild green chiles, drained, for the fresh chile peppers.

When cooking with fresh chiles, try to avoid coming into contact with the steam created while sautéing them. The potent oils are carried in the steam.

Aromatic Curried Red Lentils

Lentils are called *dal* in Indian cooking, and they form a cornerstone of that vibrant cuisine. These lentils are punctuated with cubes of delicate yellow summer squash. Serve the dish over rice, preferably aromatic basmati rice.

Yield: 4–6 servings | **Active time:** 20 minutes | **Start to finish (minimum time, slow cooker):** 3 hours in a medium slow cooker | **Start to finish (conventional):** 1¼ hours

¼ cup vegetable oil

2 medium onions, peeled and chopped

3 garlic cloves, peeled and minced

1 large jalapeño or serrano chile, seeds and ribs removed, and finely chopped

2 tablespoons curry powder

1 teaspoon ground cumin

1 teaspoon ground coriander

¾ teaspoon ground cinnamon

1 ½ cups red lentils, rinsed well

4 cups Vegetable Stock (recipe on page 86) or purchased stock

1 (14.5-ounce) can diced tomatoes, drained (*do not drain tomatoes if cooking conventionally*)

3 small summer squash, rinsed, trimmed, and cut into ½-inch dice

Salt and freshly ground black pepper to taste

¼ cup chopped fresh cilantro

1. Heat oil in medium skillet over medium-high heat. Add onion, garlic, and chile, and cook, stirring frequently, for 3 minutes, or until onion is translucent. Stir in curry powder, cumin, coriander, and cinnamon. Cook, stirring constantly, for 1 minute. Scrape mixture into the slow cooker.

2. Add lentils, stock, and tomatoes to the slow cooker. Stir well.

3. Cook on Low for 3–5 hours or on High for 1½–2 hours, or until lentils are almost soft.

4. If cooking on Low, raise the heat to High. Add summer squash to the slow cooker. Cook for 40–50 minutes, or until squash is tender. Season to taste with salt and pepper, and serve immediately, sprinkling cilantro over each serving.

If cooking conventionally: Follow the recipe to the end of Step 2, assembling the dish in a saucepan, and adding the liquid from the tomatoes to the ingredients.

Bring to a boil over medium-high heat, and cook over low heat, covered, stirring occasionally, for 40–45 minutes, or until lentils are almost soft. Add summer squash to the slow cooker. Cook for 10–15 minutes, or until squash is tender. Season to taste with salt and pepper, and serve immediately, sprinkling cilantro over each serving.

Note: Using either cooking method, the dish can be cooked up to 2 days in advance. Reheat it over low heat, covered, for 5–7 minutes, or until hot.

Variation:
- Substitute potato for the squash, and add it at the start of the cooking time.

Lentils are considered one of the healthiest foods you can eat—especially considering their low cost. Clocking in at just 230 calories per cup, cooked, they are a powerhouse of fiber, which can help to lower cholesterol, plus they are an excellent source of manganese and folate and they restore iron to your system.

Red Yam and Kidney Bean Stew

This Southwestern combination is similar to a vegetarian picadillo; it contains some raisins for sweetness, beans for fiber, and yams for substance. If you can't find yams, you can always use sweet potatoes.

Yield: 4–6 servings | **Active time:** 20 minutes | **Start to finish (minimum time, slow cooker):** 3½ hours in a medium slow cooker | **Start to finish (conventional):** 45 minutes

2 tablespoons olive oil

1 medium onion, peeled and diced

2 garlic cloves, peeled and minced

2 tablespoons chili powder

2 teaspoons ground cumin

1 teaspoon dried oregano

Hot red pepper flakes to taste

1 pound red yams, peeled and cut into ¾-inch dice

3 cups Vegetable Stock (recipe on page 86) or purchased stock
   (3½ cups if cooking conventionally)

1 (14.5-ounce) can diced tomatoes, drained

2 (15-ounce) cans kidney beans, drained and rinsed

½ cup raisins

2 tablespoons cider vinegar

Salt to taste

1. Heat oil in a small skillet over medium-high heat. Add onion and garlic, and cook, stirring frequently, for 3 minutes, or until onion is translucent. Add chili powder, cumin, oregano, and red pepper flakes. Cook, stirring constantly, for 1 minute. Scrape mixture into the slow cooker.
2. Add yams, stock, tomatoes, beans, raisins, and vinegar to the slow cooker. Stir well.
3. Cook on Low for 6–8 hours or on High for 3–4 hours, or until yams are tender. Season to taste with salt, and serve immediately.

If cooking conventionally: Follow the recipe to the end of Step 2, assembling the dish in a saucepan, and adding the additional ½ cup stock to the ingredients.

Bring to a boil and cook over low heat, covered, stirring occasionally, for 25–30 minutes, or until yams are tender. Season to taste with salt, and serve immediately.

Note: Using either cooking method, the dish can be prepared up to 2 days in advance and refrigerated, tightly covered. Reheat it, covered, in a 350°F oven for 20–25 minutes, or until hot.

Variation:
- Transform this stew to a version of turkey chili by adding 1 pound ground turkey to the slow cooker in Step 2.

A cup of cooked kidney beans provides 45.3 percent of the recommended daily intake for fiber. Kidney beans' high fiber content prevents blood sugar levels from rising too rapidly after a meal, making these beans an especially good choice for individuals with diabetes, insulin resistance, or hypoglycemia.

Cheesy Garbanzo Beans

Garbanzo beans, a favorite of many Mediterranean cuisines, are both the meatiest and nuttiest of the legumes, and they take to so many types of seasonings. In this thick and rich stew, they are joined with cheeses as well as herbs. Serve it over polenta or pasta, with a tossed salad on the side.

Yield: 4–6 servings | **Active time:** 15 minutes | **Start to finish (minimum time, slow cooker):** 6½ hours in a medium slow cooker, including 1 hour to soak beans | **Start to finish (conventional):** 2 hours, including 1 hour to soak beans

1½ cups dried garbanzo beans
2 tablespoons olive oil
1 medium onion, peeled and diced
3 garlic cloves, peeled and minced
½ green bell pepper, seeds and ribs removed, and finely chopped
2 cups tomato juice (*2½ cups if cooking conventionally*)
1 (14.5-ounce) can diced tomatoes, undrained
3 tablespoons chopped fresh parsley
2 teaspoons Italian seasoning
1 bay leaf
½ cup grated whole-milk mozzarella cheese
¼ cup freshly grated Parmesan cheese
Salt and freshly ground black pepper to taste

1. Rinse beans in a colander and place them in a mixing bowl covered with cold water. Allow beans to soak overnight. Or place beans in a saucepan and bring to a boil over high heat. Boil 1 minute. Turn off the heat, cover the pan, and soak beans for 1 hour. With either soaking method, drain beans, discard soaking water, and begin cooking as soon as possible. Transfer beans to the slow cooker.

2. Heat oil in a medium skillet over medium-high heat. Add onion, garlic, and green bell pepper. Cook, stirring frequently, for 3 minutes, or until onion is translucent. Scrape mixture into the slow cooker. Add tomato juice, tomatoes, parsley, Italian seasoning, and bay leaf. Stir well.

3. Cook on Low for 10–12 hours or on High for 5–6 hours, or until beans are tender.

4. If cooking on Low, raise the heat to High. Remove and discard bay leaf, stir in mozzarella and Parmesan cheeses, and season to taste with salt and pepper. Cook for 10–15 minutes, or until cheeses melt. Serve immediately.

If cooking conventionally: Follow the recipe to the end of Step 2, assembling the dish in a saucepan, and adding the additional ½ cup tomato juice to the ingredients. Bring to a boil and cook over low heat, covered, stirring occasionally, for 1½–1¾ hours, or until beans are tender. Remove and discard bay leaf, stir in mozzarella and Parmesan cheeses, and season to taste with salt and pepper. Cook for 2–3 minutes, or until cheeses melt. Serve immediately.

Note: Using either cooking method, the dish can be prepared up to 2 days in advance and refrigerated, tightly covered. Reheat it, covered, in a 350°F oven for 20–25 minutes, or until hot.

Variation:
- For Mexican flavor, substitute kidney beans or pinto beans for the garbanzo beans, Monterey Jack cheese for the mozzarella and Parmesan, and 2 tablespoons chili powder for the Italian seasoning.

Vegetarian Bolognese Sauce

I really wanted to create a vegetarian sauce that had the same gusto, and provided the same sense of emotional satisfaction, as my Bolognese sauce made with meat. I hope you'll agree that this sauce delivers; it has a wide range of vegetables as well as seasonings.

Yield: 6–8 servings | **Active time:** 15 minutes | **Start to finish (minimum time, slow cooker):** 3¼ hours in a medium slow cooker | **Start to finish (conventional):** 1¼ hours

¼ cup olive oil
1 large onion, peeled and diced
5 garlic cloves, peeled and minced
¾ pound mushrooms, wiped with a damp paper towel, trimmed, and sliced
1 large carrot, peeled and chopped
2 celery ribs, rinsed, trimmed, and chopped
1 (10-ounce) package frozen chopped spinach, thawed and drained
¼ cup chopped fresh parsley
1 tablespoon Italian seasoning
1 teaspoon dried thyme
2 bay leaves
2 (28-ounce) cans crushed tomatoes, undrained
1 cup dry red wine
3 tablespoons tomato paste
Salt and freshly ground black pepper to taste

If cooking conventionally:
½ cup water

1. Heat olive oil in a large skillet over medium-high heat. Add onion, garlic, and mushrooms, and cook, stirring frequently, for 5–7 minutes, or until mushrooms soften. Scrape mixture into the slow cooker.
2. Add carrot, celery, spinach, parsley, Italian seasoning, thyme, bay leaves, tomatoes, wine, and tomato paste to the slow cooker. Stir well.
3. Cook on Low for 6–8 hours or on High for 3–4 hours, or until vegetables are soft. Remove and discard bay leaves, season to taste with salt and pepper, and serve over pasta.

If cooking conventionally: Follow the recipe to the end of Step 2, assembling the dish in a saucepan, and adding ½ cup water to the ingredients.

Bring to a boil, and cook over low heat, covered, stirring occasionally, for 1–1¼ hours, or until vegetables are soft. Remove and discard bay leaves, season to taste with salt and pepper, and serve over pasta.

Note: Using either cooking method, the sauce can be prepared up to 2 days in advance and refrigerated, tightly covered. Reheat it, covered, over low heat, stirring occasionally. The sauce can be frozen for up to 3 months.

Variation:

- You can change the vegetables in this sauce to suit your taste. For example, omit the spinach and add 1 large green bell pepper, seeds and ribs removed, and diced. Or sauté ½-inch cubes of eggplant with the other vegetables.

Curried Cauliflower

This Indian dish is so visually pretty, with the pale cauliflower and cubes of potato joined with bright orange carrots in a sauce made creamy with delicate coconut milk. Serve the curry over fragrant basmati rice.

Yield: 4–6 servings | **Active time:** 20 minutes | **Start to finish (minimum time, slow cooker):** 3½ hours in a medium slow cooker | **Start to finish (conventional):** 1 hour

> 2 tablespoons vegetable oil
> 1 bunch scallions, white parts and 3 inches of green tops, rinsed, trimmed, and sliced
> 3 garlic cloves, peeled and minced
> 2 tablespoons grated fresh ginger
> 2 tablespoons curry powder
> ½ teaspoon ground cinnamon
> 1 head cauliflower, leaves discarded and cut into ¾-inch dice
> 2 large redskin potatoes, scrubbed and cut into ¾-inch dice
> 2 large carrots, peeled and sliced
> 1½ cups Vegetable Stock (recipe on page 86) or purchased stock (*2 cups if cooking conventionally*)
> 1 (14-ounce) can light coconut milk
> Salt and freshly ground black pepper to taste
> ¼ cup chopped fresh cilantro

1. Heat oil in a small skillet over medium-high heat. Add scallions, garlic, and ginger, and cook, stirring frequently, for 3 minutes, or until scallions are translucent. Stir in curry powder and cinnamon, and cook, stirring constantly, for 1 minute. Scrape mixture into the slow cooker.
2. Add cauliflower, potatoes, carrots, stock, and coconut milk to the slow cooker. Stir well.
3. Cook on Low for 6–8 hours or on High for 3–4 hours, or until vegetables are tender. Season to taste with salt and pepper, and spoon into bowls, sprinkling each serving with cilantro.

If cooking conventionally: Follow the recipe to the end of Step 2, assembling the dish in a saucepan, and adding the additional ½ cup stock to the ingredients.

Bring to a boil and cook over low heat, covered, stirring occasionally, for 45 minutes–1 hour, or until vegetables are tender. Season to taste with salt and pepper, and spoon into bowls, sprinkling each serving with cilantro.

Note: Using either cooking method, the sauce can be prepared up to 2 days in advance and refrigerated, tightly covered. Reheat it, covered, over low heat, stirring occasionally.

Variation:
- Substitute sweet potatoes for the redskin potatoes, and parsnips for the carrots for a sweeter flavor.

While the life expectancy of most dried spices is about six months, for curry powder it's only about two months. This blend of up to 20 spices and herbs loses potency rapidly because it's ground so finely.

Spicy Vegetarian Hoppin' John

Traditional Hoppin' John, a classic Southern dish, is made with ham. This vegetarian version, which should be served over rice to complete the protein, has chiles added for vibrancy.

Yield: 6–8 servings | **Active time:** 15 minutes | **Start to finish (minimum time, slow cooker):** 5¼ hours in a medium slow cooker, including 1 hour for beans to soak | **Start to finish (conventional):** 2½ hours, including 1 hour for beans to soak

> 1 pound dried black-eyed peas
> 2 tablespoons olive oil
> 2 large onions, peeled and diced
> 2 green bell peppers, seeds and ribs removed, and chopped
> 4 garlic cloves, peeled and minced
> 2 jalapeño or serrano chiles, seeds and ribs removed, and chopped
> 2½ cups Vegetable Stock (recipe on page 86) or purchased stock
>   (*3 cups if cooking conventionally*)
> 1 teaspoon dried thyme
> 2 bay leaves
> Salt and freshly ground black pepper to taste

1. Rinse beans in a colander and place them in a mixing bowl covered with cold water. Allow beans to soak overnight. Or place beans in a saucepan and bring to a boil over high heat. Boil 1 minute. Turn off the heat, cover the pan, and soak beans for 1 hour. With either soaking method, drain beans, discard soaking water, and begin cooking as soon as possible. Transfer beans to the slow cooker.

2. Heat oil in a large skillet over medium-high heat. Add onions, green bell peppers, garlic, and chiles, and cook, stirring frequently, for 3 minutes, or until onions are translucent. Scrape mixture into the slow cooker. Add stock, thyme, and bay leaves. Stir well.

3. Cook on Low for 8–10 hours or on High for 4–5 hours, or until beans are tender. Remove and discard bay leaves, and season to taste with salt and pepper.

If cooking conventionally: Follow the recipe to the end of Step 2, assembling the dish in a saucepan, and adding the additional ½ cup stock to the ingredients.

Bring to a boil and cook over low heat, covered, stirring occasionally, for 1–1¼ hours, or until beans are tender. Remove and discard bay leaves, and season to taste with salt and pepper.

Note: Using either cooking method, the dish can be prepared up to 2 days in advance and refrigerated, tightly covered. Reheat it, covered, over low heat, stirring occasionally.

Variation:
- Substitute 1 (4-ounce) can chopped mild green chiles, drained, for the fresh chiles for a milder dish.

Native to Africa, the black-eyed pea was introduced into the West Indies and from there to Virginia as early as the 1600s. Most of the black-eye pea cultivation in the region, however, took firmer hold in Florida and the Carolinas during the 1700s. The planting of crops of black-eyed peas was promoted by George Washington Carver because, as a legume, it adds nitrogen to the soil and has high nutritional value.

Vegetarian Chili Molé

Zucchini takes the place of cubes of beef in this zesty chili made with a tomato sauce given a smoky nuance from chipotle chiles and richness from the traditional combination of unsweetened cocoa and peanut butter in the sauce. Serve it over rice to complete the protein.

Yield: 4-6 servings | **Active time:** 20 minutes | **Start to finish (minimum time, slow cooker):** 3½ hours in a medium slow cooker | **Start to finish (conventional):** 1 hour

3 tablespoons olive oil

2 medium onions, peeled and diced

4 garlic cloves, peeled and minced

2 tablespoons chili powder

1 teaspoon ground cumin

1 teaspoon dried oregano

¼ teaspoon ground cinnamon

2 medium zucchini, rinsed, trimmed, and cut into ½-inch dice

2 (15-ounce) cans kidney beans, drained and rinsed

1 (14.5-ounce) can diced tomatoes, undrained

2 cups Vegetable Stock (recipe on page 86) or purchased stock (*2½ cups if cooking conventionally*)

2 chipotle chiles in adobo sauce, finely chopped

2 tablespoons peanut butter

1 tablespoon adobo sauce

1 tablespoon tomato paste

3 tablespoons unsweetened cocoa powder

1 tablespoon granulated sugar

Salt and freshly ground black pepper to taste

1. Heat oil in a small skillet over medium-high heat. Add onions and garlic, and cook, stirring frequently, for 3 minutes, or until onions are translucent. Add chili powder, cumin, oregano, and cinnamon, and cook, stirring constantly, for 1 minute. Scrape mixture into the slow cooker.

2. Add zucchini, kidney beans, tomatoes, stock, chipotle chiles, peanut butter, adobo sauce, tomato paste, cocoa, and sugar to the slow cooker. Stir well.

3. Cook on Low for 6–8 hours or on High for 3–4 hours, or until vegetables are tender. Season to taste with salt and pepper.

If cooking conventionally: Follow the recipe to the end of Step 2, assembling the dish in a saucepan, and adding the additional ½ cup stock to the ingredients.

Bring to a boil and cook over low heat, covered, stirring occasionally, for 30–40 minutes, or until vegetables are tender. Season to taste with salt and pepper.

Note: Using either cooking method, the sauce can be prepared up to 2 days in advance and refrigerated, tightly covered. Reheat it, covered, over low heat, stirring occasionally.

Variation:
- To make this a non-vegetarian chili, brown 1 pound ground beef before sautéing the onions and garlic, and omit the zucchini.

Molé sauce is a traditional food left at graves to celebrate El Día de los Muertos (Day of the Dead) in Mexico. Scholars trace the origins of the modern holiday to indigenous observances dating back thousands of years and to an Aztec festival dedicated to the goddess Mictecacihuatl. Celebrated on October 31, the religious holiday honors deceased family and friends.

Vegetarian Chili with Tofu

This chili preparation is at the delicate side of the spectrum; it contains mild green chiles and uses a restrained hand in the spicing. The cubes of tofu absorb the flavor of the sauce wonderfully in the slow cooker.

Yield: 4–6 servings | **Active time:** 20 minutes | **Start to finish (minimum time, slow cooker):** 5 ½ hours in a medium slow cooker, including 1 hour for beans to soak | **Start to finish (conventional):** 2 hours, including 1 hour for beans to soak

1½ cups dried pinto beans
2 tablespoons olive oil
2 large onions, peeled and diced
2 green bell peppers, seeds and ribs removed, and chopped
2 garlic cloves, peeled and minced
2 tablespoons chili powder
1 tablespoon ground cumin
1 tablespoon dried oregano
1 (28-ounce) can crushed tomatoes in tomato puree
1 (4-ounce) can chopped mild green chiles, drained
2 tablespoons tomato paste
½ cup Vegetable Stock (recipe on page 86) or purchased stock (*1 cup if cooking conventionally*)
1 (14-ounce) package extra-firm tofu, drained and cut into ¾-inch dice
Salt and freshly ground black pepper to taste

1. Rinse beans in a colander and place them in a mixing bowl covered with cold water. Allow beans to soak overnight. Or place beans in a saucepan and bring to a boil over high heat. Boil 1 minute. Turn off the heat, cover the pan, and soak beans for 1 hour. With either soaking method, drain beans, discard soaking water, and begin cooking as soon as possible. Transfer beans to the slow cooker.
2. Heat oil in a medium skillet over medium-high heat. Add onions, green bell peppers, and garlic, and cook, stirring frequently, for 3 minutes, or until onions are translucent. Add chili powder, cumin, and oregano, and cook, stirring constantly, for 1 minute. Scrape mixture into the slow cooker.
3. Add tomatoes, chiles, tomato paste, and stock to the slow cooker. Stir well.

4. Cook on Low for 6–8 hours or on High for 3–4 hours, or until beans are almost tender.

5. If cooking on Low, raise the heat to High. Add tofu, and cook for 1 hour, or until beans are tender. Season to taste with salt and pepper, and serve immediately.

If cooking conventionally: Follow the recipe to the end of Step 3, assembling the dish in a saucepan, and adding the additional ½ cup stock to the ingredients.

Bring to a boil and cook over low heat, covered, stirring occasionally, for 1–1¼ hours, or until beans are tender. Add tofu after beans have cooked for 50 minutes. Season to taste with salt and pepper, and serve immediately.

Note: Using either cooking method, the dish can be prepared up to 2 days in advance and refrigerated, tightly covered. Reheat it, covered, over low heat, stirring occasionally.

Variation:

- Substitute 2 medium zucchini or yellow squash, rinsed, trimmed, and cut into ¾-inch cubes, for the tofu.

Ratatouille Flan

There are few dishes that glorify the cornucopia of vegetables as well as classic French ratatouille; the combination of colors and flavors is masterful. In this easy entrée, which is also wonderful at brunch, the vegetables are bound by an egg custard.

Yield: 4–6 servings | **Active time:** 20 minutes | **Start to finish (minimum time, slow cooker):** N/A | **Start to finish (conventional):** 1³/₄ hours

1 (³/₄-pound) eggplant, trimmed, and cut into ¹/₂-inch dice
Salt
¹/₄ cup olive oil
3 medium onions, peeled and diced
2 garlic cloves, peeled and minced
1 green bell pepper, seeds and ribs removed, cut into ¹/₂-inch dice
2 small zucchini, rinsed, trimmed, and cut into ¹/₂-inch dice
4 ripe plum tomatoes, rinsed, cored, seeded, and cut into ¹/₂-inch dice
2 teaspoons herbes de Provence
¹/₂ cup tomato suce
6 large eggs
¹/₄ cup sour cream
Freshly ground black pepper to taste
Vegetable oil spray

1. Place eggplant in a colander, and sprinkle cubes liberally with salt. Place a plate on top of eggplant cubes, and weight the plate with some cans. Place the colander in the sink or on a plate, and allow eggplant to drain for 30 minutes. Rinse eggplant cubes, and squeeze hard to remove water. Wring out remaining water with a cloth tea towel.

2. Preheat the oven to 350°F, and grease a 9 x 13-inch baking pan with vegetable oil spray.

3. Heat olive oil in large skillet over medium heat. Add onions and garlic, and cook, stirring frequently, for 3 minutes, or until onions are translucent. Add eggplant, green pepper, zucchini, tomatoes, herbes de Provence, and tomato sauce to the skillet. Cook, stirring frequently, for 5 minutes, or until vegetables begin to soften.

4. Reduce the heat to low, cover the skillet, and cook vegetables for 20 minutes, or until they are soft and the liquid has almost evaporated.

Season to taste with salt and pepper, and allow mixture to cool for 10 minutes.

5. Whisk eggs with sour cream, and season to taste with salt and pepper. Stir vegetables into eggs, and pour mixture into the prepared pan. Bake custard for 45–55 minutes, or until eggs are set and the top is lightly browned. Allow to sit for 5 minutes. Serve hot, at room temperature, or chilled.

Note: The vegetables can be prepared up to 2 days in advance and refrigerated, tightly covered. Allow them to reach room temperature before baking custard.

Variation:

- The filling can be transformed to a quiche by baking it in 2 (9-inch) unbaked pie crusts. The cooking time will be the same.

Eggplant turns an unappealing brown once cut, so it should be cooked right after it is salted.

Eastern European Vegetable Casserole with Dried Fruits (*Tsimmis*)

Root vegetables flavored with spices and sweetened with dried fruits make this a homey and hearty dish. Serve it with a red cabbage slaw, and some crusty bread.

Yield: 4-6 servings | **Active time:** 20 minutes | **Start to finish (minimum time, slow cooker):** N/A | **Start to finish (conventional):** 2 hours

1 pound carrots, peeled and cut into ½-inch slices
¾ pound sweet potatoes, peeled and cut into ½-inch cubes
½ pound rutabaga, peeled and cut into ½-inch cubes
1 medium onion, peeled and diced
1 cup dried apricots, diced
1 cup pitted prunes, diced
1 cup apple cider
1 cup Vegetable Stock (recipe on page 86) or purchased stock
½ teaspoon ground nutmeg
½ teaspoon ground cinnamon
Salt and freshly ground black pepper to taste

1. Preheat the oven to 400°F, and grease a 10 x 14-inch baking pan.
2. Place carrots, sweet potatoes, rutabaga, onion, apricots, and prunes in a mixing bowl, and toss to combine. Transfer mixture to the prepared pan. Combine cider, stock, nutmeg, cinnamon, salt, and pepper in same bowl, and stir well. Pour liquid into the pan, and cover the pan with aluminum foil.
3. Bake for 1 hour, or until vegetables are almost tender. Remove the foil, and bake for an additional 30 minutes, or until lightly browned and liquid has almost evaporated. Serve immediately.

Note: The dish can be prepared up to 2 days in advance and refrigerated, tightly covered. Reheat it in a 350°F oven, covered, for 20–30 minutes, or until hot.

Variation:

- Feel free to substitute any dried fruit you like for those listed. Raisins, dried cranberries, and dried peaches all work well.

Chapter 9:
$1 Sweet Endings: Desserts That Are Easy on the Budget

When I promised that a complete meal would cost less than $3 per person, that, of course, included the dessert; those are the recipes you'll find in this chapter. All of these luscious desserts are less than $1 per serving. So when that cost is factored in with the cost of the entree and side dish, you've created a filling and sensually satisfying meal.

You'll find a wide range of treats in this chapter. Some use fruits, while others are based on other popular foods such as chocolate and cream cheese. Unlike as in other chapters of this book, there are few desserts that produce equally good results both from the slow cooker and your conventional oven; they are limited to bread puddings and a few other homey treats. But there is a whole category of desserts called "pudding cakes" that are tailor-made for the slow cooker, and don't work well conventionally; you'll find them here as well as many spectacular desserts made in your conventional oven.

Apple-Raisin Pudding Cake

This pudding cake is fairly light, and it delivers an intense apple flavor from three forms of the fruit. It's almost like an apple cobbler, with a thick sauce topping it.

Yield: 4-6 servings | **Active time:** 15 minutes | **Start to finish (minimum time, slow cooker):** 2¼ hours in a medium slow cooker | **Start to finish (conventional):** N/A

- 2 cups apple cider or apple juice
- Vegetable oil spray or melted butter
- 2 Granny Smith apples
- 1 cup all-purpose flour
- ⅓ cup granulated sugar
- 1 teaspoon baking powder
- ½ teaspoons apple pie spice (or ground cinnamon)
- Pinch of salt
- ½ cup whole milk
- 4 tablespoons (½ stick) unsalted butter, melted
- ¼ teaspoon pure vanilla extract
- ⅓ cup finely chopped dried apples
- ⅓ cup raisins
- ½ cup firmly packed dark brown sugar
- Vanilla ice cream or sweetened whipped cream (optional)

1. Bring apple cider to a boil in a small saucepan over high heat. Cook until cider is reduced by ½. Set aside. Grease the inside of the slow cooker liberally with vegetable oil spray or melted butter.

2. While cider boils, peel and core apples, and chop apples finely in a food processor fitted with the steel blade using on-and-off pulsing. Combine flour, granulated sugar, baking powder, apple pie spice, and salt in a mixing bowl. Stir in milk, melted butter, and vanilla. Stir until a stiff batter forms, then stir in chopped apples, dried apples, and raisins. Spread batter into the slow cooker.

3. Bring cider back to a boil, and stir in brown sugar. Pour mixture over batter. Cook on High for 2–2¼ hours, or until a toothpick inserted into the top cake layer comes out clean. Turn off the slow cooker and remove the cover. Allow cake to sit for 15 minutes before serving.

Note: The cake can be served hot, at room temperature, or chilled, topped with ice cream or whipped cream, if using.

Variation:

- Substitute 3 peeled ripe peaches, dried peaches, and peach nectar for the various forms of apple in the recipe. Omit the apple pie spice and add ½ teaspoon ground ginger to the batter.

For dishes like apple tarts, where the apples will be seen, the traditional method of peeling, quartering, coring, and thinly slicing them makes sense. But for a recipe like this one, peel them and start cutting off slices, turning the apple. When you reach the core, discard it. It's a much quicker method!

Classic Creole Bread Pudding

Pecans and raisins dot this rich, cinnamon-scented pudding from the New Orleans tradition; because it's a way to use up stale bread, it was a "peasant dish" until the twentieth century.

Yield: 6-8 servings | **Active time:** 15 minutes | **Start to finish (minimum time, slow cooker):** 3¼ hours | **Start to finish (conventional):** 1 hour

> 5 large eggs
> 1 cup granulated sugar
> 2 cups whole milk
> 6 tablespoons (¾ stick) unsalted butter, melted
> 1½ teaspoons pure vanilla extract
> 1 teaspoon ground cinnamon
> Pinch of salt
> ½-pound loaf French or Italian bread, cut into ½-inch slices
> ½ cup raisins
> ½ cup chopped pecans
> Vegetable oil spray or melted butter
> ½-¾ cup caramel sauce, purchased or homemade

1. Combine eggs, sugar, milk, melted butter, vanilla, cinnamon, and salt in a mixing bowl, and whisk well. Add bread slices to the mixing bowl, and press them down so that bread will absorb liquid. Stir in raisins and pecans. Allow mixture to sit for 10 minutes.

2. Grease the inside of the slow cooker liberally with vegetable oil spray or melted butter. Spoon mixture into the slow cooker.

3. Cook on High for 1 hour, then reduce the heat to Low and cook for 2-3 hours, or until puffed and an instant-read thermometer inserted in the center registers 165°F. Serve immediately, topped with caramel sauce.

If cooking conventionally: Preheat the oven to 350°F, and grease a 9 x 13-inch baking dish with vegetable oil spray or melted butter. Follow the recipe to the end of Step 1, and transfer mixture to the prepared pan. Cover the baking pan with aluminum foil, and bake in the center of the oven for 30 minutes. Remove the foil, and bake for an additional 15-20 minutes, or until puffed and an instant-read thermometer inserted in the center registers 165°F. Serve immediately, topped with caramel sauce.

Note: Using either cooking method, the bread pudding can be baked up to 2 days in advance; reheat it in a 325°F oven, covered, for 20–25 minutes, or until hot.

Variations:

- Omit the sugar, cinnamon, and pecans, and add 1½ cups white chocolate, melted, to the bread mixture. Serve with chocolate sauce.
- Substitute maple syrup for the granulated sugar, reduce the cinnamon to ½ teaspoon, and substitute walnuts for the pecans.
- Substitute ¾ cup orange marmalade for ¾ cup of the sugar, omit the cinnamon and pecans, and substitute dried cranberries for the raisins. Serve topped with ice cream or sweetened whipped cream.

While pure vanilla extract is more expensive than artificial, it's worth the extra money. You use so little of it, and the artificial one gives foods a chemical taste.

Pineapple-Coconut Bread Pudding

This bread pudding has all the luscious flavors of a piña colada; it's laced with coconut and pineapple, and scented with rum.

Yield: 6–8 servings | **Active time:** 15 minutes | **Start to finish (minimum time, slow cooker):** 3¼ hours in a medium slow cooker | **Start to finish (conventional):** 1 hour

>   5 large eggs
>   ½ cup granulated sugar
>   1½ cups whole milk
>   1 (15-ounce) can cream of coconut
>   1 (8-ounce) can crushed pineapple, undrained
>   6 tablespoons (¾ stick) unsalted butter, melted
>   ¼ cup rum (or 1 teaspoon rum extract and ¼ cup water)
>   ½ teaspoon pure vanilla extract
>   Pinch of salt
>   ½-pound loaf French or Italian bread, cut into ½-inch slices
>   Vegetable oil spray or melted butter
>   1 pint coconut or rum raisin ice cream (optional)

1. Combine eggs, sugar, milk, cream of coconut, pineapple, butter, rum, vanilla, and salt in a mixing bowl, and whisk well. Add bread slices to the mixing bowl, and press them down so that bread will absorb liquid. Allow mixture to sit for 10 minutes.
2. Grease the inside of the slow cooker liberally with vegetable oil spray or melted butter. Spoon mixture into the slow cooker.
3. Cook on High for 1 hour, then reduce the heat to Low and cook for 2–3 hours, or until puffed and an instant-read thermometer inserted in the center registers 165°F. Serve immediately, topped with ice cream.

If cooking conventionally: Preheat the oven to 350°F, and grease a 9 x 13-inch baking dish with vegetable oil spray or melted butter. Follow the recipe to the end of Step 1, and transfer mixture to the prepared pan. Cover the baking pan with aluminum foil, and bake in the center of the oven for 30 minutes. Remove the foil, and bake for an additional 15–20 minutes, or until puffed and an instant-read thermometer inserted in the center registers 165°F. Serve immediately, topped with ice cream, if using.

Note: Using either cooking method, the bread pudding can be baked up to 2 days in advance; reheat it in a 325°F oven, covered, for 20–25 minutes, or until hot.

Cream of coconut should not be confused with coconut milk. Cream of coconut is highly sweetened, and it's usually found with such drink fixings as Bloody Mary mix in the supermarket.

Indian Pudding with Ginger

Corn was introduced to the Pilgrims by Native Americans, so anything made with corn had "Indian" as a prefix at one time or another. Recipes for Indian pudding date back to the early eighteenth century. This version is enlivened with some crystallized ginger.

Yield: 6–8 servings | **Active time:** 20 minutes | **Start to finish (minimum time, slow cooker):** 3½ hours in a medium slow cooker | **Start to finish (conventional):** 1⅓ hours

1 quart whole milk
½ cup yellow cornmeal
4 tablespoons (½ stick) unsalted butter, cut into small pieces
½ cup pure maple syrup
¼ cup firmly packed dark brown sugar
3 tablespoons finely chopped crystallized ginger
½ teaspoon ground cinnamon
Pinch of salt
Vegetable oil spray or melted butter
½ cup raisins, preferably golden raisins
2 large eggs, lightly beaten
Vanilla ice cream or sweetened whipped cream (optional)

1. Bring milk to a boil in a saucepan over medium-high heat, then add cornmeal in a steady stream, whisking constantly. Reduce the heat to low, and cook for 10 minutes, or until mixture thickens. Stir in butter, maple syrup, brown sugar, crystallized ginger, cinnamon, and salt. Remove the pan from the heat, and stir for 2 minutes.
2. Liberally grease the inside of the slow cooker with vegetable oil spray or melted butter. Stir in raisins and eggs, and scrape batter into the slow cooker.
3. Cook on Low for 3–5 hours, or until center of pudding has set. Serve hot, topped with vanilla ice cream or whipped cream, if using.

If cooking conventionally: Preheat the oven to 325°F, and grease a 2 quart casserole. Follow the recipe to the end of Step 1, and transfer mixture to the prepared casserole. Bake for 1 hour, or until center of pudding has set. Serve hot, topped with vanilla ice cream or whipped cream, if using.

Note: The pudding can be baked up to 2 days in advance and refrigerated, tightly covered. Reheat it in a pan in a 300°F oven, covered with aluminum foil, for 20 minutes, or until warm.

Chocolate-Peanut Pudding Cake

This is like eating a hot, luscious Reese's cup. The overwhelming flavor is one of peanuts, but chocolate is a close second. And chances are you have most, if not all, of the ingredients right in the house.

Yield: 4–6 servings | **Active time:** 15 minutes | **Start to finish (minimum time, slow cooker):** 2½ hours in a medium slow cooker | **Start to finish (conventional):** N/A

Vegetable oil spray or melted butter
1 cup all-purpose flour
⅓ cup unsweetened cocoa powder, divided
1 cup granulated sugar, divided
1½ teaspoons baking powder
½ cup whole milk
3 tablespoons unsalted butter, melted
1 teaspoon pure vanilla extract
¾ cup chunky peanut butter
½ cup chopped roasted peanuts
⅔ cup bittersweet chocolate chips
1¾ cups boiling water
Vanilla ice cream or sweetened whipped cream (optional)

1. Grease the inside of the slow cooker liberally with vegetable oil spray or melted butter. Combine flour, 3 tablespoons cocoa, ⅓ cup sugar, and baking powder in a mixing bowl. Stir in milk, melted butter, and vanilla. Stir until a stiff batter forms, then stir in peanut butter, chopped peanuts, and chocolate chips. Spread batter into the slow cooker.
2. Pour boiling water into the mixing bowl, and stir in remaining cocoa and remaining sugar. Pour mixture over batter. Cook on High for 2–2¼ hours, or until a toothpick inserted into the top cake layer comes out clean. Allow cake to sit for 15 minutes with slow cooker turned off before serving.

Note: The cake can be served hot, at room temperature, or chilled, topped with ice cream or whipped cream, if using.

Variation:
- Substitute almond butter or cashew butter with the appropriate nuts for the peanuts. If the nut butter is not sweetened, increase the sugar in the batter by ¼ cup.

Chocolate Pudding Cake

Chocolate pudding cake is the gold standard of all slow cooker desserts, and it is open to endless permutations. It's almost like magic; the boiling water starts on the top of the batter and ends up as a sauce beneath the baked cake.

Yield: 4–6 servings | **Active time:** 15 minutes | **Start to finish (minimum time, slow cooker):** 2½ hours in a medium slow cooker | **Start to finish (conventional):** N/A

> Vegetable oil spray or melted butter
> 1 cup granulated sugar
> 1 cup all-purpose flour
> 3 tablespoons plus ¼ cup unsweetened cocoa powder
> 2 teaspoons baking powder
> ½ cup whole milk
> 3 tablespoons unsalted butter, melted
> ½ teaspoon pure vanilla extract
> ¾ cup firmly packed dark brown sugar
> 1 ¾ cups boiling water
> 1 pint of your favorite ice cream (optional)

1. Grease the inside of the slow cooker liberally with vegetable oil spray or melted butter. Combine granulated sugar, flour, 3 tablespoons cocoa powder, and baking powder in a mixing bowl. Stir in milk, melted butter, and vanilla. Stir until a stiff batter forms. Spread batter into the slow cooker.

2. Sprinkle brown sugar and remaining ¼ cup cocoa powder over the batter. Pour boiling water over the batter. Cook on High for 2–2¼ hours, or until a toothpick inserted into the top cake layer comes out clean. Allow cake to sit for 15 minutes with slow cooker turned off before serving.

Note: The cake can be served hot, at room temperature, or chilled, topped with ice cream, if using.

Variations:

- Add 1 tablespoon instant coffee granules to the batter for a mocha cake.
- Add 2 tablespoons of any liqueur or liquor to the cake for added flavor.
- Add ¼ cup fruit-only jam to the batter for added flavor.
- Add ½ cup butterscotch chips to the batter for extra richness.
- Add ½ teaspoon ground cinnamon and ½ cup toasted slivered almonds to the batter for a Mexican chocolate combination.

There are two types of unsweetened cocoa powder—Dutch processed and natural. The Dutch processed has a milder flavor, so it does not deliver as intense a chocolate "hit" as natural.

Banana Nut Cake

Banana bread is homey, but this cake elevates this popular fruit to a new level of elegance. It's also fairly quick to bake and cool, so it can be an impromptu ending to many meals.

Yield: 4–6 servings | **Active time:** 20 minutes | **Start to finish (minimum time, slow cooker):** N/A | **Start to finish (conventional):** 1½ hours, including time for cooling

CAKE:

1 cup chopped walnuts, divided
1½ cups all-purpose flour
1½ teaspoons baking powder
½ teaspoon baking soda
½ teaspoon salt
8 tablespoons (1 stick) unsalted butter, softened
¾ cup firmly packed light brown sugar
1 large egg, at room temperature
¾ cup mashed ripe bananas
¼ cup sour cream
½ teaspoon pure vanilla extract

FROSTING:

2 cups confectioners' sugar
1 (8-ounce) package cream cheese, softened
2 tablespoons unsalted butter, softened
¼ teaspoon pure vanilla extract

1. Preheat the oven to 350°F. Grease and flour a 9-inch round cake pan. Toast walnuts on a baking sheet for 5–7 minutes, or until browned. Remove nuts from the oven, and set aside.
2. Combine flour, baking powder, baking soda, and salt in a small bowl. Combine butter and sugar in a mixing bowl, and beat with an electric mixer at low speed to blend. Increase the speed to high, and beat for 2 minutes, or until light and fluffy. Beat in egg, bananas, sour cream, and vanilla at medium speed, scraping the sides of the bowl as necessary. Add flour mixture, and beat until just combined. Stir in ¾ cup nuts.

3. Spread batter evenly in the prepared pan, and bake for 20–25 minutes, or until a cake tester inserted in the middle comes out clean. Cool cake in the pan on a rack for 10 minutes, then remove cake from the pan and cool completely.
4. While cake cools, prepare frosting. Combine confectioners' sugar, cream cheese, butter, and vanilla in a mixing bowl. Beat at low speed with an electric mixer until blended. Increase the speed to medium-high, and beat for 2 minutes, or until light and fluffy.
5. Frost sides and top of cooled cake with frosting, and sprinkle with remaining ¼ cup walnuts. Serve immediately.

Note: The cake can be baked and frosted up to 1 day in advance and kept at room temperature, lightly covered.

Remember how nothing should go to waste in your kitchen? That includes overly ripe bananas! Freeze them right in the peels, and thaw them to make a cake like this or banana bread.

Peach Upside-Down Cake

Toward the end of summer, when peaches are in season, this easy cake is one of the ways I enjoy them most.

Yield: 6–8 servings | **Active time:** 20 minutes | **Start to finish (minimum time, slow cooker):** N/A | **Start to finish (conventional):** 1¼ hours

4 ripe peaches

12 tablespoons (1½ sticks) unsalted butter, softened, divided

¾ cup firmly packed light brown sugar

1½ cups all-purpose flour

2 teaspoons baking powder

½ teaspoon ground ginger

¼ teaspoon salt

1 cup granulated sugar

2 large eggs, at room temperature

4 tablespoons dark rum, divided

1 teaspoon pure vanilla extract

½ cup whole milk

1. Preheat the oven to 350°F, and bring a saucepan of water to a boil. Plunge peaches into water for 30 seconds, then remove peaches from the pan with a slotted spoon and run them under ice water. Peel peaches, discard stones, and slice each peach into 6 wedges. Set aside.

2. Melt 6 tablespoons butter in a 10-inch ovenproof skillet over medium-high heat. Add brown sugar, and cook for 2 minutes, stirring constantly. Arrange peaches over brown sugar, and set aside.

3. Sift together flour, baking powder, ginger, and salt. Combine remaining 6 tablespoons butter and granulated sugar in a mixing bowl and beat with an electric mixer at medium speed until light and fluffy. Beat in eggs, one at a time, beating well between each addition. Beat in 2 tablespoons rum and vanilla. Add ½ of flour mixture at low speed until just blended. Add milk and then second ½ of flour mixture. Spoon batter over peaches in the skillet.

4. Bake cake for 45 minutes, or until a knife inserted in the center comes out clean. Remove cake from the oven, and place it on a cooling rack for 5 minutes. Invert a plate over the skillet, and then invert cake onto the plate; replace any peaches from the pan that stuck. Sprinkle

remaining 2 tablespoons rum over top of cake. Serve warm or at room temperature.

Note: The cake can be made up to 1 day in advance and kept at room temperature, lightly covered. If you do not own an ovenproof skillet, cover the plastic handle of a skillet with a double layer of heavy-duty aluminum foil to protect it from melting in the oven.

Variations:

- Substitute fresh or canned pineapple rings for the peaches; make sure that the pineapple is packed in juice and not heavy syrup.
- Substitute 1 pound fresh apricots for the peaches.

For small amounts of liquor or liqueur, such as the rum in this recipe, it's more cost effective to buy the individual drink size, like those sold on airplanes, if you don't think you'll finish the rest of a bottle.

Cheesecake

Cheesecake is a perennial favorite dessert, appropriate for any time of the year. It's also extremely expensive when bought at a good bakery. Here's a foolproof recipe that can be made for a fraction of the cost, and feeds a crowd.

Yield: 10–12 servings | **Active time:** 20 minutes | **Start to finish (minimum time, slow cooker):** N/A | **Start to finish (conventional):** 9 hours, including 7 hours for chilling

> 1½ cups graham cracker crumbs or any cookie crumb, such as vanilla wafers or gingersnaps
> 5 tablespoons unsalted butter, melted
> 2 cups granulated sugar, divided
> 4 (8-ounce) packages cream cheese, softened
> 3 tablespoons all-purpose flour
> 4 large eggs, at room temperature
> 2 large egg yolks
> 1 teaspoon pure vanilla extract
> Pinch of salt

1. Preheat the oven to 500°F.
2. Combine crumbs, butter, and ⅓ cup sugar in a mixing bowl, and stir well. Pat mixture into bottom and 1 inch up the sides of a 12-inch springform pan. Set aside.
3. Combine remaining sugar, cream cheese, and flour in a large mixing bowl, and beat at medium speed with an electric mixer until smooth. Add eggs and egg yolks, 1 at a time, beating well between each addition, and scraping the sides of the bowl as necessary. Beat in vanilla and salt. Scrape mixture into the pan on top of crust.
4. Bake in the center of the oven for 15 minutes. Reduce the oven temperature to 225°F and continue to bake cheesecake for an additional 1 hour. Turn off oven, and allow cheesecake to sit in the oven for an additional 30 minutes without opening the oven door.
5. Cool cake in the pan on a rack, and then refrigerate until cold. Run a knife around the sides of the pan to release cake, and then remove sides of pan. Allow cheesecake to sit at room temperature for 30 minutes before serving.

Note: Cheesecake lasts forever! You can refrigerate this cake for up to 10 days; keep it tightly covered with plastic wrap.

Variations:
- Add 1 tablespoon grated lemon or orange zest to the batter.
- Substitute firmly packed dark brown sugar for the granulated sugar in the batter, and add $3/4$ cup of chopped toasted pecans.
- Mix $1/4$ of the batter with 3 tablespoons unsweetened cocoa powder, and swirl this through the vanilla batter for a marble cheesecake.

While I don't recommend freezing cream cheese if you're going to spread it on a bagel because it changes the texture, it's fine to freeze it for cheesecakes if you find it on sale.

Carrot Cake with Cream Cheese Frosting

While making sweet foods with carrots dates back to the Medieval era, and is also part of Indian cuisine, the homey carrot cake with its traditional cream cheese frosting didn't become popular until after World War II. It's a fast cake to make, and it has universal appeal.

Yield: 10–12 servings | **Active time:** 20 minutes | **Start to finish (minimum time, slow cooker):** N/A | **Start to finish (conventional):** 4 hours, including 2 hours for chilling

CAKE:

2 cups all-purpose flour

1 tablespoon ground cinnamon

2 teaspoons baking soda

½ teaspoon salt

1½ cups vegetable oil

1½ cups granulated sugar

4 large eggs, at room temperature

1½ teaspoons pure vanilla extract

1 pound carrots, peeled and shredded

½ cup sweetened coconut

½ cup finely chopped pineapple

½ cup chopped walnuts, toasted in a 350°F oven for 5 minutes

FROSTING:

6 cups (1½ pounds) confectioners' sugar

3 (8-ounce) packages cream cheese, softened

6 tablespoons (¾ stick) unsalted butter, softened

2 teaspoons pure vanilla extract

1. Preheat the oven to 350°F; grease and flour 3 (9-inch) round cake pans with 1½-inch sides.
2. Sift flour with the cinnamon, baking soda, and salt, and set aside. Place vegetable oil, granulated sugar, eggs, and vanilla in a mixing bowl and beat at medium speed with an electric mixer until well blended. Add flour mixture, and beat at low speed until just blended. Stir in carrots, coconut, pineapple, and walnuts.

3. Divide batter among the prepared pans and bake for 35–40 minutes, or until cake begins to shrink away from the sides of the pan and a cake tester inserted in the center of each layer comes out clean. Cool cake layers on a rack for 15 minutes, then invert layers onto racks, and allow them to cool completely.

4. While cake cools, prepare frosting. Combine confectioners' sugar, cream cheese, butter, and vanilla in a mixing bowl. Beat at low speed with an electric mixer until blended. Increase the speed to medium-high, and beat for 2 minutes, or until light and fluffy.

5. To assemble, place 2 overlapping sheets of waxed paper on a platter. Place 1 layer, flat side down, on the paper and spread with ³/₄ cup frosting. Repeat with second layer. Top with third layer and spread remaining frosting on the top and sides. Remove waxed paper by pulling out firmly but gently on both pieces. Refrigerate the cake for at least 2 hours before serving.

Note: The layers can be prepared 3 days in advance and refrigerated, tightly covered. The cake can be assembled 1 day in advance and refrigerated.

The pineapple in this recipe is a perfect example of a food to draw from the supermarket salad bar. The quantity is far less than even a half pineapple.

Apple Brown Betty

Apple desserts can be either haute or homey, and this colonial American classic falls into the latter category. What defines a Betty, made from any number of fruits, is the use of breadcrumbs.

Yield: 6–8 servings | **Active time:** 15 minutes | **Start to finish (minimum time, slow cooker):** N/A | **Start to finish (conventional):** 1¼ hours

> 1½ cups plain breadcrumbs
> ½ cup firmly packed light brown sugar
> ½ cup granulated sugar
> 1½ teaspoons apple pie spice
> Pinch of salt
> 2½ pounds Granny Smith apples, peeled, cored, and thinly sliced
> 6 tablespoons (¾ stick) unsalted butter, cut into small bits
> Vanilla ice cream or sweetened whipped cream for serving (optional)

1. Preheat the oven to 375°F, and grease a 9 x 13-inch pan.
2. Combine breadcrumbs, brown sugar, granulated sugar, apple pie spice, and salt in a mixing bowl, and stir well. Sprinkle ¼ of mixture on the bottom of the prepared pan.
3. Place ½ of apples in the pan, and top with ½ of remaining crumb mixture. Dot crumbs with ½ of butter. Repeat layering with apples, crumbs, and butter.
4. Bake for 45–50 minutes, or until bubbly and apples are tender. Cool on a rack for 10 minutes, then serve topped with ice cream or whipped cream, if using.

Note: The dish can be prepared up to 6 hours in advance and kept at room temperature.

Appendix A:
Metric Conversion Tables

The scientifically precise calculations needed for baking are not necessary when cooking conventionally. The tables in this appendix are designed for general cooking. If making conversions for baking, grab your calculator and compute the exact figure.

CONVERTING OUNCES TO GRAMS

The numbers in the following table are approximate. To reach the exact quantity of grams, multiply the number of ounces by 28.35.

Ounces	Grams
1 ounce	30 grams
2 ounces	60 grams
3 ounces	85 grams
4 ounces	115 grams
5 ounces	140 grams
6 ounces	180 grams
7 ounces	200 grams
8 ounces	225 grams
9 ounces	250 grams
10 ounces	285 grams
11 ounces	300 grams
12 ounces	340 grams
13 ounces	370 grams
14 ounces	400 grams
15 ounces	425 grams
16 ounces	450 grams

CONVERTING QUARTS TO LITERS

The numbers in the following table are approximate. To reach the exact amount of liters, multiply the number of quarts by 0.95.

Quarts	Liter
1 cup (¼ quart)	¼ liter
1 pint (½ quart)	½ liter
1 quart	1 liter
2 quarts	2 liters
2½ quarts	2½ liters
3 quarts	2¾ liters
4 quarts	3¾ liters
5 quarts	4¾ liters
6 quarts	5½ liters
7 quarts	6½ liters
8 quarts	7½ liters

CONVERTING POUNDS TO GRAMS AND KILOGRAMS

The numbers in the following table are approximate. To reach the exact quantity of grams, multiply the number of pounds by 453.6.

Pounds	Grams; Kilograms
1 pound	450 grams
1½ pounds	675 grams
2 pounds	900 grams
2½ pounds	1,125 grams; 1¼ kilograms
3 pounds	1,350 grams
3½ pounds	1,500 grams; 1½ kilograms
4 pounds	1,800 grams
4½ pounds	2 kilograms
5 pounds	2¼ kilograms
5½ pounds	2½ kilograms
6 pounds	2¾ kilograms
6½ pounds	3 kilograms
7 pounds	3¼ kilograms
7½ pounds	3½ kilograms
8 pounds	3¾ kilograms

CONVERTING FAHRENHEIT TO CELSIUS

The numbers in the following table are approximate. To reach the exact temperature, subtract 32 from the Fahrenheit reading, multiply the number by 5, and then divide by 9.

Degrees Fahrenheit	Degrees Celsius
170°F	77°C
180°F	82°C
190°F	88°C
200°F	95°C
225°F	110°C
250°F	120°C
300°F	150°C
325°F	165°C
350°F	180°C
375°F	190°C
400°F	205°C
425°F	220°C
450°F	230°C
475°F	245°C
500°F	260°C

CONVERTING INCHES TO CENTIMETERS

The numbers in the following table are approximate. To reach the exact number of centimeters, multiply the number of inches by 2.54.

Inches	Centimeters
½ inch	1.5 centimeters
1 inch	2.5 centimeters
2 inches	5 centimeters
3 inches	8 centimeters
4 inches	10 centimeters
5 inches	13 centimeters
6 inches	15 centimeters
7 inches	18 centimeters
8 inches	20 centimeters
9 inches	23 centimeters
10 inches	25 centimeters
11 inches	28 centimeters
12 inches	30 centimeters

Table of Weights and Measures of Common Ingredients

Food	Quantity	Yield
Apples	1 pound	2$\frac{1}{2}$–3 cups sliced
Avocado	1 pound	1 cup mashed
Bananas	1 medium	1 cup sliced
Bell peppers	1 pound	3–4 cups sliced
Blueberries	1 pound	3$\frac{1}{3}$ cups
Butter	$\frac{1}{4}$ pound (1 stick)	8 tablespoons
Cabbage	1 pound	4 cups packed shredded
Carrots	1 pound	3 cups diced or sliced
Chocolate, morsels	12 ounces	2 cups
Chocolate, bulk	1 ounce	3 tablespoons grated
Cocoa powder	1 ounce	$\frac{1}{4}$ cup
Coconut, flaked	7 ounces	2$\frac{1}{2}$ cups
Cream	$\frac{1}{2}$ pint (1 cup)	2 cups whipped
Cream cheese	8 ounces	1 cup
Flour	1 pound	4 cups
Lemons	1 medium	3 tablespoons juice
Lemons	1 medium	2 teaspoons zest
Milk	1 quart	4 cups
Molasses	12 ounces	1$\frac{1}{2}$ cups
Mushrooms	1 pound	5 cups sliced
Onions	1 medium	$\frac{1}{2}$ cup chopped
Peaches	1 pound	2 cups sliced
Peanuts	5 ounces	1 cup
Pecans	6 ounces	1$\frac{1}{2}$ cups
Pineapple	1 medium	3 cups diced
Potatoes	1 pound	3 cups sliced
Raisins	1 pound	3 cups
Rice	1 pound	2 to 2$\frac{1}{2}$ cups raw
Spinach	1 pound	$\frac{3}{4}$ cup cooked
Squash, summer	1 pound	3$\frac{1}{2}$ cups sliced
Strawberries	1 pint	1$\frac{1}{2}$ cups sliced

Food	Quantity	Yield
Sugar, brown	1 pound	2¼ cups, packed
Sugar, confectioners'	1 pound	4 cups
Sugar, granulated	1 pound	2¼ cups
Tomatoes	1 pound	1½ cups pulp
Walnuts	4 ounces	1 cup

TABLE OF LIQUID MEASUREMENTS

Dash	=	less than ⅛ teaspoon
3 teaspoons	=	1 tablespoon
2 tablespoons	=	1 ounce
8 tablespoons	=	½ cup
2 cups	=	1 pint
1 quart	=	2 pints
1 gallon	=	4 quarts

Index